B-17 Gunner

B-17 Gunner

*Charles M. Eyer,
Survivor of 59 Combat Missions
and a Year in Nazi Captivity*

CRAIG A. KLEINSMITH

McFarland & Company, Inc., Publishers
Jefferson, North Carolina

All photographs are from the Eyer family collection.

LIBRARY OF CONGRESS CATALOGUING-IN-PUBLICATION DATA

Names: Kleinsmith, Craig A., author.
Title: B-17 gunner : Charles M. Eyer, survivor of 59 combat missions and a year in Nazi captivity / Craig A. Kleinsmith.
Other titles: World War II combat airman's journey through hell
Description: Jefferson, North Carolina : McFarland & Company, Inc., Publishers, 2020 | Includes bibliographical references and index.
Identifiers: LCCN 2020027779 | ISBN 9781476683294 (paperback) | ISBN 9781476641157 (ebook) ∞
Subjects: LCSH: Eyer, Charles M., 1921–2004. | World War, 1939–1945—Aerial operations, American. | United States. Army Air Forces. Bomb Group, 99th. | United States. Army Air Forces. Bombardment Group, 447th. | Stalag Luft IV—Biography. | World War, 1939–1945—Prisoners and prisons, German. | World War, 1939–1945—Prisoners and prisons—Biography. | United States. Army Air Forces—Aerial gunners—Biography. | B-17 bomber—History—20th century.
Classification: LCC D790 .K5625 2020 | DDC 940.54/7243092 [B]—dc23
LC record available at https://lccn.loc.gov/2020027779

BRITISH LIBRARY CATALOGUING DATA ARE AVAILABLE

ISBN (print) 978-1-4766-8329-4
ISBN (ebook) 978-1-4766-4115-7

© 2020 Craig A. Kleinsmith. All rights reserved

No part of this book may be reproduced or transmitted in any form or by any means, electronic or mechanical, including photocopying or recording, or by any information storage and retrieval system, without permission in writing from the publisher.

Front cover: (top) Sergeant Charles Eyer, September 1942 (Eyer family private collection); (bottom) B-17 Flying Fortresses on a bombing run (United States Army Air Force)

Printed in the United States of America

McFarland & Company, Inc., Publishers
  Box 611, Jefferson, North Carolina 28640
    www.mcfarlandpub.com

Contents

Preface	1
Introduction	3
1. Pre-War Life	9
2. The Making of a Gunner	12
3. North Africa	31
4. New Crew and New Adventures	61
5. Return to Hell	70
6. Day of Days—May 12, 1944	87
7. Stalag Luft IV	109
8. The March	140
9. Liberation	175
10. Postwar	183
Epilogue	189
APPENDICES	
A. POW Journal	193
B. POW Postcards	199
C. Letter to Mother	202
D. Liberation Journal	203
Chapter Notes	207
Bibliography	213
Index	215

Preface

During World War II, tens of thousands of young combat airmen who flew in heavy bombers became casualties of war. Many were killed in action; some were horribly wounded; and many thousands more were shot down over enemy territory, captured, and became prisoners of war. The air war over Europe was especially fierce and costly, and it required courageous, tough, and determined men to carry out those deadly bombing missions.

Those brave young American men who volunteered to man a B-17 Flying Fortress bomber and fly it deep into enemy territory to inflict destruction upon the adversary came from every walk of life. The odds were stacked against the bomber airmen and many never completed their combat tours of duty. Their duty had to be accomplished, and it would be accomplished, regardless of the high number of casualties.

This is the true story of one of those brave young men, Staff Sergeant Charles M. Eyer, a ball turret gunner on a B-17 bomber. His is an amazing tale of survival. He could have been a mechanic in the air force and safe on the ground, but he decided he wanted to be a machine gunner and fly combat missions. So deeply did he believe in his country and the cause for which they fought that he volunteered to place himself in harm's way. He flew 59 combat missions, which was astonishing because many bomber airmen never made it past 10 missions.

Eventually his luck ran out and his bomber was shot down deep inside Germany. Now the most hazardous part of his military service began. He parachuted from a burning airplane, was almost killed by angry German civilians, and was captured, interrogated, and held in a German prisoner of war camp for nine months. When he thought things could not get any worse, they did. He had to endure and survive a horrific forced march conducted over three months and hundreds of miles during one of the harshest European winters in recent history.

I first met Charlie in 1973 when I was a young soldier in the local Pennsylvania Army National Guard unit. Charlie was the maintenance repairman at that armory. For a period of 12 years I worked closely with him almost every day, resulting in a close and enduring friendship.

Someone mentioned to me that Charlie had been a ball turret gunner on a B-17 bomber and that he had been shot down and taken prisoner. This intrigued me and I wanted to learn his story. Like many combat veterans, he didn't voluntarily share the bad memories. It took some gentle prodding and a sincere desire to know his story before he told me everything. It took some time to get him to open up, but when he did, it was like the opening of flood gates. Out it all came! This book, his story, has been years in the making. From that start many years ago and for innumerable hours and days, Charlie talked to me about his wartime service. Eventually he opened up to a few other people, but not many, and he is the main source for this book.

Charlie's children, Joellyn (Susie) and Kevin, videotaped their father a couple of years before his passing. It is an amazing video of more than 13 hours of Charlie telling them about his service during the war. Some of the video was made at a World War II event where there was a B-17 bomber. Somehow, he once again summoned the courage to talk not only to his family but also to complete strangers about the B-17 and his wartime experiences. In 2018, I, along with my son Nicholas, took a ride in a B-17 at another World War II event. That short 30-minute flight helped me to understand what Charlie experienced—the sounds, the smells, the sights—and was an invaluable source in the writing of this book.

I must acknowledge the cooperation and assistance of Charlie's daughter Susie and his son Kevin in the telling of their father's story. Without their approval and help, this story might not have been told. I must also thank my wife Lori for her many hours of proofreading, honest and candid assessment, and emotional support.

Introduction

The sun is just emerging over the eastern horizon. Staff Sergeant Charles M. Eyer is aboard and in his assigned position for takeoff. In the silence he detects a faint odor of high-octane aviation gasoline. He and his crewmates exchange only a few words as they wait for the signal to start their engines. Suddenly there is a whine as the first engine turns over, sputters and coughs, and with a small cloud of oil smoke comes to life. Then the next engine whines and starts and soon all four of the massive engines are running loudly. Within a minute or two the entire bomb group's engines rumble in the predawn air at the airbase.

The brakes are released and the engines begin to roar even louder. The noise is deafening, making conversation almost impossible. The entire bomber vibrates and shakes as the pilot guns the engines. The brakes, which are used to steer the plane, squeal loudly as the pilot maneuvers his bomber on the tarmac. Engines rev, then slow down, and then rev again as the B-17 Flying Fortress moves into position. One by one, the young men move their lethal bombers into position for takeoff. The noise is incredibly loud as the pilot pushes the throttle controls to full speed. The bomber bounces and groans as it barrels down the runway until it reaches takeoff speed of 120 mph.

The first B-17 speeds down the runway and lifts into the air. Another bomber follows, quickly followed by another and another until all bombers leave the safety of the ground. Charlie and the crew are flying toward dangerous enemy territory and ultimately into harm's way. People on the ground watch the bombers gradually grow faint until they disappear, off to face a deadly and determined enemy.

For Charlie and the other young men aboard the bomber, life consisted of flying their missions until they were either killed, captured, or completed enough missions to return home. Some had a better chance of surviving than others but, when flying a combat mission, none of them really knew for sure if they would ever complete their tour. They all had their doubts, and they all asked the same questions. Is this the day that my luck runs out? Or will it be the next mission? How long will my luck hold out? What are my odds of surviving? Are my chances influenced by bravery, skill, or some kind of personal lucky charm? They lived with these questions and struggled to find answers.

The likelihood of something bad happening was very real and disturbing. Bombers flew into each other in midair and tumbled to the earth on fire, burning the crew alive. Some, weighed down with heavy loads of bombs and fuel, crashed on takeoff and exploded or burned up. Enemy fighters and antiaircraft shot down thousands of American bombers, killing and wounding many airmen. The best Charlie could hope for if he was shot down was to escape and evade the enemy.

The B-17 Flying Fortress was registered by the United States Army Air Force (USAAF) as a "heavy" bombardment airplane. It was a long-range heavy bomber whose function during World War II was daylight precision strategic bombardment. Targets were carefully selected and their primary mission was to destroy the enemy's ability to make war, to make it very difficult for the enemy to fight by denying them materiel and resources.

A lot of discussion took place about the effectiveness of bombing during the war. In the European Theater of Operations, the USAAF focused its efforts on disrupting the German war machine by attacking factories, airfields, railroad marshaling yards, and oil installations, among other targets. Accuracy of American bombers was surely overhyped. Despite what some considered poor accuracy, postwar occupation forces discovered that German industry and infrastructure were in shambles. A large portion of that destruction was the result of the steady bombing by our forces.

High altitude strategic bombing was a new kind of warfare. The know-how needed to conduct this type of air war was not possible until World War II and, astonishingly, by the end of the war, was already rendered obsolete by jets, missiles, and the atomic bomb. In the thin, freezing air of high altitude, airmen fought and died in an environment that had never been experienced by combatants before. It was aerial combat fought not at low altitudes, as before, but at high altitudes where nature could kill a man faster than the enemy could. High in the sky the cold killed and the air was unbreathable. These new battle conditions added new features to combat, conditions that fighting men had not previously experienced.

Thousands of USAAF bomber losses in Europe were because of antiaircraft artillery fire, commonly referred to during the war as flak, which is an abbreviation for the German word *Flugzeugabwehrkanone*. Flak guns fired into the area where the bombers were expected to fly instead of targeting individual planes. This was devastating because the Norden bombsight used by the USAAF, and designed for precision bombing of targets, required that the final bomb run be made without any change in course. As a result, the bombers had to fly directly through dense flak barrages. Survival was just pure luck.

For Charlie and many other combat airmen, flying and fighting were strange. Before the war, many of the men had never been in an airplane or fired a gun. Bomber warfare was irregular, with times of inactivity followed by short periods of intense combat. The job of a bomber crew can be described as hours of boredom with a few minutes of sheer terror. Charlie, a young man in his early 20s, could be fighting for his life over Frankfurt at 10 o'clock in the morning and be drinking a beer at the NCO club that evening. Some infantrymen were envious of the airmen's comforts. This new type of bombing was explained to Americans as a quicker, more decisive way of winning the war than grinding it out on the ground, but in the end, the air war was a slow and brutal battle of attrition.

The USAAF was an elite organization and was mostly made up of volunteers. Some highly qualified men who had been drafted were quickly snapped up by Air Force recruiters before being assigned to the ground forces. Bomber crewmen came from every part of the country and from nearly every lifestyle. There were college graduates and factory workers, accountants and farmers, movie stars and famous athletes. Movie stars Jimmy Stewart and Clark Gable flew on B-17s. They fought alongside men who had built skyscrapers in Chicago or mined coal in Pennsylvania.

Just like submarine crews and Luftwaffe pilots the bomber crews battled in aerial combat, Charlie and his buddies had one of the most dangerous jobs of the war. In the fall of 1943, less than one out of four Air Force bomber crew members flying out of England could expect to complete his tour of duty of 25 combat missions. Two-thirds of the airmen either died in combat or were taken prisoner of war. By the end of World War II, the Eighth Air Force alone had more than 26,000 men killed in action. This was more than the entire United States Marine Corps suffered during World War II. Before the invasion of Normandy, 77 percent of the Americans who flew against Germany became casualties! In 1944, just during the months of March through May, 987 crews were lost. Charlie was shot down during that period.

Prior to the war, the top generals foresaw this type of warfare as a battle of machines against machines with hardly any human contact. But on every mission over Europe, Charlie and many other airmen who were shot down met the enemy face to face before a single American infantryman had set foot on the European continent. Aerial combat could be just as ugly as ground combat. In some furious air battles, opposing planes were so close to each other that they could clearly see the faces of their foes.

Charlie didn't think much about dying. He focused on what he had to do to protect his bomber and his buddies. He would try to drive everything else from his mind. Sure, he was frightened, but there's a difference between fear and panic. Panic would have paralyzed him, while fear energized him. For Charlie and many others, the chief fear they experienced in the war was the fear that they would let their buddies down.

Through experience and experimentation the bomber crews learned to fight the air war. Each flight was an opportunity to learn, and it was uniquely different from that of ground troops. During aerial combat the bombers couldn't report back to headquarters with information to change the battle plan. Aerial combat was too fast paced for that and they were too far away from headquarters. These were the reasons why the commander leading a mission had power and authority far outside his age, rank, and experience.

There were no reinforcements to send, and almost every mission was a maximum effort, with every bomber capable of flying put into the air. The airmen, after fighting their way to the target, had to fight their way back. In the air, the crew was basically alone and had to make their own decisions if the mission's plan fell apart, as it often did in combat.

Charlie's job, and that of the rest of his crewmates flying in a B-17, was to strike military targets. They did this with skill and courage. They knew fear, horror, and death. Whatever their different pre-war backgrounds, they all hated the war but loved their bomber and each other. When he was asked, he claimed the Flying Fortress "the best plane of the war." It could take unbelievable punishment and still bring them home. With wings full of holes and engines out, the tail shredded, and with pieces of its aluminum body full of holes, the B-17 brought them home. This great aircraft, shattered and torn beyond the seeming limits of the ability to fly, carried them to safety, and during a few missions for Charlie, to life itself.

Introduction

Describing the valor of Charlie and his crewmates is hard to do. After these many decades we can look back with some objectivity at what they did during the war. But whatever the arguments might be, nobody can question that the men in the heavy bombers made victory possible. They shortened the war, but paid a very heavy price doing so.

Placing himself in peril, Charlie fought many miles above the earth. He shared not only the risks that the ground troops encountered in combat but also had to contend with the elements of being in the sky. There was no ground to dig into when the shooting was hot and heavy. If his oxygen system failed or his electrically heated suit failed, he might die. And then there was gravity, the constant force pulling them downward. Many times he didn't even have the satisfaction of shooting back at those who were trying to kill him. It was a dreadful demonstration of the odds of chance as he passed through flak bursts. Despite these dangers, he and the others went up day after day. Some returned, and some didn't, but they believed in what they were doing and completed the job.

Charlie didn't believe war was heroic. He knew the war was horrible and war in the air was no exception. The air war was a deadly business and entire aircrews often went to their deaths. He and his crewmates flew missions with these facts being powerfully and violently brought home to them. On many missions he watched both friends and the enemy die in the same fight. Sitting in minus-40-degree temperatures at high altitude he saw friendly bombers and enemy fighters burst into flames and go down. He sweated under his flight suit. The sweat of fear. A bone chilling type of fear.

On Charlie's last combat mission, a strong and fierce attack by scores of German fighters came straight on and through the American bomber formation. Including his plane, he watched enemy gunfire tear into the bombers. He saw bombers catch on fire and pieces falling off. There was little left of some of the bombers, and some blew up in the sky.

It was a miracle that he and his crewmates survived as the German fighters tore their bomber to shreds, causing it to catch on fire and eventually explode in the sky. It was a sickening sight. From other bombers burning bodies fell, some falling without a parachute. In some cases crew members did not have time to put on their parachutes or forgot them in their panic to get out of a burning bomber. Many jumped to their deaths. Charlie knew some of the men on those doomed bombers that day. Back at the base the night before some may have been with him, playing cards or sharing a beer. Now they were dead or dying in the skies over enemy territory. Such was war.

Charlie and his buddies understood that war in the air meant killing or being killed. You either returned from a mission to fly another day, or you just didn't come back. I don't know if the story of these brave men has ever been satisfactorily told, but only those men who experienced it can truly tell the story of aerial combat in World War II.

It is impossible for many veterans to remember combat without some degree of emotion. Sometimes remembering the pain can help to heal. Charlie had the courage to tell us his story about his experience as a gunner on a Flying Fortress crew. His service was the most exhilarating, frightening, gratifying, and prideful days of his life, and he had shared them with some of the finest men he ever knew.

What is the ultimate purpose of remembering, knowing, and understanding the service and experiences of Charlie and the other American combat airmen in World War II? If Charlie was with us today he'd probably say that there are thousands of survival stories just as amazing as his own. I just hope that future generations never forget the dedication and sacrifice of Charlie and the other combat airmen who preserved our freedom.

Historical and technical content are important and as accurate as I could record them herein. However, the emphasis is upon Staff Sergeant Charles M. Eyer and his 59 combat missions as a ball turret gunner in a B-17 Flying Fortress. The memories of his wartime experiences remained strong. The war was the single most important and formative experience of his life and, like it or not, the memories could never be erased. Some experiences left little or no impression on him, but there were some experiences that touched his inner core, which marked and changed him for life. War experiences usually cut deep and permanently change a person's attitude and outlook on life. In Charlie's words, "I was never the same after the war. It changed me."

We must not forget what Charlie did, and his story of survival lives on with this book. This book cannot give Charlie the full recognition he deserves. His survival and war exploits are timeless and true. He is more than worthy, as are his fellow bomber crewmen worthy of having their story recorded. Charles M. Eyer was the bravest man I have personally known.

Chapter 1

Pre-War Life

Charles M. Eyer was born on August 23, 1921, in Hamburg, Pennsylvania, to parents Walter W. Eyer and Sarah Elsie Fink, the fourth of seven sons. The family lived on Franklin Street in Hamburg. Tragedy struck early in Charlie's life when his younger brother Edgar, the fifth son, died suddenly at the age of nine. The Eyer family was very close-knit, which helped them get through this tragic loss and the traumatic events yet to come.

In the 1920s and through the 1940s Hamburg was a small town, much as it is today, the kind of small town where everybody knows everybody else, a community predominately populated by folks of German ancestry, commonly referred to as Pennsylvania Dutch. The Eyer family was undeniably part of that proud heritage. Charlie had many close friends as he grew up in Hamburg, which included the Bachmans, the Henrys, the Repperts, and the Kellers, and one of their favorite pastimes was playing in the "Senny" creek. He also liked hanging out at Rip's Corner, drinking Coke and eating the best hotdogs in town.

When his father was seriously injured in an automobile accident, resulting in his inability to fully provide for the family, Charlie had to help. Because he had to work to help support the family, he only finished 8th grade. His mother, in addition to taking care of her husband, the six boys, and keeping house, washed clothes for other people in order to make ends meet.

Charlie's first full-time job came at age 16, working at a diner located at Franklin and State streets in Hamburg. Being a short order cook was something he really loved doing, and that love stayed with him throughout his life. His children and grandchildren delighted in his cooking and said he made the best French toast and egg omelets they ever tasted. His love of cooking continued long after the war, and he enjoyed cooking for the Hamburg Army National Guard unit at their annual clambake. He was always the guy behind the grill, cooking up hamburgers, hotdogs, and steaks. He loved supporting the troops in that way, and the soldiers adored, appreciated, and respected him.

The Japanese attack on Pearl Harbor was a huge shock. Politicians from both political parties, those wanting to get into the war and those who wanted to stay out of war, and people from all walks of life came together as one. The country moved from peace to war with unity seldom seen, and on December 8, 1941, President Roosevelt appeared before a joint session of Congress and asked for a declaration of war against Japan. Congress responded quickly with only a single vote against going to war. Three days later, Germany declared war on the United States, a bad decision on their part, and one that would prove disastrous for them.

During World War II, four of the Eyer sons served in the military. Raymond, the oldest, was a master sergeant and the car-master for the Hamburg unit (121st Quartermaster Car Company) of the Pennsylvania Army National Guard.[1] His unit deployed to England in February 1942, and occasionally he was the chauffer for General Dwight D. Eisenhower. Brother John was drafted at the age of 24, even though he had four children. He was assigned as a tank instructor at the U.S. Army Armor School at Fort Knox, Kentucky, and never deployed overseas. Brother Lester was also drafted, trained as an infantryman and sent to the Pacific Theater of Operations, where he was severely wounded when he was hit in the shoulder by shrapnel from a Japanese mortar round. The wound crippled his arm and he was shipped back to the United States where, after recovering, he was discharged. The four brothers never had any direct contact with each other throughout the war. The only news they received about one another was through letters with their mother who passed on any new information.

Then there was Charlie, who didn't wait to be drafted. He volunteered and enlisted in the U.S. Army Air Force (USAAF), even though he only ever flew once in his life. In spite of the extreme dangers, hundreds of thousands of young men volunteered to be combat airmen. In fact, almost all combat airmen were volunteers. He wanted to fly combat, was eager to do so, and worked extremely hard to become qualified.

Once in combat, he withstood the extreme rigors of aerial combat until he was eventually shot down and captured. He endured grave danger because of pride and comradeship. He had pride in his training and his ability to accomplish the job. These traits made him proficient in aerial combat and kept him calm in the midst of danger. But mostly, he endured all of this for his crewmates, his buddies. The extreme danger of aerial combat in World War II and the teamwork required to survive forged deep bonds and unshakable brotherhood among combat airmen.

A pilot from Reading, Pennsylvania, who owned a bi-plane came to Hamburg once a year and gave people rides. He always landed on a farm sitting on top of a hill, which today is North Fifth Street in Hamburg, and there the local townspeople came to see the airplane. One year Charlie was there with some of his friends when the plane arrived. When one of the other kids who was scheduled to take a ride chickened out, the pilot asked Charlie if he would like a ride. Without hesitation he replied, "Sure, I'll go," and climbed into the front open cockpit and enjoyed every minute as they circled Hamburg.

He could not have known on that day of the aerial exploits that awaited him in the near future. As a young man, he was about to be quickly, intensely, and forcefully thrust into full manhood. Before completing 59 combat missions and before the end of the war, Charlie learned that valor was a way of life. He also learned that his two primary objectives were to perform his job well and to survive.

CHAPTER 2

The Making of a Gunner

The U.S Army Air Force (USAAF), sometimes referred to as the Army Air Corps, was part of the Army during World War II. It was an incredible task classifying, assigning, and training hundreds of thousands of men in the first 18 months of the war. But they got it done by using assembly line production methods, and it became an elite organization with its own uniforms, badges, and insignia. The USAAF was very appealing to young men wanting to fly and those who felt drawn to the dangers of flying.

In late May of 1942, Charlie traveled to Reading, Pennsylvania, with every intention of joining the United States Marine Corps. He wanted to be a Marine, but they refused to take him because he had flat feet. However, he was determined to enlist because he knew he would be drafted very soon. So undeterred, he walked in to the Army Air Force office in the Reading courthouse and enlisted. "I figured I could be a mechanic in the Air Force, if nothing else. That was my first choice, to be a mechanic. I passed all the tests and was ready to go." Charles M. Eyer was 20 years old at time of enlistment and would turn 21 in August of 1942.

They came from nearly every town, city, and state in the country. These volunteers were the sons of the rich, the poor, and everyone in between. But regardless of their background or what part of the country they came from, they had one thing in common. They wanted to fight and win the war. Charlie worked very hard to be part of that which would achieve final victory. He trained very hard to prove himself and earn his wings. Those wings were his ticket to aerial combat.

Only men who volunteered for aerial combat were accepted for training. Recruits were not drafted and forced to be a combat airman, but somehow there never was a shortage of young men willing to risk life and limb in aerial combat. It is hard to conceive the young age of the men who performed those hazardous flying jobs, and many of them were teenagers. It was USAAF policy during the war to accept only men between the ages of 18 and 27. Anyone older than that had most likely been in the military before the war or was a high-ranking officer. Most combat airmen were in their late teens or early to middle 20s, and it was not uncommon for every man on a bomber crew to be under 21 years of age.

Charlie left home for military service on June 1, 1942. The stress on his parents was great. "I knew my mother and dad would not want to take me to Reading." A friend volunteered to take him to the train station under one condition. When the train came in to the station, there would be no long goodbyes, he would just leave. His friend knew he would break down, so he said his goodbyes before the train arrived. Philadelphia was the first stop that afternoon and where he and the other new servicemen received a very brief physical examination.

Then it was back on the train. The train arrived at Fort Lee, Virginia, about 1:00 a.m. They were taken off the train, put into a barracks for the night, and awakened just four hours later at 5:00 a.m. Fort Lee was a processing center where they received some orientation training such as military rank identification, military courtesy, and so on. Also while at Fort Lee, Charlie and the other new recruits received a more thorough physical examination.

He was ordered to remove all clothing and then processed through a series of stations where an examination of a different part of the anatomy took place. During this physical examination, Charlie was part of a gaggle of nude men who followed signs, arrows, and lines on the floor directing him from station to station where he was tapped, poked, groped, and looked at. The only verbal instructions he received were "bend over and spread your cheeks" and "turn your head and cough." Finally, after the lengthy ordeal was over, a doctor told Charlie to go to room A. As he entered the room everyone was cheering because they had passed the physical examination. The recruits sent to room B found out that they were not qualified for the USAAF.

Later, as Charlie and the other recruits were standing in formation, an officer spoke to the group, informing them that men were needed for the infantry. He told them that some men from the group would be reassigned. The officer proceeded to go through the formation, selecting recruits, men who previously volunteered for the USAAF, and pulled them from the ranks. The selected recruits were sent off to infantry school and Charlie never saw them again. He was very happy that he was not selected for the infantry.

While at Fort Lee, he and a buddy received weekend passes and decided to go downtown. While downtown they saw some men in uniform getting into a car, and Charlie noticed that the car had a flat tire. Being a brand-new recruit, and not yet quite understanding military courtesy, he approached the car and said to a passenger, "Hey, Bub, do you know that you have a flat tire?" Now, anyone knowing anything about the military and rank certainly knows that you should never call a lieutenant "Bub," which was the case here, and Lieutenant "Bub" immediately and firmly reprimanded Private Eyer, who would not make that mistake again.

Processing at Fort Lee was about a week in duration, after which Charlie shipped out by train to Keesler Field near Biloxi, Mississippi. At Keesler he underwent six weeks of basic training. Keesler Field was opened as a USAAF technical training base in 1941 but was soon expanded to include an Army basic training facility. Basic training during World War II was four weeks long, although he was there for a total of six weeks. The training included physical fitness, weapons use and care, military discipline and courtesy, first aid, and close order drill.

Charlie was quickly introduced to life in the military which included barracks cleaning. "I was on my hands and knees, scrubbing the floor, and moving in a backwards direction, when someone came tearing into the barracks and across my just cleaned floor. Not turning to see who it was, I remarked that he should find another entrance. Now I was in trouble. It was a major! After that day it seemed I was always assigned the task of cleaning the barracks."

Upon nearing the completion of basic training, and while walking around the base, he saw a tent with a sign hanging on it that said something about turrets. "Since I didn't even know what a turret was, I was fascinated and decided to find out what they were." Inside the tent Charlie talked to a sergeant who explained what a turret was and asked if he'd like to get in one and operate it. The sergeant explained to him that if he was really interested in being a turret gunner he had to put his name on a list. He replied, "I am looking for excitement and I think I'll put my name on the list." The sergeant told him that he would be contacted in two days for a physical examination. Charlie recalled, "I could have been a mechanic and stayed on the ground, and safe, but I signed the papers anyway." His buddies were amazed that he signed up to fly because they all knew the dangers involved.

Two days later a sergeant came into the barracks shouting Charlie's name and told him to immediately pack his gear and fall outside. When he got outside he was told to get on a truck with his gear, and that truck

2. The Making of a Gunner

took him and some other men to a railroad station. His destination was Tampa, Florida, and gunnery school, and he arrived there near the end of July. Bomber crewmen received individual training first and then team training. Enlisted combat airmen usually performed one of three duties: gunner, radio operator, or flight engineer.

Charlie's objective in gunnery school was to learn not just how to shoot machine guns but also how to engage moving targets. The best way to learn this and become proficient was to go up in a plane and shoot at a long cloth sleeve towed by another airplane. This was thrilling for the gunnery students. However, the pilots did not exactly consider flying a target plane good duty. Luckily, accidents were rare. In addition to gunnery training, those men designated to be radio operators and flight engineers attended those specific schools and learned their specialized jobs. Failure rates in gunnery and the specialty schools were low.

Charlie recalled, "Gunnery school was six weeks in duration, and a rough ordeal, especially for those who never flew before. We spent a lot of time skeet and trap shooting, to include shooting doubles. The instructors were teaching us timing. All gunnery training was on the ground at that point, with no flying. After the first week we all had black and blue shoulders from shooting shotguns for eight hours a day. Starting with the second week of training they took us up flying."

"We were told that anyone who threw up in the plane would have to

Private Charles Eyer at the completion of basic training at Keesler Field, Biloxi, Mississippi, June 1942.

clean it up and would be flunked out of gunnery school and not qualified to fly. The first flight was simple enough with no wild maneuvers. We just sort of flew around. During the second flight the pilot did some dives and twisting. That day I was sick, but I was determined that I was not going to throw up, even if it killed me! The vomit came up into my throat, but I just held it back. After we landed, and as soon as the plane was on the ground, I felt pretty good again. The pilot looked into my area of the plane for vomit, didn't see any, and said okay."

"During the third flight the pilot flew upside down and performed some barrel rolls. The pilot asked me if I had seen the German submarine that was sunk just off of the coast. I said I had not. The pilot said, 'Well, you'll see it today,' and just like that he dove straight down and only pulled out of the steep dive just before we would have hit the water. I felt ill, but not bad enough to throw up. I kept fighting the sick feeling until I eventually got over it. After getting through that part of the training without throwing up, I then went on to advanced training." It was very important that a combat airman not suffer from motion sickness. Throwing up inside their oxygen mask during a combat mission could prove fatal.

The planes used for gunnery training had an open cockpit, as Charlie explained. "They then removed the seat from the rear part of the plane where the gunner sat and put a machine gun in it. I wore a harness with a strap connected to a ring in the floor, and I had to stand with spread legs over that ring to balance myself. I had to stand like that and shoot. I was standing in a moving plane, and sometimes flying upside down, while firing a machine gun. We didn't aim at anything specific, just fired into the air. If you shot the plane you were in, you were out of gunnery school! This flying was done out over the water of the Gulf of Mexico."

"When we weren't flying, we were shooting .50 caliber machine guns at moving targets. They used a jeep that was protected behind an earthen berm and it pulled a wooden target airplane. Every gunner had color-coded ammunition to distinguish his hits from the other gunners firing at the target. That way the instructors could tell who was hitting and who was missing the target. If someone didn't qualify, it was off to the infantry! They would change the speed of the target. Might be 40 mph or maybe as fast as 60 mph. I fired both air-cooled and water-cooled machine guns. The first targets I shot at were stationary paper targets and used a .22 caliber water-cooled machine gun. I also fired from the air at stationary targets on the ground and from the air at moving targets. I scored well all the way through the course."

The training was long and hard. "It was fascinating doing all the shooting, sometimes for 10 hours a day. Using flash cards, we spent many hours training to identify all types of airplanes. I also had a lot of other classes and sometimes 12- to 16-hour-long days. A typical day was eight hours of flying, four hours of classes, and two hours of recreation. It was mandatory to participate in some form of recreation. Training was every day, seven days a week. It was a rough course but I graduated from gunnery school." Charlie had earned his wings.

"Upon graduation I was promoted to sergeant. My pay as a private had only been $21 a month. Being promoted to sergeant, plus getting flying pay on top of that, I was now paid $78 a month and was set. I sent some of that money to help the family back home. I was supposed to get a 10-day leave after gunnery school, but that never happened."

Equipment was pre-positioned at Orlando, Florida, for a bomber group which had no assigned personnel as of June 1, 1942. This equipment would soon belong to the 99th Bombardment Group (Heavy), which was being activated.[1] "The day after graduation I was back on a train and going to Homestead Air Force Base in Florida. There they were putting crews together at random, and we started flying. This was the first phase of combat training but was not with the crew I would eventually go into combat alongside. I was at Homestead for about a month."

It was there that Charlie found out that he would be assigned to a B-17 Flying Fortress. This made him very happy because one of the most dependable bombers was the B-17. It would become legendary for its ability to reach a target and bring its crew home in spite of severe damage.

Sergeant Charles Eyer attending gunnery school at Tampa, Florida, September 1942.

Compared to other heavy bombers, it was well designed and had very few mechanical issues. The airmen were mostly concerned about an airplane's reliability, toughness, and dependability, because those things could mean life or death to them. The B-17 had all those qualities which gave the crews a lot of faith in their aircraft.

They moved after completing their initial flying training. "From Florida we went by train to Boise, Idaho. The 99th Bomb Group was formed at Boise, and Colonel Upthegrove was the group commander." Colonel Faye R. Upthegrove was assigned as the group commander, and Lieutenant Colonel Leroy A. Rainey was the deputy group commander. Charlie was assigned to the 416th Bombardment Squadron.

Almost immediately the group commander made some changes. "A normal B-17 crew had 10 airmen, but the group commander decided to have only nine crew members. He eliminated one of the waist gunner positions because we would be flying very tight formations and a second waist gunner would be unable to engage targets. Tight formation flying was very important on missions because very little fighter escort protection was available."

The crew that Charlie would become part of was formed at that time. The nine-member crew consisted of Captain John Thistlewood (pilot), Lieutenant Steve Amundson (co-pilot), Lieutenant Jack Strasberg (navigator), Lieutenant Brayton Fisher (bombardier), Staff Sergeant Farron Daniels (flight engineer/top turret gunner), Staff Sergeant Mike Mazu (radio operator), Staff Sergeant Charles Eyer (ball turret gunner), Sergeant Charles Fallon (waist gunner), and Staff Sergeant Beauford Lippolt (tail gunner).

The positions of pilot, co-pilot, navigator, and bombardier were all commissioned officers. With the exception of the pilot, which was typically a captain, all other positions were lieutenants. The men called the pilot either "Skipper," "Captain," "Boss," or "Old Man." These were names of respect because of his status as the bomber's commanding officer. While he had to be skilled in flying the bomber, he also had to be a good leader or the crew wouldn't have faith in his abilities during aerial combat.

The co-pilot was second in command, the executive officer, and shared flying duties with the pilot. If the pilot was killed or incapacitated, he would take over as commander. During routine ground operations, he supervised the various aircrew tasks. He was the main point of contact for coordinating aircrew tasks during combat missions.

The navigator was third in the chain of command. He was responsible for plotting the course to and from a target. His job was almost as great as the pilot's, and he continually had to take readings, make computations, and maintain a log.

The bombardier was fourth in the bomber chain of command. It can be argued that his job was the most important one because he had to put the bombs on the target. He was the man who would rain death and destruction upon the enemy.

All enlisted crewmen were non-commissioned officers (NCOs). The USAAF had a rule that enlisted crewmen could not fly combat missions unless they held the rank of staff sergeant or higher. This was required because if they were shot down and captured, NCOs received better treatment from the Germans. Also, the USAAF rewarded their combat fliers with a higher rank because of their highly specialized and extremely hazardous jobs.

The flight engineer/top turret gunner was the systems specialist and typically the senior NCO of the crew. He had to possess an extraordinary mechanical ability and had to have extensive knowledge of the bomber. His secondary job was manning the top turret.

The radio operator maintained communications with the outside world. He had the most understated job of the crew. Stuck in his small compartment, with a very limited view of the outside world, he had to man the radio as aerial combat raged all around.

The waist gunner's main job was to engage attacking fighters. He also had some additional duties such as arming the bombs, maintenance of the guns, and ensuring that there was enough ammunition for the mission.

The tail gunner, located in his isolated and very tight compartment, protected the bomber from an attack from the rear. His was a very important position because many times the bomber was attacked from the rear. Rarely did they return from a combat mission without the tail gunner having engaged enemy fighters.

Then there was Charlie, the ball turret gunner. Many men considered the job of ball turret gunner the most awful position on a B-17 bomber crew, but he loved being in that tiny sphere. The Flying Fortress was equipped with a turret under the belly with the purpose of protecting the bomber's vulnerable underside. This position required a man with a whole bunch of courage, of small physical build, and who was not too claustrophobic to fly inside the tiny turret.

It also required a brave man who wasn't worried about not being able to wear a parachute while in the ball. That was Charlie. He sat in a semi-seated position on a cast iron seat, knees up, with one hand on each gun, and viewed the outside through small Plexiglas windows. His hands held onto two handles which were used to rotate the turret, and his thumbs were on the machine gun triggers.

Charlie said the ball was the best gunner position on the bomber. So cramped was the gunner's position that for many men it was impossible for them to stay in it for long flights. If the occupant didn't fear how he viewed the world far below, the ball provided an amazing vantage point. This Plexiglas ball was one of many new innovations brought about by the war. An ingenious piece of equipment, the ball turret was a heavily armed bubble just large enough to hold a grown man. There was just enough room for the gunner and two .50 caliber machine guns and nothing else.

Charlie sat curled up in a fetal position and swiveled the entire turret as he aimed the two .50 caliber machine guns. He could swiftly move the turret to locate attacking planes as he followed them with his guns. He would be in every position from lying on his back to standing on his feet. He sat between the guns, his feet in stirrups positioned on either side of a 13-inch-diameter window in front, his knees bent and no room to move anything but his hands. His flight suit provided the only padding for comfort.

Being in the ball gave Charlie a great view of the scenery below, which, by the way, included fighter planes racing skyward to kill him. To him it seemed that the attacking fighters were going after him personally rather than trying to shoot down the bomber itself. In that tiny glass sphere of the ball turret he furiously fired his .50 caliber machine guns at the enemy fighters as they tried to kill him.

Visibility in the turret was restricted, and he needed the cooperation from other crew members to provide the location of enemy fighters. An optical gunsight hung in front of his face, and a pedal under his left foot adjusted a reticle on the gunsight glass. When an enemy fighter was framed in the sight, he knew it was in range and he fired the machine guns. The shell casings were ejected through a port just below the gun barrel. The bomber carried a minimum of 250 to 300 rounds of ammunition per gun for the ball turret. The ammunition was fed down from boxes mounted on either side of the ball turret mounting inside the fuselage.

One problem of being in the ball turret was that if the bomber was hit, and the plane spiraled out of control, there was no way Charlie could have gotten out of the turret. Even if he could have, he was not wearing a parachute. While flying over the target, he often spun the ball to position the door inside the fuselage. Sometimes he opened the door to help him

2. The Making of a Gunner

to get out of the ball quickly should the bomber be hit by flak. The only movement he had was to cross his hands or his lower legs. It was really cramped, and he knew that if the bomber was hit and went out of control, there was a slim chance of him escaping.

There was no toilet in the ball, just a relief tube. If he could undo all his flying clothes, heated suit, and so on, he might be able to urinate if he dared. Many ball turret gunners just urinated inside their flying suit. If this seems like a horrible place to be, it was! But not to Charlie.

Charlie knew the stories of ball turret gunners trapped in their glass bubbles because battle damage prevented them from exiting the ball into the fuselage. Not only could the gunner be left out there with no protection, his machine guns could be out of ammunition or not working. Worst of all, he faced the prospect of the large bomber having to land with him hanging from the belly.

Charlie recalled an instance when another ball turret gunner was nearly blown out of his turret at a very high altitude. His turret door flew off and only a toe of one of his flying boots, which was hooked under the range pedal of his guns, kept the gunner from being sucked out. His oxygen and intercom cables were cut and he lost communication with the rest of the crew. Somehow he managed to pull himself back into the ball and attracted the attention of a crewman who cranked him back inside the fuselage.

Andy Rooney, a reporter for the paper *Stars and Stripes*, who actually flew on some bomber combat missions over Europe, reported on the death of a ball turret gunner who was trapped in his ball turret. "The gears that rotated the ball to put the gunner in position to shoot and then return him to the position that enabled him to climb out and back up into the aircraft had been shot and were jammed. The ball-turret gunner was caught in a plastic cage." Just before landing the B-17's hydraulic system, which was riddled with shell holes, failed, making it impossible for the pilot to put down the wheels. The emergency hand crank for operating the main landing gear had also been destroyed. The pilot would have to make a belly landing. "There were eight minutes of gut-wrenching talk among the tower, the pilot, and the man trapped in the ball turret. He knew what comes down first when there are no wheels. We watched as this man's life ended, mashed between the concrete pavement of the runway and the belly of the bomber."[2]

Besides having one less waist gunner in Charlie's bomber, other changes took place. "I was actually training as a tail gunner until we got to Boise. Sergeant Beauford Lippolt was assigned as the ball turret gunner, but he couldn't stand being in the ball during flights of eight hours or longer. He was too big for the ball. So he asked me if I wanted to switch from the tail gunner position to the ball turret. Being in the ball turret suited me just fine and I agreed to the switch. But first we had to get approval from the pilot, Captain T-Wood [John Thistlewood; Charlie and the rest of the crew referred to Captain Thistlewood as T-Wood], plus I would need special training on the .50 caliber machine guns."

"I had to be an expert at disassembly and assembly, maintenance, head-space and timing, nomenclature of all parts and components, and pass a test. I even had to be able to disassemble and assemble a .50 caliber machine gun while blind-folded. When I passed the final test, and was fully qualified, I then flew in the ball turret after that time." I can personally attest to Charlie's expertise and skill when it came to .50 caliber machine guns. He could still quickly and correctly disassemble and assemble the machine gun almost 40 years after the end of the war!

The training was almost constant for Charlie and crew. "After the 99th Bomb Group [99th BG] was formed, we spent about a month training at Boise which included night training. We flew one long practice flight from Boise to Barksdale, Louisiana, then to Chicago, Illinois, and then back to Boise. We normally flew at 30,000 feet. I liked seeing the large cities at night from above and thought it was just a beautiful sight." The training was demanding, but the airmen were treated well on the ground. "The mess hall at Boise was great, with long tables that were fully set, and the food was served to us family style."

Because there were too many bombers at Boise, the 99th BG left Gowen Field for Walla Walla, Washington, on September 25, 1942. "We took a train to Walla Walla, Washington, and when we arrived there the weather was bad." The advance party and some of the equipment also arrived at that time. With the rest of the cadre now there by the end of September the real work of the group started. In addition, more ground personnel also arrived from Salt Lake City Army Air Base Replacement Center in Utah.[3]

Espionage and sabotage were a major concern and a real threat, even in the United States. "During one training exercise as the planes were getting ready to take off, many engines started sputtering and quitting. The control tower quickly cancelled all flights and the training mission was scrubbed. The FBI was called in and they discovered that a mechanic on a gasoline truck had put sugar in the gasoline. He was a German. They had to replace many engines, but the next day we received brand new planes." It would have been disastrous had those bombers taken off before the engine failures occurred. Washington State turned out to be a very bad location for training bomber crews. "We left Walla Walla after a couple of weeks because the weather there was too bad for flying."

Because of poor flying weather, the group moved from Walla Walla to Sioux City, Iowa, to complete its second phase of training. The group was already scheduled to take its third phase of training at Sioux City. This move took place in the middle of November 1942. "Then it was off to Sioux City, Iowa, were it was snow, snow, and more snow, and very cold." Here more aircraft and crews were added to the group, and they also increased the ground crew strength to about 75 percent. By November 18, the 99th BG really became a working group. The 99th BG lost its first crew and aircraft during a training accident on November 30 when a B-17 crashed three miles from the field. "There were a lot of accidents happening at that base."

Sergeant Charles Eyer while stationed at Sioux City, Iowa, December 1942.

Regardless of accidents and fatalities, the training continued. "The second phase of training at Boise was mostly bombing and target practice, but at Sioux City, the training was mostly for the pilots. We did a lot of formation flying. The bombing ranges were in Nebraska and other places. We dropped practice bombs that were filled with colored sand for identification of hits."

"All members of the crew had to know how to fly the plane. But we never learned how to either land or takeoff the plane. Just learned enough to keep the plane in the air should the pilot and co-pilot become incapacitated. When possible, each crew member was allowed to fly the plane over their home state, and I did fly the plane over Pennsylvania. The pilot also had to be qualified in flying in complete darkness, and they would cover the cockpit windows with canvas to simulate nighttime, even though they were flying during daylight. The pilot had to rely on his instruments and a radio signal beam for navigation. Captain T-Wood passed the test."

In addition to all the other important flying instruction, intensive training in oxygen procedures was one of the most important. A failure in the oxygen supply could cause anoxia which would result in unconsciousness in a few minute and death after 10 minutes at high altitudes. Anoxia was a sneaky condition in which a crewman was often unaware that it was happening to him, because the early stages made the victim feel elated and overconfident. Charlie especially took the oxygen training seriously. Being enclosed in the ball turret prevented the crew from seeing him should he come down with anoxia. He was all alone in that sense.

Another serious problem was extremely cold temperatures when flying at high altitudes. Temperatures were often 30 to 40 degrees below zero, and the windows frequently froze up due to the severe cold. The inside of the fuselage resembled the inside of a freezer, white with frost. The B-17 was an unpressurized aircraft, and the extreme, piercing cold was a constant source of misery and concern. If Charlie did not dress warmly enough, he could get frostbite or even freeze to death. For bomber aircrews in the European theater, warm, layered clothing was absolutely necessary to protect them from the extreme cold.

Charlie chuckled, "The government turned over an airplane to basically a bunch of teenagers! What could go wrong?!" The purpose of the third and final phase of training was to combine individual and collective training to create a crew that would function as a team. This transformation was as much a psychological process as it was advanced technical training. The development of a crew identity required that the airmen come together. Coming together as one was crucial in order to develop trust in the judgment and performance of the other crew members during difficult and dangerous circumstances.

The crew was not afraid of pushing the limits of both the bomber and their authority. "One day a month they would let us fly what was called 'free flying.' We could go anywhere we wanted to for an eight-hour time period. One day we were kidding each other about going down and landing on a four-lane highway. T-Wood said let's go down and look the situation over. So he dropped down to about 50 feet above the road, which caused cars to go in all directions. He pulled up quickly and got out of the area before anyone could get the plane's tail number and report us to headquarters." A B-17 is a large airplane and surely would cause a commotion by flying low over a major highway.

Most of the training during this phase focused on high-altitude formation flying, long-range navigation, target identification, and simulated combat missions. However, sometimes Charlie and the rest of the crew preferred flying low to the ground. "We had to do an airspeed calibration, and to do that you had to fly 50 feet off of the ground. I was in the ball turret one day while we were flying over flat terrain. We were doing airspeed calibration when we flew over a house with a flat roof. When I looked down I saw a woman sunbathing in the nude on top of that flat roof. I got T-wood on the intercom and told him to swing around and take another pass over that house and to look for the naked woman. Well, by the time we came in for a second pass, she was up and running for cover, but not fast enough, and the crew got a glimpse of her as she was running."

"Another time we flew low over a farmer in a field. He had a horse drawn wagon and was picking corn out of the field. We spooked the horse which took off running and taking the wagon along with it. The last sight I saw was the farmer shaking his fist at us as we flew away." Besides the boys having some fun when they flew alone was the overriding instruction drilled into each crew that he must never become a loner. Protection is with your squadron and group. Fly alone and you are easy prey for the enemy.

The weather was very snowy while they were training at Sioux City. The excessive snow presented some challenges to flying and was a serious danger. "The plowed snow alongside the runways at Sioux City was piled high. During one practice flight while we were coming in for a landing in windy conditions, a wing dipped, and when it dipped it hit a snow pile and bent the landing gear back. Captain T-Wood quickly gunned the engines and gained altitude. But when he tried to put the landing gear back down, it wouldn't fully extend. We were ordered to fly to Barksdale, Louisiana, and we started flying in that direction. After flying for a few hours we received a radio message telling us to proceed to Middletown, Pennsylvania, where they would be able to repair the plane. I was excited about going to Middletown, because home was only 30 minutes from there, and I thought that perhaps I could briefly visit home. But that was soon changed and we were ordered to fly back to Sioux City, where we circled, using up as much gasoline as possible. Better to crash land with little fuel on board to prevent fire."

"T-Wood asked me if I could shoot off the damaged landing gear with my machine guns. I was concerned and told him so, because I was afraid the bullets might ricochet off of the steel landing gear. He wanted me to try anyway. I gave it one burst of four or five rounds and didn't even scratch the surface. I told T-Wood that it didn't work and said that I believed the damaged landing gear would probably break right off when we hit the runway. I climbed out of the ball turret and into the fuselage and went into emergency landing seating with some of the crew. Sergeant Mike Mazu [the radio operator] was facing backwards, sitting on the floor with his back firmly against the radio room door, and the rest of us lined up, sitting in front of him. Everyone's back was facing the front of the plane, with our heads cocked to the sides. Heads alternating so that the crewman in front and behind you did not have their head cocked in the same direction as yours. This prevented heads from smashing into each other."

"When we hit, the snow was flying, dirt was flying, and the engines were steaming. T-Wood had pulled the undamaged landing gear up before landing, figuring the damaged landing gear would snap off and then we would do a belly landing. But it didn't break off! Our landing speed was about 120 mph, and it was a rough ride as the plane spun across two runways. When the plane finally stopped, we hurried to get out of the plane and ran as far and as fast as we could to get away from the plane because of the possibility of fire and explosion. Fire trucks and ambulances came rushing towards us and I was afraid I would be run over by one of the emergency vehicles. Luckily there was no fire and none of the crew were injured, but the plane was junk." Charlie was lucky and he knew it. This crash-landing drove home the point of just how dangerous this job was and that he could have been killed. All this and they hadn't even flown their first combat mission!

Accidents continued to occur. Nobody was immune to being a victim of a tragic training accident, and Charlie witnessed them more than once. "One day after a full day of flying, we landed and were walking back to the barracks when another plane crashed straight down into a field and blew up in flames. I saw it come down and crash. I could hear the crew screaming and watched as one man crawled upwards towards the tail which was pointing straight up, trying to get away from the flames. When he got close to the tail, he just let go and fell back into the fire. The whole crew perished. Another time, a plane hit the base water tank and crashed. We got seasoned there at Sioux City, because of all the accidents."

Finally their training was complete, and the crew received passes to go on leave. "I got leave for six days after the final training. It was supposed to be 10 days, but we were called back early. We sort of expected to get called back early because we were an entire bomb group ready to go, and they needed bombers desperately in England and North Africa. I called Milt Starr [neighbor of the Eyers] to have him tell Mom that I was coming home. Mom didn't have a phone, so Milt went and got Mom to come to the phone." This would be Charlie's first return home since enlisting back in June.

After a short six days at home, Charlie returned to the airbase at Sioux City. "The weather was bad at Sioux City—cold, windy, fog and rain. The snow was the worst. We were in Sioux City for over a month, and this was the final training before deploying overseas." This was not the last time Charlie spent time in Sioux City. He would pass through there once again, assigned to a new crew for his second combat tour of duty.

The equipment was packed and ready to go and between December 31, 1942, and January 4, 1943, the ground crews took trains to airfields at Mitchell and Watertown, South Dakota. The air crews went to Salina, Kansas.[4]

Sergeant Charles Eyer back home in Hamburg, Pennsylvania, on leave, January 1943.

"We left Sioux City on a train for Salina to pick up a brand-new plane. At Salina, there were B-17s parked wingtip to wingtip, five miles long and one mile deep! These brand-new B-17s had been flown in directly from the factories by pilots and co-pilots made up entirely of women. Ground personnel took us out by bus to find our plane and the number of bombers were so great that the bus driver needed a chart to find our assigned plane. It was quite a sight when we took off and I looked down and saw all those planes. We were there only one day [January 5, 1943] while the 99th Bomb Group received their 36 planes. We flew the new plane to Homestead, Florida." America truly was the arsenal of democracy.

The flight from Salina to Homestead started a feud between the crew and an unnamed major that would not end until their tour of duty was complete. "A major flew our plane from Salina to Homestead, because our crew had gotten drunk a few times. The major said that Captain T-Wood

The crew of Shanker Ali while at Sioux City, Iowa, in 1942. Standing (from left to right): Flight Engineer/Top Turret Gunner Staff Sergeant Farron Daniels; Radio Operator Staff Sergeant Mike Mazu; Tail Gunner Staff Sergeant Beauford Lippolt; Waist Gunner Staff Sergeant Charles Fallon; and Ball Turret Gunner Staff Sergeant Charles Eyer. Kneeling (from left to right): Pilot Captain John Thistlewood; Navigator Lieutenant Jack Strasberg; Co-Pilot Lieutenant Steve Amundson; and Bombardier Lieutenant Brayton Fisher.

couldn't handle his crew and, therefore, the major said he was taking over and flying the plane and he would get the crew into shape! So T-Wood moved over into the co-pilot's seat."

Charlie and most of the sergeants did not tolerate trivial harassment, otherwise known as "chickenshit" that officers sometimes dealt out to enlisted soldiers in the ground forces. This didn't happen very often among the bomber crews, although sometimes ground officers attempted to disrupt the more laid-back environment in which combat fliers functioned. Charlie's crew had one such ground officer, "the major," who tried very hard to break up their little rank-less clique.

"At Homestead Air Base there were tall telephone poles painted yellow with black stripes around them. These poles were very important to the base commander, and he didn't tolerate anyone hitting any of his poles.

2. The Making of a Gunner

So the major landed our plane and is taxiing through the poles which are on both sides and clips one with a wing! I and the crew got out of the plane and hurried to the damaged wing and started laughing. This made the major so angry that he turned bright red."

"The base commander, a colonel, came out on the field and wanted to know who hit one of his poles! He chewed out the major, telling him he was lucky that he was going where he was going, because otherwise he wouldn't be in uniform anymore! They gave us a new plane that was already there at Homestead."

"When it was time to leave, the major wasn't flying as a pilot anymore. Captain T-Wood was back in the pilot's seat. But that major had it in for us after that. He always gave us the worst position in formation, and whenever he needed a plane to be 'Tail-End Charlie,' the last [and sometimes the most dangerous] position in a formation, that's where he assigned us. The major thought he was going to get rid of us, but we finished our tour of 50 combat missions anyway!" Charlie and crew were not deterred by the major and never hesitated to enjoy themselves at every opportunity.

"Before departing for North Africa, we spent a few days at a luxurious hotel in Homestead. One night we were at a nightclub where we met a guy who came to our table. He told us to eat and drink whatever we wanted until tomorrow morning, and it was all on his tab. So we did. The tail gunner, Staff Sergeant Beauford Lippolt, didn't want to leave, even though we were scheduled to fly out that morning. Three times I got him on the bus and three times he jumped off and I had to chase him down the street and put him back on the bus. If I wouldn't have, we both would have been AWOL [absent without leave]. We got back just in time to get on the plane, still somewhat drunk. We put on our oxygen masks which sobered us up." Lippolt and Charlie grew very close and were the best of friends throughout their North African tour of duty.

The enlisted men of the crew were often inseparable because of the brotherhood and trust they had for each other. They went everywhere together, drank together, and took their passes together. If one got into a fight, they all got into the fight. This closeness led to a great deal of sharing among the crew, and they shared almost everything with each other. They loved to tease and taunt each other in a good-natured way. But when things got serious, they did whatever they had to do to comfort and help each other.

The 99th BG departed the United States from Morrison Field, Florida, in February 1943. They flew the southern route via Borinquén, Puerto Rico, Georgetown, British Guiana, Belém, Brazil, and Bathurst, Gambia, to their destination at Marrakech, Morocco. The ground and support personnel and equipment would eventually make the trip by ship.[5]

It truly was a marvel that the USAAF could take thousands of civilians and turn them into combat airmen with some of the most challenging jobs in the military. Men who had never flown before were taught to operate the most advanced aircraft of the time and then had to take part in extremely difficult operations. This in itself was no simple task. Charlie and crew went about their work as if danger and heroics were common, everyday things. They surely performed great deeds while flying.

Chapter 3

North Africa

After returning from a short leave back home, the bomber crews of the 99th Bombardment Group (Heavy), the "Diamondbacks," departed for North Africa. They left from Morrison Field, Florida, and took a route that went through Borinquen, Puerto Rico, Atkinson Field, Georgetown, British Guiana, Belem Brazil, Yumdum Field, Bathurst, Gambia, and finally to Marrakech, Morocco.[1]

Charlie didn't know where the final destination would be and recalled, "We departed Homestead, Florida, on February 3, 1943. At Homestead, one hour before departure, we received a sealed envelope and were not allowed to open it until we were one hour off of the coast. We had no idea where we were going until Captain Thistlewood opened the envelope. The orders inside said we were to proceed to England, via North Africa. We learned later that we would be staying in North Africa." This was because the Army was desperate for heavy bombers to support operations in the Mediterranean Sea region. "We were not allowed to tell anyone back home where we were going. We could only tell them that we were deploying, but not when or where."

"We flew to Puerto Rico, where we landed. The perimeter guards at the base were all Puerto Ricans who did not speak English. We found out there was a club close by, not too far from the base. So we went to the club and drank rum and coke for hours. After a while I was tired and left the club to return to the base. But I had forgotten the password. I ran into a perimeter guard, who hollered at me to halt, but I kept walking until I heard the guard click off the safety of his rifle. I sobered up real quick! I backed away, turned around, and went back to the club where I asked the guys for the password. I then went back to the base and gave the password. The next morning we sobered up enough by the time for departure."

The trip continued from Puerto Rico. "The next day we landed in Georgetown, British Guyana, and they weren't ready for us. There were no meals, but they did have plenty of bananas—green ones. We ate them and they were good, but we were warned about spiders sometimes hiding in the banana bunches. Later we found some canned goods and did our own cooking and KP [kitchen police] duty. We stayed in Georgetown overnight. I was amazed at the size of the mouth of the Amazon River as we flew over it. It had to be 50 or 60 miles across."

During World War II, navigating and flying across the Atlantic Ocean was not as easy and safe as it is today. "We had two gas tanks installed in the bomb bay, and they held a total of 1,700 gallons. The tanks in the wings held another 1,700 gallons of gasoline. On the last leg we took off at daybreak and it was pretty near night when we reached the coast of North Africa. Captain T-Wood was nervous and said to the navigator that he better soon find the coastline because we were just about out of gas. According to the navigator's calculations, we should soon see the coastline, and in a few minutes we did." They finally made it to North Africa. "Marrakech, Morocco, was on the coast, and when we arrived at Marrakech, we thought we were still on our way to England."

As Charlie recalled, the 99th BG was assigned to the 12th U.S. Air Force during the North African campaign. The 99th came to be known as the Diamondbacks due to the diamond insignia painted on the vertical stabilizer of their B-17s. While assigned to the 12th USAAF, they conducted both tactical and strategic missions. They supported land forces but also bombed the harbors and shipping in and around North Africa, Sicily, and Italy. As Allied ground forces pushed the German Afrika Korps into Tunisia, the 12th Air Force flew missions cutting off German supplies coming from Italy and Sicily. The 99th flew missions mainly across the Mediterranean Sea, attacking targets primarily in Sicily and Italy.

After arriving in North Africa, Charlie and crew named their bomber "Shanker Ali." But before they had named the B-17 Shanker Ali (a name for an alley where houses of prostitution were located), they had named the plane "Poon Tang." Well, the major that always gave the crew a hard time knew what poon tang was (a certain part of the female anatomy below the waist) and made them remove the name. The major was unaware of the origination of the name Shanker Ali or he would have made them change the name once again. Charlie also had "Wun Hung Low" painted on the side of his ball turret.

The official serial number of a bomber was not a very good way of identifying a plane, so aircraft nicknames were allowed on the bombers'

3. North Africa

Shanker Ali in North Africa in 1943. Staff Sergeant Charles Eyer is standing on the left and a Sergeant Peters next to him.

noses in most combat units. Individual bomber names were popular and an easy and more personal identification within the unit. Charlie recalled, "Shanker Ali had quite a few accidents and hits through the course of 50 missions."

The group arrived in Marrakech in February 1943, soon after the defeat of the Allies at Kasserine Pass on the frontier of Algeria and Tunis. "We stayed at Marrakech for five weeks. After we landed the officers were called into a meeting, and after the meeting they informed us enlisted men that we would be staying in North Africa."

The group was held at Marrakech while the Allied commanders revised their North African strategy. Marrakech was an interesting city and had kept much of the original North African culture. "There was no airfield ready for us, and we stayed in Marrakech

Staff Sergeant Charles Eyer in North Africa in 1943, kneeling next to his position on the B-17, the ball turret, which he nicknamed "Wun Hung Low," as can be seen painted on the side.

Shanker Ali in North Africa in 1943.

until a new airfield was constructed near Constantine, Algeria. Rommel and his Afrika Korps were still in North Africa when we arrived. We didn't fly any combat missions while at Marrakech."

Charlie and the crew did get some time off while at Marrakech, and he had some excitement one day while at the beach. "I was swimming in the ocean close to the base, and there was a cove that had a strong undertow. I heard a guy hollering who had waded out too far and the undercurrent got him. I swam out and pulled him back in. He had to weigh almost 180 pounds and I became very tired and thought for a while that I might drown. But my feet finally touched the sandy bottom and I pulled him all the way to the shore. He was a local guy and his whole family witnessed this. He owned a local hotel and told me that I and the entire crew were invited to his place and could eat and drink for free. We never went."

After the Allied commanders finally completed their revised strategy, it was decided that Charlie's outfit, the 99th BG, would be officially assigned to the North African Theater and not sent to England. The 99th then proceeded to the La Senia airfield, which was close to Oran, Algeria, where the crews received their final briefings, various lectures, and other training to get them ready them to fly combat missions.[2]

In March 1943, after the work was completed on the group's own airfield at Navarin, Algeria, located near Constantine, the 99th relocated once again.[3] They moved to a brand-new airfield right in the middle of a farming district. "We got to Constantine in mid–March 1943 and our ground crew went to England." Immediately upon arrival the crew set up their tents and dug fighting positions because there was a threat of German air attacks.

The airfield was approximately 25 miles south of the city of Constantine. Constantine was founded by the Emperor Constantine during the Byzantine Empire, and Charlie and the other men were able to visit Constantine, which at that time was full of Allied soldiers. They traded soap and various other available items with the Arabs for eggs, chickens and fruit.

"We were many miles from the base to town. We would take a horse drawn taxi to town. Most of the taxis were old cars or part of a car pulled by horses. I got to town pretty often since I often drove the officers into town, and I had to carry a sidearm to prevent the Arabs from stealing the jeep. Also had to be careful of German booby traps along the roads, including piano wire being strung across a road that would decapitate someone if the windshield was down, which we had down most of the time. We were soon ordered to keep the windshields up, and eventually they installed a steel bar to the front of the jeeps, which would catch and cut the wire."

The crew of Shanker Ali lived in tents at the remote airfield. They had a roof over their heads, and even if it was only a tent, it was still more than their counterparts in the infantry had. Knowing this, Charlie considered himself fortunate for the shelter, even if it was not perfect. "Constantine was up in the mountains, and during the day the temperature could be 105 degrees, and at night, down to zero. At night we had a pot-bellied stove in our tent and burned briquettes."

There was no alcohol to be found at the air base. Booze was one of those items that the crew desired, and since there was none to be found anywhere, they decided to make their own. "We had a still in our tent. To make it, we removed a de-icing tank from one of the wings of our plane, and we also took the copper tubing it was hooked up to. Using the potbellied stove in our tent and charcoal bricks, we could get that stove cherry red and that's how we rigged up the still."

They needed something to put the moonshine into and quickly solved that problem with the help of one of the locals. "A little boy would sell us two bottles of wine every day until we had enough empty bottles to start the still up. Using the empty wine bottles we had saved, we ran off the first batch. Well, Fallon said we can't drink it like that; good whiskey is brown, not white. So Fallon went to the mess hall and scrounged some caramel candy. He stirred the caramel candy into the booze and it turned brown. We tried it and it was pretty good, but powerful! We didn't know you had to run it through the still twice. We only ran it through once. It was pure alcohol!"

The enlisted men weren't the only airmen that liked a sip or two of booze, as Charlie and the guys discovered. "We had a captain who was the officer of the day, and his duty was to check on the guards on each plane every day. He drove a weapons carrier vehicle and came out to us one evening. We were boozing it up pretty good at the time. He stuck his head inside the bomber door and we invited him in. He sat on the catwalk with us and we asked him if he wanted something to warm himself up, and he said sure. After one sip of our booze, he wouldn't leave and sat there with us for hours. We're drinking this stuff, and when it was time for the captain to leave, he couldn't even back up his vehicle. He was so drunk that he couldn't even put it into gear. So I got out of the plane and I backed it up for him and pointed it toward the taxi strip. I threw it in to second gear, and off he went. We told him not to try and walk because he wouldn't be able to walk all the way back. After that night, the captain was out there with us almost every night."

Tents resembling a pyramid in shape were spread throughout the base area. The mess and kitchen tents along with the mail shack were located in the center of the base. Far away and out in the sandy desert were the straddle trenches which were used as latrines. The tents gave some protection by providing shade during the daytime, when temperatures often got as high as 115 degrees. Charlie and the others slept on cots under mosquito nets, with homemade mats covering the sandy floor. Stacked ammo crates were used as storage for clothing and other items.

For lighting they had one low wattage light bulb that hung in the center of the tent. Gasoline fueled generators provided electricity and the constant hum of the generators was a part of camp life. The showers were constructed using a wooden frame and a slotted grate as the floor. The frame had a 50-gallon drum mounted on top which the water trucks filled every day. During the day the water became too hot to shower, and the men had to wait for it to be cooled down by the cool night air.

The Arabs seemed strange to Charlie and the other American airmen.

"The Arabs knew we had chocolate and gum, and the women wanted some but wouldn't come close because their men would not allow them to. We would throw stuff toward them, which they would pick up only after we moved away. The women were always fully dressed in either black or white outfits that covered them from head to toe, with only their eyes exposed. The Arabs would also drive their camels right across the airstrip. They would also steal our bed sheets if nobody was on guard. We started to shoot over their heads to scare them off, and after a few times of doing that, they stopped coming around."

The living conditions were very primitive, and Charlie and the other American airmen found themselves in a strange environment of a completely different culture. "A little boy of about 12 years old who understood some English would come around the base. We got him to bring us chickens, and vegetables, and wine, and we always paid him for the stuff. One day we convinced him to take us to a remote village which was through the jungle."

"All five of us enlisted men went, even though there were orders not to leave the base, but we did, and we never told Captain T-Wood. After a long walk we came to a 20-foot-high bamboo fence, and we figured we were finally at the village. There were two guards at the gate, and they opened the gate and we walked right in with the boy. The interior was filled with huts. The middle of the village was like a hub where meat was hanging. Not sure how they preserved the meat, or if it was fresh, or if they ate it right away. Nobody bothered us and we just sat there a while and watched the people and their activities. The people were very interesting to look at since they wore these very large rings in their noses and ears and also those big flat lip plates."

"The boy took us to the hut where he lived. The hut was large and round. It was just one room with thatched rugs on the ground." Things became a bit tense when the men decided to leave, but they all stayed cool and calm. "After a while we decided to head back to the base. When we began to leave the natives started jumping into our way, like they were trying to stop us. I told everyone not to draw their pistol, and soon the natives opened the gate and let us out."

The 99th BG, and some of the other bomb groups, started operations severely handicapped. The flight element was separated from the ground element, and when the flight crews deployed to North Africa, the ground crews were still back in South Dakota. Initially, Colonel Upthegrove had only the aircrews of the 99th BG present in North Africa. There were a few temporary units assigned to the group for maintenance of the bombers, processing supplies, and administration.[4]

This meant that Charlie and crew had to perform most of the work that the ground crew would have accomplished. "When we first got to North Africa we didn't have any ground crew. We had to fuel, maintain, and load bombs ourselves. We had to fuel the plane by hand, using a hand pump, and pumping gas from 55-gallon drums. It took 1,700 gallons of gasoline to fill the plane. Immediately upon returning from a mission we started pumping gas, which normally took us one half day to do. Sometimes we worked 16 hours a day, which included both flying and doing ground crew duties."

The aircrew personnel had to do all the ground work on the base after flying all day. Everyone pitched in, and when they moved in even the group commander helped dig the first latrine at the new airfield. Until the ground crews would arrive, the aircrews fueled the aircraft, loaded the bombs, and performed maintenance on the bombers, machine guns, and other equipment. Bomber maintenance was especially difficult because sand and dust infiltrated the working parts of the engines. It was quite a task, but they kept the bombers flying. On May 24, 1943, the flight crews and grounds crews were finally united again after a long separation.[5]

After flying all day, the aircrews loaded bombs at night for the following day's mission. One time Charlie and another crewman decided to have some fun at the expense of a few soldiers on guard duty. "Before the ground crew arrived, we had to load our own bombs. Lippolt and I played a trick on some of our perimeter guards. These guys were walking their post and three or four of them came over to watch us load the bombs. Lippolt told them that if one of the bombs slipped and hit the ground that it would explode. So we went up into the plane where we had a 1,000 pounder in the sling. Lippolt cranked one side and I cranked the other side. You had to keep the bomb level as it was cranked all the way up, until you snapped it into the bomb bay. I asked Lippolt if he wanted to scare the perimeter guards, and he was in favor of doing that. So we got the bomb up part way and all of a sudden it tilted and down it went! Forgetting where he was [under a wing], one guy squatting under the plane jumped up so quickly that he knocked himself silly. He laid flat on the ground with his legs still running. A couple of them hurt themselves when they ran away, including the last guy when he came to. We never had anybody come around to watch us again."

The enlisted men spent much of their time at the bomber, rather than sitting in the tent. "We had a little generator that we used for the plane and we could turn the lights on in the plane. Because of the possibility of moonlight reflecting off the glass, all glass on the ship was covered with

A B-17 bomber in North Africa with its glass covered to prevent the enemy from spotting it by the moon's reflection at night. The names of the airman are unknown.

tarps so that Germans couldn't spot it at night while flying over. We'd sit in the radio room and Mike Mazu would tune in radio programs from the States, and we listened to them. The bands and stuff like that. We had our own stuff to drink and eat, and we'd usually spend the evening in the plane. We were in the plane more than in the tent. We'd find out how the war was going and listen to good music, especially on a Saturday night."

"We had guard duty 24 hours a day on the plane, and what we did to keep warm was to put on our heated flying suits. All five of us enlisted guys would stay in the plane overnight. When it got too cold, we went back to the tent and took turns guarding the plane."

There were many real threats while Charlie was in North Africa. One such instance occurred when some Germans attempted to steal a bomber. "Two German officers who had been shot down near our base tried to take one of our planes and fly out. Lippolt [who was on guard duty] heard them sneaking in and hollered at them. He fired a couple of rounds at them and they froze and were captured. That's why there were guards on the planes. When our ground crew finally made it there, they took over guard duty, and we didn't have guard duty for anything after that."

Every military unit had at least one member who was good at scrounging up those items the military didn't provide. Well, Charlie's crew was no different and one of the crew proved to be a very good scrounger. One item needed for the enlisted members of the crew was food. Food was important and what was being provided to them from the mess wasn't all that good, so they decided to provide for themselves.

"One of our enlisted men was our scrounger, and whatever we needed, he got. One day he went into the port of Oran and watched as the ships came in and unloaded their cargo, observing how things were distributed. He came back to the base and told us that we could get a whole truck load of food! We just needed an officer to sign for it. So we found one of our officers who said he would go along and sign for the food. But before we did, we removed all insignia, except for rank, that identified us as an aircrew. The food rations were stacked on the docks and marked with the unit designation for whom the rations were meant. So we told the guy operating the ration distribution point that we were from company so-and-so and we were there to pick up our rations. Our officer signed, not using his real name, and we loaded up all the rations and got the hell out of there real fast before the real company showed up to get their rations!"

Now where to hide an entire truckload of food? "The scrounger got us some lumber and nails and tools and we built boxes inside the bomb bay of our plane, where we stored this truckload of food. We had to keep it out of sight and be able to fly with it when we finally would depart. We quickly stored the food after the boxes were constructed. We had canned hams, canned fruit, powdered eggs, powdered milk, etc. We had enough food for an entire company! But we didn't eat any of it while we were at that base. When we got to our next base, which was Constantine, we dug deep pits inside our tent. We placed the wooden boxes into the pits to hold all the food. We also had some stashed in 55-gallon gas drums with the bottoms cut out, which we kept right outside our tent. The major was suspicious while we were at Constantine, because we weren't eating in the mess hall every meal. He nor anyone else ever found the stash of food."

Once again, the major suspected something about the crew, but just couldn't seem to catch them red-handed. "One day the major came to our tent. He knew something was wrong, but just couldn't find anything. He always carried a big stick and he'd jam it into the sand floor of our tent. But we had the food box buried too deeply for him to find. The box was filled with all canned food like peanut butter, jam, Spam, etc. We had so much food that I got sick one night eating peanut butter and pineapple sandwiches."

The major was persistent and took great pleasure in tormenting the crew and making their lives harder. "The major came in one day and said he was going to check our rifles. Well, heck, we had just thrown our rifles behind our cots and there they lay in the sand for months. We never bothered with them and they were covered with sand. So we had to get them out of the sand and the major gave us a good lecture. He really chewed us out but there was nothing he could really do to us. So we cleaned our rifles and put them in bags and hid them."

Charlie recalled that during the early days in North Africa, a serious shortage of spare parts made bomber maintenance crucial. Sometimes shortages grounded aircraft for long periods and required some airmen to fly missions in bombers assigned to other crews. Aircrew personnel were rarely switched between squadrons to fill an empty crew position for a combat mission, but if maintenance problems were particularly acute in one squadron, planes from another would be used by its crews.

Although they lacked combat experience, Charlie and his fellow crewmen wanted to prove themselves in battle. Sometimes in the confusion of aerial combat many gunners fired at a single enemy fighter. If that enemy fighter went down, more than a few gunners might make a claim in the belief that he was the one that shot it down. Most of the gunners didn't intend to deceive. It was difficult to know for sure who hit it when an enemy fighter closed in at 500 miles an hour. Sometimes when an enemy fighter flipped belly-up after firing a burst and plunged straight down, their exhausts gave off a trail of thick black smoke. A gunner might have believed the smoke and violent evasive maneuvers of the fighter as damage he caused. Charlie rarely claimed any enemy fighters.

For the bombardier, his first combat mission was also his first time he dropped bombs at a very high altitude. The Norden bombsight was a challenge to operate, even during perfect weather. During the heat of aerial combat, the bombardier had to stay calm and focused even while planes were going down all around him. But first, the navigator had to find the target.

On March 31, 1943, the first combat mission of the 99th was against the Villacidro Aerodrome in Sardinia. Colonel Upthegrove was flying in the lead B-17. The 97th, 301st, and the 94th Bomb Groups also took part in this raid. It was the largest number of B-17s used in the war to date.[6] "My first mission was on March 31, 1943. The target was the aerodrome at Villacidro, Sardinia. We bombed a lot of aerodromes. The first mission was scary and anybody that wasn't scared had something wrong with him. That feeling never left me. I was just as scared on the 50th mission as I was on the first."

A briefing was conducted before every combat mission. The briefing informed the crew about their mission and the kind of enemy opposition they might encounter as well as any other important information. The entire crew attended the main briefing. After the main briefing, there were separate briefings for the pilot, navigator, bombardier, and radio operator, where those men received specific information related to their position on the bomber. The briefing was stressful for Charlie and crew because it gave them the location where they might be killed, seriously wounded, or captured.

Charlie continued, "Briefings were in the early morning. We usually got up at 3:00 a.m. I got dressed and then went for breakfast. After breakfast we all went to the briefing. We were briefed and then they would brief the officers some more as we enlisted men went out to the ship and did our pre-flights and got everything set and checked out. This was all completed about the same time as the officers arrived at the ship. It was always cold in the morning, windy, and dust storms. We usually took off at daybreak. We never bombed at night, only during the day. For each mission we got special instructions about our submarines picking us up in the event of ditching into the sea [Mediterranean Sea]. We knew the submarine pick-up locations. I had a map and a compass in the survival vest of my flight suit."

As Charlie related, eating the wrong foods before a mission could be extremely dangerous. "You dared not eat anything that gave you gas. If you had a tiny amount of gas in your stomach when you got up to 30,000 feet, it would greatly expand. It could kill you, and we had no doctor on the base until the ground crew arrived. I don't know where they took the injured, perhaps to an Army infantry base close by. I ate anything I felt like eating and sometime took the chance because I got tired of eating carrots. We had carrots for most meals. The only meal we ever ate before flying was breakfast, and we always ate the same stuff in the morning. Our crew was lucky because we had our own food [the food that they had scrounged] and could eat ham or anything we wanted. But none of us got up in the morning to cook, so we always ate breakfast in the mess hall. It was mostly powdered eggs and corned beef. Sometimes they baked the eggs and corned beef together to make it different. The coffee was always good."

After Charlie's fifth combat mission he was awarded the Air Medal. This warrior decoration was important to him. He was very proud of his silver wings and air medals. He suffered great hardship and danger for the medals that affirmed his bravery. Before he finished his 50th combat mission he would be severely tested, and these decorations symbolized dangerous missions.

One of those extremely dangerous missions took place on May 3, 1943. The 99th BG was tasked with bombing ships in Bizerte Harbor, but on the way there flew into some nasty weather. The mission was aborted and the formation scattered, and each bomber had to find its way back to the base. Crash landings were made in the sea and in the mountains, and men parachuted from their bombers. Five bombers were lost. One ditched into the sea, killing some of the crew. The four other bombers either crash-landed or bailed out over land. It was several days before the survivors were once again flying. One bomber landed with a full load of bombs and an engine on fire. The crew succeeded in getting out of the bomber and ran about 200 yards and dived behind a sand dune just as the bombs exploded. The crew was uninjured. Seven airmen were lost in the sea. Some airmen journeyed down steep mountainsides on mules and camels after having bailed out in the darkness over mountainous terrain. The casualty toll for May 3, because of bad weather, was two dead, 12 wounded and five missing.[7]

On another dangerous return from a mission, Charlie didn't know if he would survive. "Sometimes we flew into darkness, especially when coming back from a long mission over Italy. It would be dark, but not too dark that you couldn't land. During one mission while coming back there was a thunderstorm over North Africa. When we were coming back there was nothing but clouds, dark and rain, and nobody knew where we were going. We had to rely on the navigator. Some of the planes hit a mountainside, and some flew into a cliff."

"We were coming in and our navigator said to the pilot that we should be over the airfield. Right now! Well, we couldn't see a thing, so the pilot called down to the airfield and asked them to put all vehicles they had along the runway and turn on their headlights, and maybe we could find the airstrip. We circled and circled and were getting very low on gas. But suddenly a hole opened up in the clouds and down below we could see the runway and the lights. Well, old Captain T-Wood was an old truck driver, and he just peeled off and down we went and landed all right."

"Another plane from our squadron that couldn't see lost their tail wheel when they clipped the top of a mountain and belly landed on a flat part on top of that mountain. The ship was still loaded with its bombs and it caught fire, but they escaped and jumped into a gulley before it exploded, and nobody was hurt. Some Arabs rescued the crew using little donkeys and it took them two days to get back to the base. We lost quite a few, perhaps four, planes. That was my eighth mission."

Charlie had been in the noisy bomber for a long time, but now, on the ground, things were quieter. The nonstop rumble of the engines and the thunderous booms of flak had stopped, but the sudden silence could be unsettling at times. It was normal on a combat mission for him to be extremely uncomfortable for many hours. He was cold, cramped, and wearing very uncomfortable gear. But eventually he relaxed a bit when he realized that he could have died today. He never felt he was out of danger until his feet were on solid ground.

During one combat mission, Charlie got quite a scare. "The only time I was out of the ball was during takeoff and when the group was forming. Once started on our way to the target, I would get into the ball, check everything out, and get hooked up. On one mission over the Mediterranean Sea to Italy, it was an exceptionally cold day, and I was in the ball. When we were over Sicily, I had to be in the ball because sometimes the enemy fighters would come up to attack us. But after we passed Sicily, I shut the ball down and was watching the waves. Nearing Italy, I went to turn the ball on, but it wouldn't move. The hydraulic system got cold and the oil thickened up. I kept moving the controls to heat it up, and finally it let go and started working just as we reached the Italian coast. It wasn't too long before German fighters came up to battle."

Frostbite and freezing to death were a constant danger with air temperatures as low as 40 to 50 or more degrees below zero Fahrenheit. The piercing cold was very painful. It crept into a crewman's entire body, freezing any sweat, and could quickly kill him. If Charlie would have removed his gloves and touched anything made of metal, his fingers would have immediately became stuck to it. Removing his hand would have torn the skin from his fingers.

Charlie, in the ball turret suffered greatly from the biting cold. It provided almost no protection from the elements, and the numbingly cold air penetrated through cracks in the turret. His exhalations through the oxygen mask froze and formed a thick mass of ice on his chest, and even his eyebrows and eyelashes would freeze. His feet were also numbed by the cold. Even with the electric heat suit and all the heavy clothing he wore, he barely kept from freezing to death.

It was so cold that windows and gun sights got frosty, bomb bay doors iced up, and other mechanical equipment froze and broke. Flying in temperatures as brutally cold as the Arctic and Antarctic caused a lot damage and casualties. An airman who started a mission wet from rain or sweat was most likely going to be frostbitten. Many airmen were hospitalized for frostbite.

Frostbite was big trouble for a wounded airman, especially if his electric heat suit or oxygen supply were damaged by bullets or shrapnel. One heartbreaking ordeal occurred when a crewman's oxygen mask had been punctured by a flak blast that blew a large hole in the nose of the bomber. His oxygen supply was damaged and he was unconscious for a full hour. Six weeks later, his hands, feet, ears, and nose were amputated and his frozen eyeballs removed. He lived.[8]

Airmen were removed from bombers with cases of frostbite at the end of almost every mission. Within a day or maybe two the frostbite wounds turned purple and then black in extreme cases. Airmen were typically grounded for up to two weeks for the milder cases. A third of frostbite victims were hospitalized. Many of the severe cases weren't returned to duty for months, and some never returned to duty.[9]

To prevent frostbite and freezing to death inside the ball turret, Charlie's outfit was slightly different from the other crew members. He wore long underwear, wool slacks, and a wool long sleeve shirt. On top of that he wore an electrically heated suit made of a thin, lightweight nylon-type material. It was sort of like an electric blanket and had small electric wires embedded in the fabric. The suit was similar to bib overalls with a long-sleeved jacket, and it had a connection at the ankle to plug in his electrically heated shoes. There was also a plug connection at the wrist for the heated gloves. A third connection was on the collar for his heated goggles, which had small wires in the lenses that prevented fogging.

Next he wore a nylon-type jumpsuit that zipped in the front which had numerous pockets, then finally a flight jacket over everything. On his head he wore a leather helmet with ear phones. It also had side tabs to attach his oxygen mask. His hands were protected by silk gloves, then electrically-heated gloves, then fur-lined leather gloves on top of those, and finally bulky cloth mittens. His feet were covered with wool socks, an electrically-heated felt shoe, and then an insulated cloth over-boot. His survival gear was located in his jumpsuit. On top of everything he donned a bulky rubberized suit called a "Mae West." It could be inflated by pulling a cord that triggered a small pressurized cylinder. Last but not least was his parachute harness with straps over his shoulders, around his chest, and through his groin area.

The cold could and did cause equipment problems, in addition to making things uncomfortable for Charlie. "It was typically 40 to 50 degrees below zero. The suits were heated but your hands and feet froze. The heat suit would double up at my belly when I was in the ball, causing a burn, and I was always red around my waist. The inside of the plane was covered in heavy frost and looked like the inside of a freezer. We would take along a five-gallon pail filled three-quarters of the way with water. When we came down it was frozen like a rock and then we had ice water. I didn't mind being in the ball."

Going to the bathroom was extremely difficult. In the bomb bay was a funnel with a tube that went outside of the bomber. If Charlie wanted to use it, he first had to carefully walk across the narrow bomb bay catwalk, sometimes with bombs hanging on both sides. Then he had to undo himself in the extreme cold and bouncing plane, aim into a funnel, and urinate. If he was the first to use it, no problem. However, if someone had used it before him, and if their urine had frozen and blocked the tube, Charlie's urine splashed right back onto him. He didn't use the tube very often. Like most of the crew, if he really had to go, he just unzipped and peed on the floor or out a waist window. Sometimes the urine froze before going out the waist window, and clattered around as little yellow ice cubes.

If he had to defecate, he had only two choices. Go in his clothing or use the metal bucket that was located in the waist section. Even if he had the time to go, it meant removing much of his clothing in sub-zero conditions. If he would have placed his butt down on the frozen metal of the bucket, it surely would have removed some of his skin when he stood back up. Like most of the crew, he did not use it, and if he absolutely had to go, which wasn't very often, he just defecated in his suit. The smells and mess that greeted the ground crew after they came back from a long and dangerous mission were just awful.

When the Allies directed their attention to Sicily, they used a combined Allied air force to eliminate the threat from enemy air forces stationed on the island of Pantelleria. The island was in the path of the route to Sicily, and the enemy fighters based there would be in a position to attack the Allied forces when they invaded Sicily. In June of 1943, the 99th BG conducted heavy raids on Pantelleria, and after many days of devastating bombardment, Allied troops took the island without a single loss of life.[10]

Charlie recalled, "At Pantelleria Island there were hangars where the Germans kept their planes underground, with 50 feet of concrete over top of them. We used block busters, but they never penetrated the concrete.

But the concussion of the bombs going off smashed the planes together inside the hangars."

This was a case of strategic bombardment taking an objective without the use of either sea or land forces. When Pantelleria surrendered, all Italian air force aircraft remaining on the island were destroyed. Charlie said, "That took out a lot of the German and Italian air force. We knocked that thing silly for days in a row. It was the most important hangar around, and headquarters wanted it hit, and they got it!" Now the way was open for the invasion of Sicily, which would be the Allies first foothold into Europe.[11]

On another mission, "we made a raid over Italy but couldn't find the target because everything was overcast. At a time like that, the group commander called all planes and told everyone that we couldn't find the target, so we would turn around and each plane should head back to the base on their own. So then all bombers dispersed to avoid flying into each other. No fighters came after us, or ack-ack [flak], because of the limited visibility. We had been over Italy before, so I had seen some possible targets of opportunity. What we were supposed to do with the bombs, if we couldn't hit the target, was to drop them in the Mediterranean Sea and not bring them back. We never dropped them in the water."

On every mission Charlie always made note of anything with a red cross on the roof or castles and bridges. He firmly believed that buildings with a large red cross on the roof and castles were possibly German military headquarters locations, and bridges were always a high priority target. If they couldn't locate any of those targets, then they would drop their bomb load on anything that looked promising.

"One time over Italy we couldn't hit the primary target. We turned to head back and saw a railroad and two highways all crossing one bridge. It was big and long, and I had seen it previously. We hit that bridge and down it went! Another time we bombed a castle on top of a mountain. It was beautiful with high walls. So where else would you find the generals living? None of these counted as combat missions because they were aborted runs. We were over Italy numerous times and often we couldn't hit the target because of weather."

There were some very tense days in June of 1943, when intelligence information was received that an Arab uprising may occur. Because of the possibility of an attack by the Arabs, the men were required to carry firearms at all times for a few days. The uprising never took place and was soon forgotten. However, there were acts of sabotage, including a small nighttime German paratroop drop over Oudna Field, Tunisia, that resulted in the capture of three Germans. Even though not a serious danger like an attack, summer dust storms made life miserable for the men. They were a great nuisance while in North Africa and substantial amounts of dust settled on everything.[12]

June 25, 1943, was the 99th BG's 37th mission, and this one was to Messina, Sicily, to cut the flow of supplies. They encountered very tough opposition from both flak and fighters, but the marshaling yards and warehouses were hit hard. However, the enemy took a toll of the group's men, killing two and wounding eight.

Charlie could see the flak everywhere with its black bursts and red centers. There were many hundreds of bursts as far as he could see, and the bomber rocked and bounced from the never-ending explosions. Sometimes the bursts were very close and he could hear the sounds of tearing sheet metal. He often described flak as being "so thick you could get out and walk on it."

He really hated and feared the flak because he could not fight back against it. Flak was frustrating because there was nothing they could do except fly through it and drop their bombs on the target. Charlie called the airmen who became jittery and nervous because of it "flak happy."

Sometimes the flak was so heavy that Charlie could smell it through his oxygen mask. Intense barrages exploded with such force that the concussions bounced any crewman around inside the bomber who wasn't buckled in. All they could do was sit and take it as they flew through the flak. Sometimes it was so nerve racking that it caused Charlie to break out in a cold sweat, even at 40 degrees below zero.

Flak was very deadly. On a B-17 during another mission, a flak shell burst just outside a waist gunner's window. The waist gunner had on a flak suit and a flak helmet, but they didn't save him. A piece of shrapnel hit him in the forehead and took off the top of his head, and some of his brains flew forward and splattered against the radio room door. The flak suit did protect his torso and vital organs, but both legs were severed. They stayed with the body because the flying-suit had been tucked into his electric boots.[13]

Damage and losses were routine, and "almost every time we came back from a mission, we or the ground crew were patching holes. Sometimes the ship looked like a sieve. When an entire crew was lost, they'd send in another crew. There were always extra planes on hand."

Charlie and the crew of Shanker Ali were lucky and only suffered one casualty during his 50 combat missions in North Africa. "The only one of our crew that was injured on a mission was Lieutenant Strasberg. I had loaded all the weapons, which was my job as well as cleaning them. At mission time I put each gun in its position. Each man was supposed to set their own headspace on their machine gun, but Strasberg forgot to set his. We were over the coast of Italy when fighters attacked, and when he fired, the brass bullet casing blew straight down and ripped him open. He screamed and cried over the intercom, and we didn't know how badly he was injured. Captain T-Wood asked each of us if we wanted to turn back. Turning back could be a court-martial offense. We each said yes, and so we turned back to Africa. They took him to the hospital and luckily he was not hurt as bad as we thought. But if we would have continued on the mission, he may have bled to death. He was the only one hurt in all the missions we flew."

The following day, although no missions were carried out, saw more loss of life. Sixteen men were killed outright and four more sustained critical injuries when a load of 500-pound bombs exploded while being unloaded. The men killed and injured were from the Ordnance Company and the Service Squadron.[14] Fortunately for Charlie, although he was close, he was not close enough to sustain an injury from the explosion.

"The bombs were brought in by train. There were wooden stakes on the sides of the flatbed railroad cars, and they piled the bombs on top of each other, up to a peak. The only thing holding them on the railroad cars were the stakes. Forty-seven guys from our gang went down with trucks and started unloading. They pulled the stakes out and rolled the bombs off. One on top of the other, clink, clank, clink, clank, and suddenly one bomb went off! It killed many men of the ground crew. Behind the railroad station was a fenced area that was a French prison for AWOL French soldiers. The station was built out of brick and was nice looking. They had guards up in possum houses [guard towers], and the compound was full of prisoners. After the explosion there was nothing left! Nothing! The whole thing went up and all that was left was an immense crater. The whole works went!"

"I was about a mile from the station, and it was late afternoon. We had 50-gallon drums that were cut in half. One had soapy water and one had rinse water, and that is where we cleaned our eating utensils. I was there and had just soaped up my stuff and was kneeling down to rinse my stuff when the explosion occurred. The concussion sent me flying over the rinse tub and I ended up in the sand on the other side. Every tent in the area collapsed. One guy was driving a truck towards the railroad station when the blast occurred. It picked up the truck, turned it completely around facing in the opposite direction, and sat it back down. The driver was so stunned that he couldn't even talk. He didn't know what happened. That was one of the worst accidents we had."

On July 4, 1943, there was another explosion at the ordnance dump, and this one started a large fire in nearby wheat fields. It took a great effort extinguishing the fires in the wheat fields. Fortunately there were no casualties this time.[15]

Not every day was dangerous, unless you happened to be a chicken. "Captain T-Wood had a pet chicken named Esmerelda. When it got to be the right size we enlisted guys decided it was time for some chicken noodle soup. So I got some noodles and gathered up Esmerelda, killed it and cooked it, and we had chicken noodle soup. The captain never found out what happened to Esmerelda."

On July 5, 1943, the 99th attacked the airfields at Gerbini, Sicily. The group was led by Colonel Upthegrove and caused a great amount of damage.[16] The flak was heavy, intense, and accurate all the way from the IP (initial point) to the target. It rattled Charlie inside the ball turret as the explosive concussions shook the bomber hard and bounced him around within the tight confines of the ball. With every flak blast he expected a piece of red-hot shrapnel to come tearing through the Plexiglas and kill him. That piece of shrapnel never came, and Shanker Ali flew on through the dark black clouds left by the bursts. After what seemed like an eternity with flak exploding all around, he watched the bombs fall and felt the lightened bomber rise slightly higher.

During this raid on Gerbini, the group suffered a heavy loss when an entire flight of three B-17s from the 348th Bomb Squadron was shot down during ferocious fighter attacks. The Germans attacked with more than one hundred Me-109s and FW-190s plus other enemy fighters. Charlie and the other men watched as air crews bailed out over enemy territory. Another B-17 was seen making a crash landing on a beach. The 99th Bombardment Group would receive a Distinguished Unit Citation for this mission.[17]

The B-17 Flying Fortress was designed, built, and armed to defend itself against enemy fighters. However, when alone, it was very vulnerable to enemy fighter attacks. Just as he had to on this mission, Charlie and the other gunners often had to fight for their lives during a combat mission. The speed and aggressiveness of enemy fighter attacks left a deep impression on him. Typically and with little warning an enemy fighter attack quickly materialized, with machine guns and cannons firing at them. Often the enemy fighters dived out of the blinding sun and tore through the bomber formation with guns blazing.

Near Gerbini, the enemy fighters suddenly attacked the bomber formation. The first line of enemy fighters tore through the formation. The fighters approached from head-on. The weapons mounted in their wings flashed like blinking headlights. Suddenly everyone was on the intercom broadcasting the location of the enemy fighters. "Fighters at twelve o'clock high, fighters at three o'clock level, fighters at ten o'clock low." Charlie felt the B-17 shake as the .50 caliber machine guns returned fire. He could see the glowing tracer rounds as they flew in every direction as the battle raged miles above the earth. Attack after attack came, and they were lucky that their bomber was still in one piece afterwards.

Through the intercom Charlie could hear the others firing. Then in a flash enemy fighters went past him as they dived downward. He focused his sight on one of the fighters. His gunsight jumped about, and when he knew the enemy fighters were in range, he squeezed both triggers. Pop, pop, pop, pop ... pop, pop, pop, his twin .50 calibers roared and made the ball turret rock. It was hard to stay on a target for long as he fired and followed the enemy fighters until out of range. Then he looked for the next enemy fighter.

He saw some of the enemy fighters smoking, and others had flames coming from their engine cowling. Somebody nailed those fighters, but Charlie didn't know if it was him or some other gunner. He didn't have a chance to watch because more fighters attacked from every direction. His ball turret was filled with a gray smoke from his guns. Spent ammunition belt links bounced around the inside of the ball turret. His machine guns were red hot by the time the enemy finally had enough and left.

By this time he was wet with sweat as he rotated the ball turret still searching for more enemy fighters. He also looked over the underside of the bomber for any damage. He saw some holes, but good old Shanker Ali was still in one piece and flying! He slowly rocked the ball back and forth and pushed the machine gun belt links out through the link chute slot. As he looked around, he noticed that some bombers from the formation were gone.

Charlie recalled that many fighter attacks during his tour of duty in North Africa were not as powerful or as lengthy as the Gerbini mission. However, such enemy fighter attacks happened often enough to tire him and the other crew members. He remembered that flak brought down more bombers than the fighters did and that flak posed a considerably greater threat than fighters. But conversely, he recalled that a bomber hit by flak had a better chance of making it back to base than one attacked by fighters.

In July 1943 the Allies assaulted Sicily. Charlie may just have bumped into the top brass at his air base, and he thought that perhaps they were there finalizing the plans and coordinating for the invasion of Sicily. "One day as I was approaching the mess hall, five generals came walking toward me. One was Ike [General Dwight D. Eisenhower] and one was British field marshal Montgomery. The other three I did not recognize. It was a thrill to salute them, and they returned my salute. This was just before the Sicily invasion."

On July 9, 1943, the day of the invasion, a special invasion mission was flown to Sicily.[18] "The invasion of Sicily was my most memorable mission. Being a ball turret gunner, I could not have had a better seat to look down on the Mediterranean Sea and watch the ships circling and firing their guns at the coastline. The infantry came in on little boats and dropped the gate and charged the beach, and I could see them! We were going there to bomb the big pill boxes. The pill boxes were made out of concrete and had railroad tracks and large guns inside. They would roll them out and fire at the boats. We were to knock them out and used 1,000-pound block busters and hit them several times. It was a sight to see."

Recalling the bomb types they used, Charlie said, "We mostly dropped three different types of bombs. The 1,000 pounders known as blockbusters were used for penetrating fortifications, buildings, factories, etc. The 500 pounders were for anything on the surface because they could not penetrate very deeply. We also dropped anti-personnel bombs [cluster bombs] to kill personnel. Fifty or 60 to a cluster. These were used against troop concentrations in an area and against factory workers. We never mixed bomb types."

The first raid on Rome took place on July 19, with the 99th BG dropping 108 tons of 500-pound bombs on the marshaling yards and railroad buildings in the area.[19] The crews were careful to avoid dropping any bombs on the Vatican City and the ancient Roman ruins. Charlie was part of that raid. "We went to Rome to bomb the marshalling yards, and they had plenty of ack-ack [flak] there. All the railroad tracks came into Rome, and it was immense. The reason for the mission was because the Allies were preparing to invade Italy."

"At the briefing they told us that anybody who was Catholic and did not want to make this mission would be excused. Not one man stepped out. The Vatican wasn't too far from the marshalling yards. When the lead bomber dropped their bombs, all planes dropped theirs as well. For this mission they took our bombardier and put him in the lead plane with Colonel Upthegrove. Our bombardier, Lieutenant Fisher, was the best bombardier in the whole outfit. Well, we made the mission, but boy, was that chaotic because we had ack-ack all over the place. The fighters we faced were Göring's special fighters with the noses painted yellow. They were the only German fighters with yellow noses, so we knew who we were up against. They were hot shots and the best pilots you could find in Germany." Charlie had a fearful respect for that particular group of German fighter pilots. The yellow-nosed Germans fighters were Reichsmarschall Hermann Göring's hand-picked pilots.

"Three weeks before that mission, we flew over Rome and dropped leaflets telling the citizens when we were going to bomb. It was a touchy situation. If we would have over-shot the target, we could have hit the ancient buildings or the Vatican. So we warned them that we were coming so the people could get out. We hit the marshalling yards good! This was July 19, 1943. Rome missions were 12-hour missions, and we had to start those missions early so we could get back in time to find the field before darkness."

On July 22, their mission was over Foggia, Italy, and their target was the marshaling yards. The group met heavy enemy opposition and lost one bomber and crew, with several other bombers damaged.[20] On August 1, 1943, the raid was against the docks and shipping at Naples.[21] Charlie recalled, "We hit the harbor at Naples, Italy, just as loads of troop-carrying ships were there. I could see the troops on the gang planks getting off of the ships. Intelligence estimated that many thousands of German troops were killed by the bombs. We also sank some of the boats."

During the Naples mission they had P-38 fighter escorts. The Lockheed P-38 Lightning was the first American-built fighter to escort B-17s on a mission, and they played an important role in the North African theater.[22] Charlie recalled that the bombers were aggressively attacked by German ME-109s and Italian fighters, but the P-38s eventually chased them away after shooting some down.

Initially, enemy fighters had been attacking B-17s from the rear where some of the bombers' guns could hit them. Luftwaffe experiments soon discovered that the nose of a B-17 had practically no defensive firepower, and regardless of the dangers of very high closing speeds, it was soon considered the best way to shoot down a B-17. It was dangerous because a tiny error in judgment could mean a useless pass by the fighter or result in a mid-air collision.[23]

It didn't take long for the B-17 crews to improvise and correct this danger. "In North Africa we flew the B-17F model which did not have any machine guns in the nose. The German fighter pilots soon learned that coming in at us straight on from the front was best. So we countered that by installing one .50 caliber machine gun in the nose that the bombardier could operate."

The German fighters would move out of machine gun range on one flank and follow the B-17s to determine their exact course, altitude and speed. Then they quickly moved ahead of the bomber formation and turned around for a head-on pass. When they attacked from dead ahead the closing speed was around 550 mph. The extreme speed made it very hard to engage a bomber for more than a brief moment. Normally while using a head-on approach, the angle of attack was from 12 o'clock high. Because the best way to shoot down a bomber was to kill both pilots, this was found to be the most effective attack method.[24]

Charlie and the other combat airmen respected German fighter pilots and were impressed by the courage they displayed. It appeared to him, and others, that it was almost suicidal for them to attempt head-on attacks against the massed firepower produced by the bomber formation. "Colonel Upthegrove had us flying very tight formations, and that made it very hard for the German fighters to penetrate our formation. However, on one mission a German Messerschmitt ME-109 came flying straight up, so close that he passed between our front and rear wings. As that fighter twisted, he was so close that I could see he had blue eyes. I did not get a shot off after him because I was too busy shooting at another ME-109."

On August 5, 1943, the 99th relocated to Oudna, Tunisia, which was a few miles south of Tunis.[25] There they once again set up a tent city to include foxholes, outdoor latrines, and antiaircraft defense. They were now closer to a major city than had been the case at Navarin, and Charlie and the guys were sometimes able to visit the city of Tunis. "We didn't get passes. If you had a day off, you could go into town, unless there was some kind of restriction."

Even though they were now closer to a larger city, things weren't any safer. "For a period of time while flying out of Tunis, I had to be in the ball during both takeoff and landing because the Germans would attack us as soon as we came off the coast. They also would follow us back to the base. I had to be ready all the time until they were finally chased out of Africa. I normally was not in the ball during takeoff and landing, and when not in enemy territory, I could be up in the plane."

Their first mission from the Oudna airfield was to Messina, Sicily, and it was very successful. On August 13, 1943, the target was the San Lorenzo marshaling yard at Rome.[26] Luckily it turned out to be an easy mission. The big event on August 14 was the Bob Hope show at the 301st

Bomb Group airfield. Many personnel of the 99th BG went to that field to see the show, which included the lovely Frances Langford.[27]

Charlie didn't get to see the show, but "in Tunis, I saw Bob Hope and Frances Langford. Lippolt and I went sightseeing into Tunis one afternoon and checked out the town. We were walking down a street and I heard a voice and I thought to myself, 'I know that voice.' It was Bob Hope and Frances Langford coming out of a hotel. We yelled at them as they got into a waiting car and Bob waved to us. They were there to put on a show. I never got to any of his shows."

Rest and relaxation was never long enough, and soon it was back to flying dangerous combat missions. "One time on a mission over Italy, flak hit us and cut the main wing spar. We had to feather one engine and drop out of formation. We headed back, but Captain T-Wood told us that we were not going to make it all the way back to our base in North Africa, so

Some of the men on pass in an unknown North African city in 1943. From left to right: Mike Mazu, Charles Eyer, and Jack Strasberg.

he was going to try for Sicily. Half of Sicily was still being held by the enemy, and we could not use the radio because the Germans would have located us and shot us down. The captain flew as low as possible. There were mountains on both sides of us, and boy, were they close. Captain T-Wood saw a landing strip, and he said, 'Boys, I don't know if it's American or German, so here we go because I got to get down.' It was an American fighter base."

"We landed and got out of the plane as their ground crew came out to meet us. They used big poles to push the wing up. They then took some of the underside of the wing off and climbed up inside to weld it and put it back together. We were there at least two days, maybe three. Finally we were ready to go, but we were afraid that the welding job wasn't going to hold. We took off and made it back to our field. There our ground crew checked it out and said, 'If you flew it here, you can fly it some more.' I finished all those missions in Shanker Ali."

On August 17, the 99th carried out their first mission to France. The target was the Istres–Le Tubé airfield near Marseille.[28] They surprised the enemy and destroyed numerous aircraft that were caught on the ground. The enemy had their planes lined up wing tip to wing tip. The bombers also caused damage that day to hangars and flak batteries. Fortunately the flak was light and there was no fighter opposition.

On August 19, 1943, Charlie and crew hit the marshaling yards at Foggia, Italy.[29] There was no fighter opposition and the flak was moderate. On August 25, Foggia was again the target for the 99th.[30] They destroyed 41 enemy aircraft on the ground and damaged 28 others. One bomber and crew from Charlie's squadron, the 416th, was lost. The August 28, 1943, target was the marshaling yards at Terni, Italy.[31] There were enemy fighters in the area but the P-38 escort made short work of them. The flak was accurate but light. On August 31, 1943, the targets were the marshaling yards and industrial area at Pisa, Italy, where they did encounter some enemy fighters.[32]

Often the hardest part of a mission was the return home, especially in a damaged bomber. "Returning from a mission to Italy we saw one of our planes go down and make a forced landing in the Mediterranean Sea. Their life boats did not come out and they were down there swimming around. I was in the ball and could see them and told Captain T-Wood what was going on down below. He decided we would swing around and drop our life boats for them. We made a big circle and the bombardier took over flying the plane to drop them as close as possible. He dropped them and I watched the downed crew get to the life boats. We dropped two life boats which is all we had. We got into trouble for doing that because we broke formation and you weren't supposed to break formation for any reason. As usual, we were called on the carpet. We got called on to the carpet pretty often for doing things like that. So we took our verbal lashing, but at least those guys had life boats."

Sometimes the ground personnel and the air crews did not get along or see eye to eye. "A Lieutenant O'Rourke was the flight officer for Operations. He was part of the ground crew. We nick-named him the '90-Day Wonder.' Nobody liked him. So the first night he was Officer of the Day [OD] he came out to check the airplanes and us guys to see if anyone on guard duty was sleeping. We had all seen on the bulletin board that he was going to be the OD, so we put together a plan. All the guys in all the planes, which were parked in a circle, and he would have to come in, and then we would take out our sub-machine guns. We would let him come out so far, and then we were going to give him a celebration. So when he came out we were all ready and everybody opened fire when he got close enough. We all shot up into the air. He spun the jeep around and went back, and he wouldn't come out anymore. They had to put other officers on as OD. Lieutenant O'Rourke was kept on other duties and never messed with us again."

However, the troubles for Lieutenant O'Rourke were not quite over. "We were landing after a mission, and as we approached the area, somebody, probably a ball turret gunner, opened fire on Lieutenant O'Rourke's tent. If the lieutenant would have been sitting in his chair! A round went through that chair and there was a row of holes through the tent. All ball turret gunners along with the pilots were called in. They questioned the pilots first. None of the pilots heard any firing. Then they came to the ball turret gunners. They questioned and lectured us. They wanted the guy that did it to step forward. Nobody stepped forward. Then we were asked individually if we fired our guns. No, sir! Wasn't anything they could do because all the guns had been fired in combat. So how would they check? They couldn't find out who did it, but, whoever did it, we praised him. The next day that lieutenant was gone. They shipped him out."

On September 9, 1943, the raid targets were bridges and a highway over the Volturno at Capua, Italy, where the bombers were met with light flak and no enemy fighters.[33] The September 10, 1943, target was a highway at Isernia, Italy,[34] and it was clogged with German trucks and vehicles when American bombers attacked. The group met only light flak on September 11, 1943, when they bombed a highway bridge at Benevento, Italy.[35] On September 12, 1943, the target was the airfield at Frosinone, Italy.[36]

About 60 German JU-52 transports were parked on the airfield and many were destroyed. The September 14, 1943, target was Torre Annunziato, Italy.[37] This was a significant mission and was carried out to obstruct the flow of German reinforcements to the Salerno area.

Finally Charlie reached his 50th combat mission and completed his tour of duty. "My 50th mission was on September 16, 1943. The target was a highway/railroad bridge at Benevento, Italy." The group encountered some flak on this mission while attacking the highway and railroad bridge at Benevento. "I flew a lot of missions that didn't count toward the total. Sometimes I had to fly with another crew if they were short someone, but most missions were with Shanker Ali and my crew."

Combat fatigue, or, as it is known today, PTSD, affected most of the men at some time during their tours. "There was one time [at the base] I couldn't get out of bed. I was paralyzed due to battle fatigue. I woke up one morning and couldn't move. The guys picked the cot up with me in it and carried me down to the dispensary to see the doctor. The doctor said, 'He'll be all right—he's just tired and battle fatigued and this is what happens.' They took me back and he gave me something to take, and I rested for a few days. He checked me out three days later. So I missed three days. When you were sick they put a substitute in your place. That's how we got to fly with different crews when required. Our whole crew didn't finish at the same time."

Staff Sergeant Charles Eyer. This photograph was taken in North Africa just after he completed his 50th combat mission in September 1943.

At the time, Charlie didn't realize that all those missions took a serious psychological and physical toll on him. He knew that some men would break under the stress and come down with battle fatigue, but never himself. But when it happened to him, he felt he just needed a rest from combat missions, the same way an infantryman would need a rest if he could no longer fight. He had seen other combat airmen removed temporarily from flying status and knew that most of them usually returned to combat duty.

Upon completion of his 50th combat mission, Charlie remembered the airmen who sadly lost their lives. He remembered all of the close calls he had and from which he escaped unharmed. Now those memories seemed like a bad dream to him. The many hours he was unable to fall asleep on the night before a mission. The anxious moments he spent thinking about dying. Now, for the moment, anyway, all this was part of the past. Today he was alive and in one piece, and it seemed almost too good to be true.

Much anxiety and care just fell from Charlie's shoulders. "After finishing up my last mission [50th], I was sent to a beautiful hotel in Algiers. They had little two-person villas. Before the war couples paid to stay in these places, and they were really nice. We had a cleaning woman who came in every day and cleaned. We spent most of our time in the hotel. There they had a barroom, and we could eat there in the cafeteria. I was sent there to rest for three weeks. They used to bring in truckloads of girls, with their parents, who had to stay with the girls. They had an orchestra and would have a big dance in the hotel. It was really nice and almost like being at home. That is where I met Audrey. She was there with her mother and they didn't dance, and neither did I. So we sat at a table and talked. The mother could speak English. We had a nice time and once a week they were there on a Saturday night. They did that just for us. This was for the guys who finished their 50th mission."

Even at a rest camp, excitement seemed to find Charlie. "The officers went to some other place to rest. It was a beautiful hotel and a beautiful beach where we could swim. They had a horse that could be ridden. It was a big black stallion. The French caretaker asked if I wanted to ride the horse, and I shook my head yes. He saddled the horse, and I got on him and started following a road from the hotel. I got into a little town and it was all cobblestone roads. As I approached the town the stallion started acting crazy, with his ears up, prancing. I knew something wasn't right, but I wanted to go into the town, and I did. I got into town and there was a guy with a buggy pulled by a mare, and she was in heat. That's what was on the stallion's mind. I had a hell of a time because he was trying to mount her right on the street and while she was attached to the buggy! The other guy had her by the reins and was trying to walk away with her, and he was hollering bloody murder as the stallion tried mounting her. I was trying to turn and control the stallion. Finally I got him away and turned around and rode him back to the stable. I'm not sure if we damaged that buggy, but I never did get to see the town."

Finally it was time to return to the United States, but not before he witnessed one final tragedy. "I had orders to come back to the States on a boat. I didn't want to return on a boat. I wanted to fly. Me and another guy got a truck and went to a nearby airfield to get a plane ride. The colonel at the base looked at our orders and said we didn't have to take a boat, we could fly back. At the end of the three weeks I had to report back to the airport. Everything was scheduled, so we just waited. We were standing outside waiting and there was a bunch of women there, WACs [Women's Army Corps], and they were all pregnant. They were sending them back to the United States. We talked to them until their plane arrived. They loaded onto their plane and taxied away. The plane revved up and started going as we waved at them. What happened next, I don't know. But as the plane was lifting off it suddenly dropped down, nose first, flipped over and blew up! That was the end of all of them. The plane had been full of fuel and they couldn't get the fire out quickly enough. And here we stood, waiting for our plane to arrive."

CHAPTER 4

New Crew and New Adventures

The difference between ground combat troops and combat airmen was at some fixed point their combat days would come to an end. Men in ground combat units were typically in the war for the duration, if they had not earned enough points to be sent home. But most combat airmen flew a tour of duty and when completed they were shipped back to the United States. This rotation system provided Charlie with some hope of survival and motivated him to fly his assigned missions. Like most combat airmen, he desired to honorably complete his tour of duty.

The length of a crewman's tour of duty depended on the unit and the location. Early in the war, when missions were difficult and very hazardous, they generally flew fewer missions to complete their tours. In England, for bomber crews, a tour of duty consisted of between 25 and 35 missions. In North Africa and then in Italy, bomber crews had to fly 50 combat missions.[1] Charlie felt great joy when he completed his 50 combat missions as the many months of stress seemingly disappeared in the excitement of his survival and triumph.

As Charlie worked his way through the dangerous combat tour of duty, he went through different states of mind. He knew how many missions he had to complete, and he knew he could become a casualty on any mission. Casualties among the heavy bomber crews in the European theater were very high, and in the first six months of 1944 alone, they suffered a casualty rate of more than 88 percent.[2] Most of the casualties were either men killed in action or taken prisoner of war.

Early in his first tour Charlie believed that his chance of survival and completing it were good. But after a few close calls and seeing other bombers shot down, his confidence wasn't quite so high. As more bombers went down so did his hope for surviving long enough to complete his tour of duty.

Sometimes during combat Charlie found temporary relief from his fears. This occurred when his job required him to think of nothing else besides the task at hand. Sometimes he had very little time to think about his fears while he fought to survive. But at other times while in aerial combat, he could not shake the feelings of fear.

He tried very hard just to stay focused on his job and not think about how many more missions he had to complete. He didn't dwell on negative thoughts and tried to stay positive and upbeat as much as possible. Even though men he knew had been killed, he was glad that it wasn't him or any of his crew. But he also knew that it was a very dangerous business and something disastrous could strike him at any time. Sometimes he thought about the odds and realized he was playing against a stacked deck. Nearing the end of his tour in North Africa was a time of some anxiety for Charlie.

Between Charlie's first and last mission, he had to go about trying to survive long enough to complete his combat tour. Seeing so much death and destruction, he sometimes wondered why some men died and others didn't. He fought to control something that was mostly uncontrollable: life or death.

His extremely dangerous job affected him. Experiencing some level of fear was understandable considering the dangers he faced. Just as ground combat soldiers did not hesitate in admitting their fears, so did Charlie. He and many other crewmen were very suspicious of anyone who claimed not to be afraid. He believed that anyone like that was either a liar or crazy.

Still in North Africa, Charlie's transport plane finally arrived and the first leg of his return to the United States began. However, his return trip was also dangerous, but in a way that Charlie did not anticipate. "They flew us from Algiers to Dakar [Senegal], which is in the jungle. There I had to stay overnight. There was mosquito netting over the cots, and each cot had a pump sprayer to kill the mosquitos. I got in and tucked the screening in around the bottom of the cot. Then I took the sprayer and sprayed all about. I laid down and put a blanket on me, and the next thing I heard was buzzing mosquitos. Somehow they were getting past the netting. I finally fell asleep and sometime during the night was bitten by a mosquito."

Charlie's long-awaited journey home was in trouble. "The next morning everybody got on the plane. I was the last to get on and a sergeant stopped me. He told me there was a lieutenant who has been there for a couple of days already, so I would have to wait overnight. I was getting sick now. The first odd thing I noticed was when I lit a cigarette. I threw it away because it had the most horrible taste I ever had in my mouth. I did not feel well, but I didn't know what the heck was going on. I kept getting worse, and by the evening meal, I couldn't eat. I went back to the tent and really started feeling badly. Somehow I realized it might be malaria."

"I went to see a doctor. I saw a lieutenant first and he told me that I had malaria. He also told me that I would be going to the hospital there and that I would be delayed at least two weeks. Oh no! The doctor finally came in and asked me what the problem was. I just told him that I hadn't gone in a while and I needed a laxative or something. The doctor fixed me up with something and said that should help. So I just left and went back to my bunk and slept. By the next morning I felt rotten, but I got up and got ready to depart."

Charlie was determined to make it home, no matter what. "The plane came in and I got on it. Just one more stop and I'd be in Florida! Flying the first stretch to Jamaica, I felt like I was going to die. I was so sick. Before getting off of the plane, they fumigated it, and that was awful. Getting off the plane there were two nurses at the bottom of the stairs, taking temperatures and checking people. I thought, 'Oh no, now I'll end up having to stay there.' A nurse put a thermometer in my mouth, took it out, and asked me if I was feeling all right. I said I was just airsick, but I'll be okay. She questioned me some more, and I told her I'd be all right, and she let me go." Did the nurse not see the wings on Charlie's uniform or know he was a combat airmen? Airsick?

The journey home continued. "On the flight to Florida I felt so bad that I thought I would die. We landed in Florida and trucks were there to transport us. I asked a sergeant how long we would be there. He replied that I would be on my way home tomorrow morning. So I thought, 'If I'm going to die, I'm going to die at home.' They gave me my orders and took me to the train station. I arrived home and started thinking that I was not that sick, and I kept fighting the illness."

He continued to struggle with the malaria and tried very hard to enjoy his leave with family and friends. "Halloween arrived and so did the Halloween parade in Kutztown. Some family friends came and picked up Mom and me, and we went to the parade. I was okay watching the parade, but while I was standing there, I got worse. I started to sweat, and the water just ran off of me. Finally the sweating stopped but then the chills started. I stood behind Mom so she couldn't see me, and that's how I watched the parade. After the parade we walked down the street to a relative's house. I felt so poorly that I could not eat anything. When it was time to leave, I was too sick to drive. When we got home I went straight to bed, and all night it was sweat and chills, sweat and chills."

He had a very rough night and the next morning something had to be done. "The next morning Mom telephoned the doctor. Dr. Potteiger came to the house and checked me out. I told him that I thought that I might have malaria. It was then that he remembered that I had been in Africa. Dr. Potteiger called the Reading airport, where there was an army hospital. They came to the house and picked me up. They piled four or five blankets on me to keep me warm because I was shaking so badly that my teeth were rattling. By the time we got to the hospital, they could have wrung those blankets out from all the sweat."

In the army hospital, "two nurses fought over which one would get to take care of me. The bed was close to the wall, and when I got the chills, it banged against the wall. The nurse had to keep pulling the bed into the middle of the room. My condition got worse, and I became delirious and didn't even know where I was. But finally I woke up and felt better from whatever they were doing to me. It took about two weeks until I felt well enough to get up and move around."

"One day the nurse asked if I minded doing some work, and I said I didn't. So they gave me some cleaning chores. At the end of three weeks they were ready to discharge me, but before I left, I got a lecture from the doctor. He told me not to drink alcoholic beverages, but I would drink anyway. I took quinine pills when I was on flying status. But they didn't give me any after that, includ-

Staff Sergeant Charles Eyer recuperating from malaria at the air force hospital located in Reading, Pennsylvania, in November 1943. The nurse is unknown.

ing while I was at the rest resort in Algiers. I probably would have never come down with malaria had they kept supplying me with the quinine."

After his three-week stay in the hospital, it was time for Charlie to report to his next duty station. "My orders said that I was to report to Salt Lake City. Because of my recent illness, I asked for a time extension. I received a telegram from a captain, and his message was not completely clear, and a person could get two different meanings. So I figured I'll take the meaning I liked and just act stupid. So I stayed home three more weeks, when I was supposed to only stay the amount of time I had already spent in the hospital. A delay en route."

Finally he was on the road again and traveling to his next base. "When going to Salt Lake City, I took a Greyhound bus out of Reading. When the bus stopped in Arizona, I and another guy got off. I went into a bar and got drunk. The bus driver would not let me back on the bus because I was too drunk. The next day I was still not allowed on a bus, for the same reason. Finally on the third day I was sober and allowed to get on the bus. But now I had lost two days." Charlie didn't know of the trouble that awaited him because of those lost days.

"When I finally got to Salt Lake City, I had to report to this captain. The captain lectured me about being AWOL. I showed him the telegram and told him what I thought it meant. He said no, that he knew what it said because he was the person who wrote it! So he called the military police, and two MPs came and the captain instructed them to take me to the brig. So I went to the brig."

Life in the brig wasn't too hard for Charlie. "The brig was just a barracks with bars on the windows. The MPs turned me over to the sergeant in charge there. The sergeant told me that if I wanted to go to the movies or anyplace to just let him know and he'd cover for me. He said the charge against me was ridiculous. The captain had me up for a court-martial for being AWOL."

"A lieutenant was assigned to defend me, and we talked and I gave him the telegram. The lieutenant read it and said that he thought he would have stayed home too! He told me not to worry about it and that he would work on my defense. A couple of nights later the prosecutor came to see me. I gave him the telegram and he started laughing. He said that he would have done the same thing! He then said, 'Here's what we're going to do. I'm going to ask you one question: why did you come back two days early? I don't want you to answer.'"

On the day of the court-martial: "two MPs, one on each side of me, came and took me away to the court-martial. I stood up in front of the court-martial board and stated my name, rank, and serial number. The officer defending me then made a statement. Then the prosecutor asked me the question 'Why did you come back two days early?' As previously instructed, I didn't answer, but I'm thinking, 'What's going to happen?' A lieutenant colonel on the court-martial board stood up, as did I, and said that I was acquitted. The MPs took me out and told me that a captain [not the captain who preferred the AWOL charge] wanted to see me. They took me to him, and this captain said he wanted me to hear something. He telephoned that captain that sent me the questionable telegram and chewed him out!"

"They took me to my new barracks, and I was the first man assigned to that barracks. I went to the mess hall and was standing in line when one of the mess personnel started the line moving into the building, stopped it, and yelled out my name. He told me to come ahead of everyone. When I got up on the porch at the entrance, this mess person said, 'Guys, this is the sergeant who flew 50 missions and just came back.' I got into the mess hall first, and for every meal they always wanted me to go first."

"They asked me what I was going to do now. Laughing, I said, 'Well, as long as I'm not in the brig, I want to go back overseas and fly some more.' They wanted me to teach the new gunners, but I didn't want to be an instructor. Lippolt did become an instructor." Charlie requested to be assigned as a gunner in a B-29 Superfortress in the Pacific theater, but his request was denied. He wanted to fly combat, and the air force would honor his request by sending him back to combat in the European theater in B-17s once more.

As much as Charlie wanted to survive and be at home, he was very proud of his duty as a combat airman. He never avoided combat and never shirked his duties and obligations. Handling the incredible stress and exhaustion of aerial combat and still having such an attitude was not easy. Surviving a tour of duty and dealing mentally with the effects of combat were not easy to do. Even though he had risked his life as a matter of routine, and suffered some of the worst horrors of combat, still felt that he had made the right choice volunteering for aerial combat again.

"I was sent back to Sioux City, and they knew I was coming because they had my photograph posted around the base. I got a Class-A pass and could do as I wanted, so I went into town. I didn't know that a Class-A pass was only good for three days. New ones were issued in different colors so you couldn't stay out for more than three days at a time. Well, I was out for a week and when I came back to the base the MPs grabbed me and told me that I was AWOL. They took me to a first sergeant, where

4. New Crew and New Adventures

I was required to sign some papers and told that I would be hearing from them."

"I waited a couple of days and didn't hear from them. So I got a new pass and went into town and stayed there again for nearly a week. Coming back to the base the MPs grabbed me, and here we go again. The same first sergeant says, 'Not again?!' I signed some papers again and he told me again that I would hear from them."

"I also had a rough time with some lieutenant who chewed me out and threatened to take my stripes if I kept going AWOL. I told him that he could have my stripes if he wanted them. The lieutenant finally gave up on me and told me to report to the post commander, a colonel."

"I had a ball living it up. I knew that I was going back into combat so I spent my free time the way I wanted to. If someone didn't want to be either an instructor or go back into combat, they would assign you to something else until your time was served. I was the only man from the Shanker Ali crew that went back and flew more combat missions."

"The colonel started in on me about my AWOLs. I told him that I was waiting to be assigned to a new crew. He said, 'Okay, but that doesn't mean you can do whatever you please or excuse the AWOLs.' He asked me if I could drive a car and I lied and said, 'No, sir.' He suggested a couple of other things I might do, and I kept saying no, 'can't' or 'never did that.' The colonel was turning red and becoming angry. 'All right, sergeant, I have one thing that I know you can do. You report to the mess hall for KP [kitchen police] duty.' I responded, 'Yes, sir, I can do that!'"

"The next morning I got up and put on my Class A dress uniform with all my ribbons, wings, and stuff, and I went to the mess hall. I reported to the mess sergeant and told him I was reporting for KP duty. He said, 'You're what?!' I said, 'I'm reporting for KP duty.' He said, 'You get the hell out of here. If I put you on KP none of these guys are going to fly. They'll all quit after they've seen what happened to you. Don't worry about the commander, just get out of here.' So I left and thought to myself, 'Well, I'm all dressed up, so I might as well go to town!' That was the last AWOL for me and the one that Captain Van Every saved me from punishment."

"I went AWOL for a total of seven times, until Captain Van Every heard the first sergeant talking to me. Van Every asked who I was, and when I told him, he informed me that I was going to be his ball turret gunner. He told the first sergeant that he would take care of this. At this time, Van Every's crew was in their last phase of training. He asked me why I went AWOL and I told him that I had been going AWOL ever since I arrived at Sioux City because I had nothing to do. All I had been doing was waiting for the others to finish their training. That first sergeant, well, he had just put the paperwork for all seven of the AWOLs in his desk. He never did send any in and wouldn't, so these AWOLs were never put on my record."

Just who was Captain Van Every, besides the man that saved Charlie from some serious military punishment? Harold Van Every was from Minnesota and quite an athlete and, according to Charlie, a natural born leader. During the period of 1936–1939, as an all-conference halfback, he had an outstanding career with the Golden Gophers football team at the University of Minnesota. As a sophomore for the Gophers, he received All-American mention in 1937. He was a member of two Big Ten championship teams.

Dubbed a "triple threat" for his ability to run, pass and kick, he was named team MVP in 1939, the year he led the entire nation with nine interceptions. After graduation, Van Every was selected by the Green Bay Packers in the first round of the NFL draft. He played for two seasons under coach Curly Lambeau until the outbreak of World War II.

The crew was finalized and consisted of Captain Harold Van Every (pilot), Lieutenant Oran Richardson (co-pilot), Lieutenant Rudy Jacob (navigator; later killed in action by friendly fire while flying with another crew), Lieutenant Leonard Jankes (navigator), Lieutenant Nicholas Scholz (bombardier), Sergeant Anthony Rakiewicz (flight engineer/top turret gunner), Staff Sergeant Ralph Hough (radio operator), Staff Sergeant Charles Eyer (ball turret gunner), Staff Sergeant William Finch (waist gunner), Sergeant Charles Hathaway (waist gunner), Staff Sergeant John Prendergast (tail gunner; wounded in action and replaced), and Staff Sergeant Robert Jackson (tail gunner).

After the new crew was trained and ready to go, Charlie was granted one last trip back home. "I got a 10-day pass to go home before departing Sioux City. I took the train going home, but only got six days because I received a telegram telling me to return to the base immediately."

"We departed Sioux City for England in April of 1944. We left Sioux City on a train for Salina, Kansas, where we picked up a new plane. From there we flew the new plane to Bangor, Maine. When we were getting close to Bangor, we got a radio message that they were having a terrible snowstorm there. We landed but then got snowed in. We spent a couple of days there until they opened up the runway and we could take off again. From there we flew to Iceland and then to Ireland."

"We flew into Ireland, where they kept all the new planes. When a crew was shot down, they'd fly a plane from Ireland to England to replace the one that was shot down. That's how they shuttled them over. They

4. New Crew and New Adventures

were protected in Ireland from German bombing."

"We were in Ireland a couple of days. Then they put us on a little boat and took us across to England. There we were picked up by trucks and taken to the base. The English countryside was covered with air bases. The plane we would fly was already at the base. We got a brand-new plane that had been flown to the base earlier. We didn't know what squadron or group we would end up in yet. We ended up in the 447th Bomb Group, 710th Bombardment Squadron."

The same as inexperienced men in ground combat units, new combat airmen and crews had to prove themselves in combat before winning the respect of the veteran airmen. The new crew knew they were not part of the original unit, and being a replacement crew was a lonely thing. They were expected to take over for a bomber crew that may have been loved and respected. The crew they were replacing was either returning home, sitting in a prisoner of war camp, or dead.[3] Charlie now found himself as the only veteran crewman in a B-17 filled with inexperienced and unproven men.

Staff Sergeant Charles Eyer back home in Hamburg, Pennsylvania, on leave in March 1944.

Charlie knew the shock of combat and knew what it was like to have a heart beating so hard that breathing was difficult. He knew about a tight throat and a mouth so dry he couldn't even swallow. He knew what it was like to sweat inside a heated suit so much that it gave him small electrical shocks. He knew in aerial combat that the instinct to survive takes over and made him react to the situation by doing what was necessary, what he had been trained to do. He knew what it was like getting an adrenaline rush which gave him added strength and drive. All these things Charlie knew about because he had experienced them many times.

Chapter 5

Return to Hell

Many American combat airmen in the European theater were stationed in England. Large formations of heavy bombers attacked Germany from there and helped to pound them into submission using powerful strategic bombing. None of that would have been possible without the dozens of American airbases located in East Anglia and southern England, filling the region with American planes and airmen.

At that time, East Anglia was an area of very old farms, meandering rivers, and low, flat marshland. It stretched northward from Cambridge to the town of Norwich and eastward to Great Yarmouth on the North Sea. It essentially is a piece of land that pokes out into the water and points directly at the European continent. Its fields were ideal for airbases from which the Americans could strike deep into enemy territory. It was changed by the war into one of the greatest battlefronts of the world, a battlefront unlike anything seen to that point in time. It was an air front.

Charlie and crew were assigned to the 447th Bombardment Group (Heavy), which was part of the 8th Air Force. The group headquarters and all four subordinate bombardment squadrons were located at Rattlesden. It was situated between Stowmarket and Bury St. Edmunds and was built in 1942 as a bomber airfield. The airfield had three intersecting concrete runways, perimeter track, hardstands for 50 aircraft, and hangars. Barracks and dining facilities were located on the east side of the field.

After arriving at Rattlesden on April 13, 1944, Charlie and crew were assigned to the 710th Bomb Squadron of the 447th Bombardment Group (Heavy). They had a short period of orientation training before flying their first combat mission. During this time the crew attended classroom briefings and completed some cross-country training flights. These were flown to familiarize the crew with the lay of the land and to learn the landmarks unique to their airfield. But the most important thing they did was practicing close-formation flying.

Training missions, just like combat missions, were often dangerous. The first task of either mission required a successful takeoff, and this was sometimes hard to do because of the excessive weight of the aircraft. Bombers were typically overloaded with thousands of gallons of fuel in addition to the bombs for their mission and then required to takeoff from cramped airfields with short runways. These conditions always made Charlie a bit nervous.

Two crews were located in a non-commissioned officer (NCO) barracks, with 12 men, all sergeants, in each hut. The huts were made of corrugated steel in the form of a half-dome with a wooden wall and door at the front. They were set upon a concrete slab. Inside the hut were bunks, homemade shelves, and one single bare light bulb dangling from a wire in the center. A small coke stove was in the middle of the hut, but it didn't provide much heat.

Charlie slept on a straw mattress covered with "ticking," which is a very heavy canvas-like material. Sheets and pillowcases were not provided, but they did have the thick, itchy army-issue woolen blankets. The base and living conditions were somewhat comfortable. He knew he was very lucky to be able to return to a safe base after a dangerous mission and find a bed and hot chow waiting for him.

He discovered that the standard of living was lower in England than it was back home. But he understood that because of the war, the accommodations couldn't really be any better. He clearly knew that many other troops were living in much worse conditions and that made Charlie thankful for having a roof over his head. Above all, he appreciated living in England, a nation very similar to America, because it was much better than living in a dusty tent in North Africa.

"We arrived at the base with all our duffle bags and stuff with us. We grabbed our stuff and got off of the trucks. They had Quonset huts as barracks. This is where I met Sergeant Northrup, whose crew had been shot down some time before we got there. He came running out of the barracks, waving his arms and yelling that we didn't want to go into that hut. When we asked him why, he said every crew that had stayed in that hut had been shot down. We told him we weren't superstitious and we were moving in."

Northrup's warning may have seemed superstitious to Charlie and crew, but it may have been a premonition of bad things to come. "We moved in and it was the third or fourth mission we're flying, with Northrup's plane in our formation. Coming back over the coast of France and headed for

England, they [the Germans] had the flak guns on us and pumped the stuff up at us. Northrup's plane was hit and went up in flames. I didn't see any chutes from his plane. So when we got back and went to the debriefing, where the officers asked questions—like, did you shoot anything down, etc.—we reported the lost plane [Northrup's]. We kept flying our missions after that, and of course, we go down on our ninth mission."

Briefly jumping ahead in time, Charlie recalled meeting Northrup again, after believing he had been killed. "After being captured they took us to Frankfurt where there was a big holding building. We were taught that if you got into a place like that, you don't know anybody and nobody knows you. The Germans watched for that. So I walked into the building and into an immense room filled with guys, and there sat Northrup, in a cast from his feet to his waist! I couldn't believe it when I saw him, but I didn't look directly at him or anything. I waited a long time and then just eased my way over to him and sat down next to him. When no guard was looking, we talked a little."

"He had gone down in the English Channel. He and two others lived. One of those guys would go insane later in the prison camp, and the other guy was hurt worse than Northrup. When they took us to the prison camp he was with us. He was one of the crippled guys that the Germans put in each boxcar so we wouldn't try to escape. They knew we wouldn't escape without taking everybody along. We had another guy with a broken back in the same car." Northrup would survive the war.

Back at Rattlesden, all training flights and combat missions were flown following a standard briefing. After the briefing the crews moved out to their assigned bomber and conducted various preflight procedures. Once ready, the airmen waited for the firing of a green flare which signaled the mission would proceed. For Charlie, waiting for clearance to start their engines was one of the hardest parts of a mission. Having prepared himself mentally to face another dangerous combat mission, the wait allowed for boredom and anxiety to creep in and increased tension.

"We started flying almost immediately after arriving in England because they wanted as many planes as possible in the air. Usually we took off at daybreak. In England it was always raining and foggy, but when we got up through the clouds we would be in the clear. Sometimes it took two or three hours to form up. Twice, out of eight missions, we had to return because of bad weather. Some missions were 12 hours long. As soon as we cross the Channel, we were over enemy territory."

England is known for its rainy and foggy weather, and clear days in England were few and far between. The pilots had to handle dangerous

5. Return to Hell

weather conditions and fly in them, like it or not. Frequently the foggy and rainy English weather was not bad enough to cancel a mission, which meant flying in very dangerous conditions.

Predicting the weather was difficult, and the main problem was all the moisture. The weather often changed rapidly and Charlie and crew rarely found themselves flying in really good weather. A mission would only be scrubbed for very bad weather over England or over the primary target. He realized that the scrubbed mission would have to be flown another day but still felt a sense of relief, for the moment.

Charlie and the other airmen disliked the weather not only because it made for dangerous flying conditions, but also because it caused lousy living conditions. To heat the hut with the small stove provided, they only received a coke ration every three days, and if it was a bitterly cold and damp evening, they could burn up their entire supply in one night. Because they never received enough coal or coke, the men regularly helped themselves to some from the base coal pile.

The crew was usually concerned about the weight to be carried, but weather was the greatest problem that affected takeoff and assembly in the air. Thick fog, low cloud ceilings, and rain were common problems. Those conditions might require the bombers to increase their takeoff intervals from the normal 30-second span in good weather to a one-minute interval when not so good. Bad weather caused numerous incidents of bombers crashing into each other on the ground and in the air.

For takeoff, Charlie and the other three gunners in the rear part of the bomber gathered in the radio room. They gathered there because it was the safest place if there was a crash, plus it also moved the weight nearer the center of the bomber making control easier for the pilot during takeoff and climb. Once the bomber was in the air, the crewmen returned to their assigned positions.

On the bad weather days when they could not fly, Charlie and the men just laid in their bunks for much of the day, smoking, writing letters home, reading, or just doing nothing at all. Some rode bicycles into the local villages to pubs for some beer, whiskey, and some civilian companionship. They enjoyed England because of its familiar traditions, culture, and the same language, and they had excellent relations with the British people.

For the most part Charlie and crew ate well and received reasonably good food compared to the food served to other troops. The combat airmen ate in special mess halls reserved exclusively for combat personnel, usually had hot meals, and they rarely had to eat C-rations or K-rations, unlike the ground troops who often had to eat cold prepackaged rations.

On days when no missions were planned, a typical breakfast consisted of powdered eggs and sliced ham. Fresh eggs served at breakfast confirmed that a combat mission was scheduled. Fresh eggs were scarce, valued, and served only to combat crews who were scheduled on a mission. Charlie recalled, "For breakfast we got regular eggs, when nobody else did. Only the crews that flew. Everybody else was eating powdered eggs." The powdered eggs were prepared in large pans and for some strange reason always appeared to be green in color. Not very appetizing, but he ate them anyway.

Breakfast was prepared to eliminate stomach problems at high altitude and was very bland. The coffee tasted rusty and the cereal had to be eaten using lumpy powdered milk. Sometimes Charlie ate oatmeal and powdered milk, sometimes hot cakes with molasses syrup, and not because he liked them, but because they were warm and filled him up. He knew that breakfast might be his last meal for a long time, especially if he was shot down. After drinking some juice or coffee, the chow usually was easier to swallow. On very long missions, sandwiches were prepared, but they quickly froze solid in the extreme cold temperatures and couldn't be eaten.

There was no shortage of food on the airbase, nor was there a shortage of alcohol. During the war combat airmen had the reputation of being hard drinkers, which was somewhat true. Charlie and the crew drank great amounts of alcohol when off-duty. They had easy access to bars on the base and in the pubs and restaurants off base, and they also had plenty of money to spend on booze.

To temporarily escape the horrors of combat, he and many others drank large quantities of alcohol. The majority of the drinking didn't take place at parties, but rather night after night at the enlisted men's clubs on the base. After a terrifying day in the skies, he drank as a release. When casualties were heavy during a particularly rough mission, it affected morale and resulted in many airmen becoming extremely drunk. They also drank just to relieve the boredom. Charlie recalled, "That's what we did at night. We drank." As he laid in his bunk smoking a cigarette on those nights after returning from a particularly dangerous mission, he could see a lot of cigarettes glowing in the dark.

Operation Overlord (D-Day) was planned for the spring of 1944. Allied leaders were worried that their air forces would not have enough time and strength to gain air supremacy. General Dwight D. Eisenhower thought air supremacy necessary for the success of what would be the largest amphibious invasion in history. For this reason alone the bomber offensive could not be suspended, regardless of the high number of aircrew casualties. The invasion would depend upon the success of the bombers. In the cruelty of total war, it was considered far better to lose hundreds of bombers than to have entire ground force units destroyed on the beaches of enemy-held territory.

The USAAF completed a crucial duty. In the five-month battle for air supremacy that made D-Day possible, the American air forces in Europe lost more than 2,600 heavy bombers and 980 fighter planes and suffered 18,400 casualties, including 10,000 combat deaths.[1] Charlie commented, "We bombed and bombed and bombed, but if not for the ground forces, it didn't mean a thing. The infantry had to come in and take the land. The bombing we did was to soften up Germany. Hit them where it hurt most."

Casualties increased at an alarming rate in 1944, too fast for the airmen to even track them. A replacement crewman arrived in England in time for dinner, climbed into his bunk, and vanished the next morning over enemy territory. No one ever learned his name. His personal belongings were hurriedly tossed into bags and his bunk stripped. In no time at all there was no indication that he had even existed.

By 1944, more aircrews than bombers were available, and Charlie and crew would fly three different B-17s during their overseas tour of duty. Thousands of 8th Air Force aircraft were shot down or damaged beyond repair. The B-17s that he flew in while stationed in England were nameless, nor did they have any nose art. Most of their B-17s didn't last long enough for anything to be painted on the fuselage.

Charlie's first combat mission was flown on April 24, 1944, to Friedrichshafen, Germany, as a replacement with another crew. The briefing was at 6:30 a.m., and the target was an aircraft plant on the shore of Lake Constance which separated Germany from Switzerland. The bombers carried 48 tons of general purpose and 19 tons of incendiary bombs. They took off at 8:50 a.m. and the journey across France and southern Germany was uneventful. Flak over the target was heavy but caused no serious damage on his bomber. The bombing results were considered good, and they returned to base at 5:47 p.m. Of the 243 B-17s dispatched, nine were lost and 119 damaged. Casualties were seven killed-in-action (KIA), four wounded-in-action (WIA), and 71 missing in action (MIA). A fighter escort had been provided.[2]

The flak gradually stopped on the way back to Rattlesden, and the alert for enemy fighters was called off. Soon they were past the French coast and down to 10,000 feet. Now that they were out of danger, Charlie removed his oxygen mask, unplugged his electrically heated suit, and climbed out of the ball turret and into the fuselage. He relaxed for the first time since the mission began. The intercom was alive with chatter to determine how everybody was doing. The bombardier and the navigator crawled out of the nose and stretched out in the waist and chatted with the gunners. The radio operator turned the intercom to music from home, and they listened to some big band music.

As he looked out of one of the waist gunner windows while over the channel, Charlie saw the White Cliffs of Dover and then Rattlesden. The bomber slowly circled as the landing gear was lowered and the tail wheel was locked into position. The bombers ahead of them in the landing pattern with wounded aboard fired red flares to alert the base medical personnel. The tires squealed as they touched down, and they slowly taxied back to their hardstand. Opening the waist hatch, he and the other gunners piled out with all their gear. Charlie was a little shaky from all the hours confined in the ball turret and because of the oxygen he had been breathing.

The ground crew arrived and disassembled all the machine guns. The bomb bay was opened and all the releases were checked. The guns went back to the shop for cleaning and maintenance in preparation for the next mission. The spent brass was picked up and then it was off to the debriefing hut.

The intelligence officers asked the crew the usual series of questions, which took about 30 minutes. The Red Cross gals offered Charlie and the men a shot of whiskey and peanut butter sandwiches—not a good combination on an empty stomach. Back at the lockers he turned in his parachute and hung up his flying clothes. Then it was back to the hut where he just fell into bed. He was too tired to think or eat anything at the moment. Later, he got up and checked the bulletin board to see if the crew was on the roster for a mission the next day.

Charlie walked with some of the other crewmembers to the mess hall for dinner. After dinner, it was either a trip to the NCO club to listen to some good music and drink or maybe catch a movie at the base theater, and then it was back to his bunk to write a letter back home as he listened to the radio. He was careful about what he wrote because it might be censored. He was tired, but the weariness was mixed with anxiety because he knew tomorrow or maybe the next day he'd go through this same routine. With every mission the odds against coming back got worse and worse. Charlie had seen bunks left empty when a crew did not return. He had watched as personal effects were removed. He often pondered if he would be next and wondered when all this would come to an end.

5. Return to Hell

Charlie's second combat mission took place on April 27, 1944, to Le Culot, France. The briefing was at 1:30 p.m., and the planes were loaded with 60 tons of bombs, with takeoff at 4:00 p.m. The bombing altitude of 18,000 feet was reached as the group crossed the French coast. However, the primary target, which was a V-weapon site, was covered by clouds so an airfield in Le Culot was bombed instead. Results were fair and landing started at 9:00 p.m. One hundred and twenty B-17s were dispatched. Two were lost and 29 were damaged. Casualties were one KIA and 20 MIA. A fighter escort had been provided.[3]

The Germans had a chain of radar stations that stretched from Norway to northern France, and they typically knew when Allied bombers were coming from the moment they started assembling in the air over England. Charlie recalled, "From the time we hit the French coast we got ack-ack [antiaircraft] fire. And that is the thing that worked on my nerves the most. More than anything else at all. With the fighters I stood a chance because I could shoot back at them. With flak I had no control. We tried to avoid it if possible, but we were always patching flak holes on the plane."

His third mission was on April 29, 1944, to Berlin, Germany. Briefing was at 4:30 a.m. The bombers were loaded with 52 tons of incendiary and general purpose bombs, and their target was railway facilities.[4] "We got to the mess hall about 3:00 a.m., ate breakfast and then went to the briefing. They told us our mission and where we were going and all the details. Then we enlisted men went out to the plane and conducted the pre-flight. The officers had to stay and get their briefings—what course, what altitude, etc. When they were finished they came out to the plane and by that time we had the plane warmed up and ready to go. The sun wasn't up yet."

The formation reached the bombing altitude of 22,000 feet as they crossed into enemy territory. On the way to the target they encountered heavy numbers of enemy fighters. The formation was attacked by an estimated 350 German fighters and several bombers were lost to the Luftwaffe. A force of about 100 to 120 single engine fighters, mostly ME-109s, attacked with a fierce determination.[5]

Charlie watched as the German fighters came head on through the bomber formation and shot down three bombers on the first pass. The enemy was relentless and the attack lasted for more than 30 minutes. After the first couple of concentrated attacks, they bore in with four to eight fighters at a time. Then, when the bombers reached the target, they encountered heavy flak and lost some more aircraft. Once more the German fighters attacked, right in the middle of an intense flak barrage, which caused the bomber formation to become scattered. They eventually left the enemy coast on course and broke up the formation on orders from the wing commander.

Charlie and crew were in serious peril on this mission to Berlin. From the time their bomber crossed the French coast, they had been peppered by bursts of deadly black flak. Then, before reaching the Berlin target, more serious trouble developed. Just before opening the bomb bay doors, the No. 2 engine quit, and Captain Van Every was unable to feather the propellers. To feather an engine means that the propeller blades are turned so that they are aligned with the airflow to create minimal air resistance. This is done when an engine is shut down to prevent the propeller from creating drag and possibly causing the engine to tear itself apart.

They couldn't keep up with the formation on three engines so Van Every ordered the bombs dropped. They dropped their bomb load but then the bomb bay doors failed to close, which slowed them down some more. "We were making a run to Berlin, and just as we got close to the target, a fighter knocked one engine out," Charlie recalled. "With losing that engine we couldn't keep up with the formation. The Germans would try to knock an engine out and then the plane had to bank off to get out of the way of the other bombers behind it. And when it banked, the fighters were all over it. There we were, helpless, with no protection at all."

German fighters raised hell with them the entire time. Part of the oxygen system was shot out so Van Every had to drop down to a lower altitude. They were now entirely away from the protection of the group formation and knew they were easy prey if a German fighter saw them. There was only one thing to do, and that was to try to make it home alone.

The ship couldn't do more than 135 miles an hour, so Van Every asked for everyone's attention. He told them they must lighten the load! Get rid of everything! They threw out all the guns and ammunition and dropped the ball turret, which landed somewhere in Germany. "We peeled off and Van Every called everyone and said throw everything out. The guns, everything! He said we were down to two engines now. Throw everything out, radios, everything. He called me and said, 'Do you think you can drop the ball, Charlie?' I replied that I could drop it, and he said, 'Do it.' With my feet hooked around the catwalk so I wouldn't get sucked out, I removed the bolts and down it went. There were four bolts that held the ball in. I loosened all four of them, and when it went, it was a good thing that I had my feet hooked in because it really pulled me, but I hung on and stayed in the plane."

"I then laid on the catwalk, and just as I was getting up, I felt something go through my hair. I quickly looked toward the back of the plane

5. Return to Hell 79

and saw a piece of red-hot flak shrapnel. It had lifted my hair and went out the back of the ship somewhere. When that happened, I instantly dropped flat to the floor and it's good I did because a fighter came in and put a row of 20mm rounds right over me. The bullets striking the fuselage sounded like typing on a loose piece of paper. I laid flat on the catwalk as did the two waist gunners, and so was the tail gunner. That's all we could do." They no longer had any machine guns with which to return fire. They had no way now to protect and defend themselves or the bomber. It would be up to Van Every to get them home, somehow.

There was a thick overcast and they couldn't tell where they were going. They flew right over a German city which turned out to be Hannover and as they did the Germans really threw the flak at them. The Germans must have thought that their bomber was a whole formation. Somehow they managed to keep going. Finally they saw two or three American fighters. The fighters saw that they were going to make it and left. The coast of England looked mighty good to Charlie that day.

"We made it back to England and landed on an emergency field. We came in low over the White Cliffs of Dover, and right there was a runway for emergency use. They had fire engines and everything there. We landed and the ground personnel told us they knew we were all okay because they could count us walking around inside the plane. There were that many holes in the plane! They hauled us back to our base in a truck, and the next morning we had a brand-new plane."

Back in England, Charlie and crew took stock of what happened. There were more than 100 flak holes in the bomber. The gunners claimed five German fighters destroyed. It had been a long trip back from Berlin all by themselves. The overcast had saved them. If the German fighters would have spotted them, they would have been a sitting duck. They were lucky and glad to be alive. They learned a lot that day. It had been a bad day for the group. A total of 228 bombers were dispatched. Ten bombers were lost and 150 damaged. Casualties were one KIA, seven WIA, and 100 MIA. A fighter escort had been provided.[6]

The discovery the Germans had made previously about the B-17's nose being the most vulnerable place to attack was put to good use by the enemy during the missions over Germany. To exploit this weakness the German fighters would fly parallel with the bombers and stay just out of range of the B-17s machine guns, but close enough for Charlie and crew to see them. Then they quickly moved approximately a mile ahead of the bomber formation before making a sudden turn. Then, as they flew wingtip to wingtip, they ripped into the lead bombers of the formation with wave after wave of fighters. Each enemy pilot held his fire until he was close enough to see the spinning propellers of the bomber. Then he would fire all his guns and dive away just before crashing into the bomber. German fighter pilots described flying into the bombers' defensive machine gun fire as like flying into a shower.[7]

His fourth mission was on May 1, 1944, to Noball [sic], France. Briefing was at 1:30 a.m. and the target was a V-1 rocket site. Takeoff started at 4:19 a.m. but in the process of assembling the planes created a vapor trail cloud. Because of this, the group had to increase their altitude to get into clear air. After travelling only 16 miles, the contrails were so thick that the mission was aborted, and they started landing at 10:30 a.m.[8]

Charlie's fifth mission took place on May 7, 1944, to Berlin, Germany. Briefing was at 3:30 a.m., and the main target for this mission was the Luftwaffe itself. The bombers were used primarily as bait to bring the Luftwaffe to battle. The bombers were loaded with 53 tons of 100-pound incendiary bombs. Takeoff was at 6:00 a.m., and the group crossed the continent as they reached their bombing altitude of 23,750 feet.[9]

This was a new method. Typically in the past, bombing raids had included deceptive missions to confuse the enemy. But this time there weren't any tricks. The bombers flew predictable routes, which placed them in harm's way, and that was part of the plan.[10] With greater numbers of long-range P-51 Mustangs now in England, the USAAF was itching for a fight.

The flak was very heavy and accurate over Berlin, which caused the bomber to shake and bounce. Charlie heard the shrapnel hitting the bomber and it sounded like sleet pelting against a metal roof. Occasionally he heard the sound of metal tearing when a flak round exploded really close. Flak could tear big, ragged holes in the wings and fuselage and was capable of tearing a B-17 in half. Fortunately there were no losses in Charlie's group, and they landed at 2:45 p.m. Six hundred B-17s were dispatched. Eight bombers were lost, two were damaged beyond repair, and 265 were damaged. Eight were KIA, 14 WIA, and 83 MIA. Fighter escort had been provided.[11]

This was a very dangerous and nerve-wracking mission for Charlie and the rest of the crew. "At the debriefing, we all sat together at a long table and talked to an intelligence officer and told him what we saw, what we shot at, and whether we thought we hit anything. I never claimed any planes, but I know I shot some down. I fired on the fighters coming in at us until they turned away, and then I was after the next one coming in. I don't know if they turned away because I scared them, or if I hit them and maybe the pilot was dying. I never claimed them. There were a lot of guns firing at the same fighter. So who really hit? It wasn't a contest to me. I wanted to live. I didn't watch to see if an enemy fighter went down. They had bottles of scotch with shot glasses, and we drank as much as we wanted when we sat down for the debriefing. Tell them what you know and relax. After that debriefing I couldn't even go to eat. None of us wanted to eat."

The USAAF continued to take the fight to Germany, sent out the heavy bombers on huge raids, and dared the enemy to come up and fight. Sometimes in overcast weather, which made accurate bombing impossible, they still sent out large formations of bombers on baiting missions just to kill enemy fighters. In April of 1944 alone, Charlie's first month in England, the 8th Air Force lost 409 heavy bombers. That was the most it lost in any single month of the air war.[12]

Even though these missions to Berlin were sometimes suicidal, the fact that American planes had reached Berlin in daylight was very significant to both the Allies and the Germans. Early in the war, Hermann Göring had pledged to Hitler and Germany that not a single enemy bomb would drop on the capital, Berlin. After the war Göring was asked at what point had he realized that Germany was doomed. He replied, "The first time your bombers came over Hanover [sic], escorted by fighters, I began to be worried. When they came with fighter escorts over Berlin, I knew the jig was up."[13]

Mission number six for Charlie was flown on May 8, 1944, again to Berlin. The briefing was at 3:30 a.m., and the bombers carried 45 tons of general purpose bombs and takeoff started at 6:15 a.m. The targets were aircraft factories and targets of opportunity. Landing started at 2:15 p.m. Five hundred B-17s had been dispatched. Twenty-five B-17s were lost, one was damaged beyond repair, and 169 were damaged. Casualties were one KIA, seven WIA, and 261 MIA. Fighter escort had been provided.[14]

Everywhere Charlie looked he saw trails of smoke and balls of fire, and many, many parachutes from bombers going down. On the way in and over the target he sweated it out inside the ball turret as he listened to the thump of each shell exploding. No matter how cold he had been before the bomb run, he was warm now. While going through flak on the bomb run, there was little or no talk. But the instant bombs were away, everybody talked on the intercom, saying, "Let's get the hell out of here!"

After Charlie settled down into the routine of flying back to the base, he felt a flicker of happiness. Once again he and the rest of the crew had gone through hell without any injuries. Shot up as it was, the B-17 was still flying smoothly.

These suicidal missions gave Charlie a feeling that the odds of him surviving the war were getting worse. "I wrote a letter the night after the second bad mission. I went back to the Quonset hut and sat down and I had a funny feeling so I wrote a letter. I had a New Testament, a little one that I kept in my luggage. If things turned out the way I felt they might, they would find my letter inside the Bible. Maybe Mom would find the letter as she went through my stuff. So I wrote the letter which stated that I didn't feel as if I would be killed, but that I just felt something was going to happen. I failed to remember that if you go missing in action, the army will not send your stuff back home. They hold on to it until you return. And one day after the war I was back home and a box came in the mail, and there was the New Testament and my letter, and I read it to Mom."

His seventh mission took place on May 9, 1944, to Laon/Athies, France. The briefing was at 3:30 a.m. and the target was an airfield. This was the start of the air offensive against enemy airfields one month before the invasion of Normandy so that the Luftwaffe would not have time to recover before D-Day. This airfield was about 50 miles northeast of Paris. The bombers were loaded with 1,118 100-pound general purpose bombs and takeoff started at 6:00 a.m. The bombing altitude of 22,000 feet was reached as the group crossed the French coast near Calais. The flak was light, and the mission was mostly uneventful, but not for Charlie and crew. Bombing results were good and at 10:50 a.m. they started landing. A total of 242 B-17s were dispatched. Two B-17s were lost and 44 damaged, and one was KIA, one WIA, and 20 were MIA.[15]

Recalling this mission, Charlie said, "On the seventh mission, Sergeant Prendergast was hit. It was a rough mission, and the one side of the radio room was shot away. Prendergast was hit in the head, when a bullet got inside his helmet." Because they were returning with a wounded crewman, they broke formation upon approach at the air base. They fired a double red flare alerting other aircraft of the wounded man and their priority to land first. The ambulances raced to meet the bomber at the end of the runway and sped Prendergast away to a nearby medical facility.

A wounded crewman often had to hold on for hours during the return trip to their home base, and sometimes this was aboard a seriously damaged bomber. For a wounded crewman, the main thing was to make it back to a base. If he could do that, his chance of survival was good. When they approached the base, bombers with wounded aboard shot special flares in to the air to alert the tower. They then received first priority to land where an ambulance and trained medical personnel were waiting.

5. Return to Hell

Ambulances moved the wounded airmen to medical facilities that were usually located on or near the airbase.

There were many ways an airman might meet his fate. He might be killed by enemy fighters or flak or from other causes such as anoxia. There were no trained medical personnel available until the bomber made it back to a base. It was common for a badly wounded airman who was not going to survive a long journey home to be pushed from the bomber with his parachute. They did that hoping the enemy would provide medical care and save the crewman's life.[16]

In aerial combat death was horrible, brutal, and violent, and many combat airmen suffered tremendously. It wasn't glorious or romantic like in the movies. It was grisly and shocking. Bombers fell from the sky in flames. Often they spun out of control, trapping the crew inside. Occasionally one pulled out of a dive and crash-landed, but too often they blew up in the air. Charlie witnessed crewmen falling through the sky on fire; some fell because their parachute didn't open. He saw pieces of airmen and pieces of bombers fall to earth.

"On Saturday, Captain Van Every got a truck from the motor pool and we went to London to see Prendergast. We had to be back Sunday night. He had the 20mm chunk of metal and the helmet. A 20mm round had entered and spun around inside his helmet and laid him open. We never got back to see him again because we had too many missions tearing the guys apart. It was a rough time. We got a replacement but really never got to know him [Staff Sergeant Robert Jackson]. Nobody on the crew was hurt except for Prendergast."

The air base had a dispensary and sick quarters building with beds for the patients. The slightly injured men were kept in sick quarters until fit for duty, which was usually no more than a few days. Men who were seriously injured were evacuated to a general hospital some miles away from the air base.

Often crewmen who were badly burned or mutilated in a bomber crash were beyond help. A young officer had the bad luck of witnessing the death of a B-17 near his base and had a close look at the wreckage. The top of the cockpit was gone and it was all out in the open, piled up higher than the rest of the other debris.[17]

This young officer just stood there looking at the wreckage. It was covered with foam from the fire hoses and was lumped into one large blob. His eyes soon spotted something. It was the co-pilot sitting in his seat. He could just make out the body as it stuck out from under the foam. The body sat upright, the head was gone, and its right arm was at its side and its left arm raised and bent, protecting the face that was gone. Immediately behind the co-pilot's seat was another burnt body. It was the top turret gunner at his post between the pilot and the co-pilot. Then the young officer saw the form of the pilot, lying on what was left of the cockpit floor. All that was left of the pilot was a bent arm without a hand protruding above the foam. Soon the young officer had seen enough and departed the horrible and sickening scene.

Another officer who came upon another scene of destruction of a bomber couldn't believe his eyes. Wreckage was strewn over a large area, and he was the only person there except for the bomb disposal squad. He ignored the roped off area and walked to within a few feet of one of the craters caused by a bomb. Not all the bombs had exploded and there were still several live bombs lying about. The bottom of the crater was filled with melted aluminum from the intense heat of the burning bomber.[18]

Three men had a rope around the trunk of the body of one of the dead crewmen. The dead pilot and co-pilot were still sitting in their seats. Their arms and legs had been burned to stumps, and their entire bodies including their heads were burned black. The crew assigned to clean up the wreckage gave a tug on the rope, attempting to extract the body, but instead the upper body just pulled apart.

He didn't see any other bodies, but he did see an unburned electric flying glove. The aircrews always needed extra clothing so he thought he'd pick this one up and keep it as a spare. But as soon as he picked it up, he dropped it when he realized that it still had a hand in it. One of the other men pointed to the officer's feet and told him to look down. Looking down he saw that his foot was on top of a man's skull, which had been cut off at the hairline. He had seen more than enough. It was sights like these that Charlie and the others could never forget.

Charlie remembered the damaged bombers. "We had a lot of planes tore up, and I wonder how we got through. We brought two planes back in two days that were junk. They couldn't fix them. There wasn't enough left of the plane to fix. They were shot to pieces. In nine missions we lost two planes, plus the one we left in Germany, which blew up."

Mission number eight was on May 11, 1944, to Malines, Belgium. The briefing at 12:30 p.m. revealed that the targets were railroad yards in eastern Belgium, Luxembourg, and northeastern France. The bombers were loaded with 1,000-pound general purpose bombs and takeoff began at 3:00 p.m. The formation was at bombing altitude of 18,700 feet as they crossed into Belgium. Because of bad weather, the group bombed a railroad junction at Malines, Belgium, as a target of opportunity. Flak was light and the bombing results were fair. Landing started at 8:00 p.m. Six hundred Nine B-17s were dispatched. Eight B-17s were lost, one damaged beyond repair, and 172 damaged. Casualties were two KIA, 23 WIA, and 83 MIA. Fighter escort had been provided.[19]

There was no rest for Charlie and crew, and even if they had a bad day flying, they'd be right back up there fighting for their lives the next day. "It got harder to get in the plane every day. The next day we had to fly again. They would not let us stay on the ground, not if you had a bad experience. Because if they let you stay down one day, you'd never go back up again. That night we were on the list to fly again tomorrow. They took our navigator and tail gunner, and we got a replacement for each. These two replacements needed only one more mission to finish up their tour, so they put them with us." This would be their last mission, but not in the way they hoped for it to end.

Charlie's ninth and final mission flown out of England took place on May 12, 1944, target Zwickau, Germany. This would be Charlie's 59th combat mission overall. His B-17 was flying the number four lead position. He was in the lead flight of a 295-strong bomber formation. The crew for the mission was Captain Van Every (pilot), Lieutenant Richardson (co-pilot), Lieutenant Jankes (navigator), Lieutenant Scholz (bombardier), Sergeant Rakiewicz (top turret gunner), Staff Sergeant Hough (radio operator), Staff Sergeant Eyer (ball turret gunner), Staff Sergeant Finch (left waist gunner), Sergeant Hathaway (right waist gunner), and Staff Sergeant Jackson (tail gunner). The briefing was at 6:00 a.m. and the target was an aircraft repair depot at Zwickau, about 40 miles south of Leipzig. The bombers were loaded with 500-pound general purpose bombs and the first plane took off at 8:20 a.m.[20]

There were approximately 700 German fighters within interceptor range of the bomber formation. The formation headed for Frankfurt which pulled the Luftwaffe in that direction. As the bombers crossed the Rhine, there was only one friendly fighter group escorting them. Two hundred German fighters attacked and overwhelmed the American escort and scored heavily on the bombers. Another American fighter escort joined the fray and was able to get control. The German fighters reorganized and attacked the bomber formation again, but the fighter escort handled them.[21]

Things got tense when the bombers' "little friends" tipped their wings. This was the signal that the escort had to turn back because they were at the end of their range. Now the entire crew searched the sky for German fighters, "bandits." The frontal attacks by German fighters were terrifying, and they were a great danger to the bombers during violent air battles. Charlie, like many other combat airmen, respected and feared the German fighters.

The relay system that the American fighters used to protect the formations gave the enemy plenty of opportunities to shoot down bombers. Each group of escort fighters made contact with the bomber formation at a designated point. They then provided protection until their fuel was low, and then turned over escort duty to another group of long-range fighters. Typically, Thunderbolts and Lightnings took the bombers across the Rhine, and Mustangs ferried them to and from long-range targets such as Berlin and Munich. Up to a thousand fighters could be needed just to keep a few dozen covering the bombers at any given time. On Charlie's final combat mission they suffered heavy losses because there was a time period when they had little or no fighter escort coverage.

At 12:27 p.m., Charlie's group, the 447th BG, was attacked by FW-190s. The attack was head on and very intense, and about 15 B-17s were seen going down during this attack. Several of the bombers blew up. Enemy fighters attacked again at 2:34 p.m. when another B-17 went down. The 447th BG dropped their bombs with good results. A total of 295 B-17s were dispatched. Forty-one B-17s were lost, one damaged beyond repair, and 162 damaged. Casualties were three KIA, eight WIA, 377 MIA.[22] Charlie's bomber never got a chance to drop their bombs because they were shot down by enemy fighters before reaching the target. The odds finally caught up with Charlie.

Chapter 6

Day of Days—May 12, 1944

"On our ninth mission, we never made it to the target and were shot down before reaching it. We weren't the only one that went down that day. The Germans were out to get us."

Charlie couldn't know that May 12, 1944, would be the day of days for him and his fellow crewmates. On that day, after one more roll of the dice, Charlie's luck ran out. From the very beginning the odds were stacked way too high and were never in his favor.

Charlie ended up in Germany the same way thousands of other American airmen had before him and many more would after him. He got onboard a Flying Fortress, which flew into enemy territory to bomb a critical target, and never made it back to the safety of his base. As his bomber fell so did Charlie's hopes, faith, and efforts. Everything he had trained for and worked for during the past two years ended on that fateful day.

The B-17 Flying Fortress that Charlie bailed out of on that terrible day was serial number 42-97815. It had been delivered to the USAAF on March 5, 1944, and had only been delivered to Rattlesden airbase on April 22, 1944. The official report lists it as being knocked out of the air by German fighters with a wing on fire. According to the German Missing Air Crew Report #4770, what was left of the bomber crashed at Stockheim near Frieberg, which is about 20 miles east of Frankfurt.

On May 12, 1944, General Jimmy Doolittle sent 886 bombers against a group of synthetic oil plants in central Germany. This brought on a terrific air battle in which the Americans lost 46 bombers and the Germans more than 60 fighters. With improved German defense forces, nearly a thousand enemy fighters were positioned inside Germany on that day. They were in place to savagely attack the bomber formations using tightly massed assaults. It was a battle of mass against mass. This aerial battle, like many others in the months just prior to D-Day, was incredibly costly in men and planes.[1]

It was 3:00 a.m. when Charlie was awakened by a light shining in his eyes. It was the charge of quarters runner with a flashlight. He went to each bunk and told each member of the crew, sergeants Jackson, Finch, Hathaway, Rakiewicz, Hough, and Eyer, to get up because the mission was on.

Charlie was sleepy but he arose right away and got dressed. He grabbed his towel and personal hygiene kit and walked to the latrine in the cool, dark morning. In addition to men from other bomber crews, his five crewmates were there to wash up and shave. There was very little talk and within a few minutes he was on his way back to the hut.

He returned to the hut to stow his kit before putting on a cap and heading for the mess hall. Just like every mission he flew before this one, he wondered where the target would be this time. The mess hall was well lit and very warm and full of airmen wanting breakfast. His appetite was not too great because of the early hour, but more because he was concerned about the mission. Most of the combat airmen were quiet as they drank their coffee and ate the chow.

Then he went back out into the cool, dark morning, and walked back to the hut. He then dressed himself for the flight. He left his wallet and a few other personal items inside his locker because he didn't want them to be lost or found by the enemy should he not return from the mission. He wanted those items to be sent home to his mother if tragedy struck. Once dressed he and the rest of the crew walked to a building to be briefed on the mission for the day. After the briefing, he would return briefly to the hut to get his oxygen mask, goggles, and flying boots. Finally he picked up a parachute and an escape packet that included a compass, map, German phrasebook, and some German money.

The group commanding officer walked briskly down the aisle and ascended the stage. Behind him on the stage was a large map covered by a curtain. He gave a pep talk to the men and then turned the briefing over to the intelligence officer. The intelligence officer raised the curtain covering the area of operations map. Charlie and the others saw a string of red yarn which started at the airbase and ended at the target. A groan arose from the men when they saw where the target was located.

The crew briefing completed, the officers were then briefed on their individual and specific mission information. Charlie and the other airmen rode a jeep over to the bomber which was parked on the hardstand. The sky slowly got brighter as dawn approached. When they arrived at the B-17 the ground crew was loading the bombs.

6. Day of Days—May 12, 1944

He walked around the bomber and climbed on board through the waist door and placed his parachute near the ball turret. Then he conducted his pre-flight checks. His twin .50 caliber machine guns were properly installed and ready for action. The oxygen-pressure dial showed full. The dial next to it showed the little lips moving up and down which indicated that oxygen was flowing. He checked the emergency bottles and the large oxygen tank located inside the fuselage, making sure they were full. He plugged in his intercom and conducted a communications check to be certain that he could hear and that his throat mike was working properly.

After the sun was up, Charlie and the other enlisted crewmen helped the ground crew pull the props to clear any oil out of the cylinders. That tasked completed, he boarded once again through the waist door, and soon the entire crew was aboard.

Staff Sergeant Jackson, the tail gunner, Staff Sergeant Finch and Staff Sergeant Hathaway, waist gunners, and Charlie sat on the floor in takeoff position. The radio operator, Staff Sergeant Hough, took his position in the radio room. The top turret gunner/flight engineer, Sergeant Rakiewicz, went forward to his position behind the cockpit, where he checked out his turret, the airplane instruments, and fuel and oil pressures.

The pilot Captain Van Every, co-pilot Lieutenant Richardson, navigator Lieutenant Jankes, and bombardier Lieutenant Scholz came aboard through the front hatch. They completed pre-flight checks of their equipment and the entire plane. With nothing to do, Charlie sat quietly in the waist and was tense as usual. Suddenly the quiet was broken with a whine as an engine started.

Captain Van Every gave the command "Clear, contact!" A member of the ground crew stood next to the engine with a fire extinguisher. The prop spun slowly until the engine caught. Smoke came out of the exhaust as the engine started humming. This was followed by the other three engines until all four were running. Van Every then released the brakes and the B-17 moved from the hardstand and got in line with the other squadron bombers. In short order all bombers were lined up along the taxiways. They sat and waited for the green flare from the control tower signaling that the mission was a go, or possibly a red flare signaling the mission was scrubbed.

After the green flare was seen, each bomber moved up for takeoff. The brakes loudly squealed and the engines revved up and down. Within minutes they were lined up for takeoff. Along the runway a green light blinked. Captain Van Every moved the throttles and the four powerful engines revved and made the entire bomber shake. The noise was deafening.

With brakes released the bomber rolled forward slowly at first and then picked up speed until it reached approximately 120 miles per hour. Slowly it lifted from the runway and the wheels came up. As they flew into the clouds, Rattlesden gradually disappeared below them.

The big bomber bounced, lifted, fell, and then went up again as Charlie held on. He hoped they were soon out of the turbulence. On many takeoffs he worried that they might hit another aircraft or crash. They were caught in the prop wash of the bombers in front of them. Then, just as quickly as it started, it stopped, and the plane continued to climb. Finally they came out of the clouds into bright sunlight and assembled on the squadron's lead bomber.

Higher they climbed and circled as the group slowly formed. Once assembled the group met the rest of the wing and soon hundreds of bombers were headed for the English coast. Hundreds of white contrail streams from the bombers' engines filled the clear blue sky. When they reached 10,000 feet, Van Every told the crew to go on oxygen.

Now it was time for Charlie to get into the ball turret. He rotated the ball until the guns were pointed straight downward, bringing the turret door inside of the fuselage. To do this he had to take a hand crank and attach it to a manual operation shaft. He then shifted the elevation clutches from power to manual operation and loosened the brake. With the turret door in entry position, he switched the power on again and removed the hand crank.[2]

Before entering the ball, he hooked up his oxygen mask and plugged in his electrically heated suit. One of the waist gunners helped Charlie open the ball hatch and watched as he wiggled and squirmed his way into it. The waist gunner then closed and locked the hatch. Charlie then hooked up his intercom system and connected his safety belt. He carefully positioned his oxygen tube to prevent it from being pinched off and also checked the rheostat of his heat suit, making sure it was turned on and working. He checked in with the waist gunner on the intercom and did that from that moment until the mission was over.

He turned on the main power and the whine of the ball motor could be heard. Once in position, Charlie gripped the handles and spun the ball fully through its rotations, testing its movement. He had to make sure that the turret was ready for action because German fighters could suddenly appear. Everything was "OK." Satisfied that everything was in order, he settled in. There was nothing for him to do but sit and wait. He hoped he wouldn't get any cramps.

Charlie was hunched in the ball turret with his back against the door

6. Day of Days—May 12, 1944

and his legs bent and spread with his feet on the rests on each side of the 13-inch diameter armored glass panel. Through that small window he had to scan for enemy fighters. His face was 30 inches from that panel and hanging in between was an optical display of the computing gunsight. A pedal under his left foot adjusted the reticles on this glass, and when an enemy fighter was framed within it, he knew it was in range.

To sight he had to look directly between his feet. There were two handles above the sight which made the turret move. In the end of each handle was a firing button for the machine guns. His arms were bent and his hands were positioned above his head to control movement of the turret and fire the machine guns. The two .50 caliber machine guns were only a few inches away from his head. The hunched position wasn't too uncomfortable, but the real suffering was that he couldn't stretch.[3]

Over the English Channel, Van Every came on the intercom and told all positions to check and test-fire their machine guns. Charlie and the other crewmen fired their .50 caliber machine guns into open airspace. The entire bomber shook when they all fired at the same time. He watched the tracer bullets (every fifth round) streak through the blue sky. The noise was deafening and the smell of gunpowder was very strong. He felt good firing the guns. It was something he was an expert at, and it gave him a sense of control during combat. With his guns he could defend himself and the rest of the crew.

Before long it started getting colder and soon the bomber reached temperatures of 40 or 50 below zero. The only sound now was the monotonous roar of the engines. Everyone was ready, and Charlie prepared his mind for combat.

Captain Van Every told the crew that they were over Germany and to watch out for German fighters. The protection of friendly fighters peeled off, leaving them unprotected. The first flak appeared as small black puffs that seemed to follow them. Charlie heard it and felt it as the B-17 rose and fell because of the explosions. The flak sounded like hail hitting against the bomber. There was nothing they could do about the flak but endure it. With flak all around, the ball turret felt very lonely.

Van Every told them they were now on the IP (initial point) of the bomb run. A bombing run was the time and distance it took for the bombers to fly from the designated IP to the target. While on the bombing run, the bombers were not allowed to change course to avoid enemy flak or attacking fighters. Even a slight deviation in the flight path caused the bombs to miss the target. The running of a flak gauntlet was the greatest cause of fear for the bomber crews. The bomb runs were usually very dangerous and violent, and every successful return to the base seemed like a small victory over death.[4]

Charlie checked his oxygen mask and broke up the ice that had formed from condensation. Van Every handed the bomber over to the bombardier because they were on the bomb run now. Charlie recalled, "We turned at the initial point to start the bomb run. We had fighter escort up until that point. But then there was a 15-minute lapse until the next fighter escort caught up with us."

He liked the P-51 Mustangs. They could escort the bombers to their targets and back again and were very effective against the German fighters. But on this mission even they were powerless to prevent the German fighters from causing large scale carnage. Charlie recalled that soon after their escort turned back, the bomber formation was hit with a massive German frontal attack.

Someone came on the intercom and said, "Bandits at 12 o'clock!" Van Every got on the intercom saying, "The sky is black with enemy fighters ahead, so get ready guys!" Charlie, along with everyone else, searched the sky. "In those 15 minutes, in all the flights I made, I never saw a group of enemy fighters like this at one time. They were up ahead of us." There was too much going on for him to be scared. He just wanted to shoot his .50 caliber machine guns and feel that he was doing something, anything.

"I turned the ball around and looked toward the front of the formation, but I didn't see the German fighters. Just then the nose of our plane bounced up and I could see all the German fighters coming toward us. I knew we were going to take the worst of it. I shot the antenna off of the bottom of our plane because I pulled very hard on the controls to get a shot at the incoming fighters. I fired as they came in from 12 o'clock high. They dived down and in and made it hard for me to engage them, but I kept firing at what I could see. There were hundreds of them!"

Charlie recalled that the German fighters were lined up many rows deep, and the bombers flew directly into a wall of bullets. Eleven B-17s went down almost immediately. "After I turned the ball facing rearward, I started to feel heat on my back. I turned the ball around and saw that fire was coming back under the belly to me. I hit the intercom button and told Van Every that we were on fire! I said hit the button [bail-out button]. I once had told Van Every that if I ever called and told him to hit the button, hit it! Because I knew the difference between an engine fire and something else like the gas tanks burning. Well, I made the call and that's the only reason we all made it out."

6. Day of Days—May 12, 1944

The main danger was from fire caused by a fuel tank igniting. Fire was their greatest fear and the main threat. It ranked above all other dangers for striking absolute fear into the hearts of the airmen. Most airmen would have chosen to die rather than being permanently disfigured or disabled by fire. Enemy fighters, flak, the open sea, bad weather, and mechanical problems were nothing compared to the danger of fire.[5]

A B-17 in distress would try to limp back to England before crash-landing or parachuting into enemy territory. Many bombers that didn't make it back to their base ditched into the North Sea or the English Channel. The inflatable life rafts weren't all that good, and the flares, K-rations, and first aid packs weren't waterproofed. Plus, the bombers were not built for easy escape in water landings.[6]

Their situation was now critical and Van Every flipped on the emergency bell and the steady ring meant abandon ship. Charlie climbed out of the ball turret and picked up his chest chute, and he quickly, but carefully, snapped each ring onto the harness. "I turned the guns straight down so I could open the hatch and get out of the ball. My chute was hanging on the side of the plane. I had a harness on and I snapped the chute on to my harness." He then turned and made his way to the door. "By the time I got to the rear door, the flames were flashing by it." Three main fuel tanks were burning, and Charlie experienced the sick feeling that came with the realization that their bomber could not get them home.

Charlie had to find a way to escape the dying bomber. He preferred to parachute to the ground instead of crash landing. At 20,000 feet, and 70 degrees below zero, Finch, one of the waist gunners, kicked open the back door and threw himself out of the burning plane. Like the rest of the crew, this was the first time he used a parachute.

Many airmen didn't wear a parachute all the time because they were bulky and the bomber was cramped. However, they did wear the harness at all times. The parachute itself was often folded up in a neat little bundle that could be quickly clipped onto the harness if needed. Most airmen wore their chutes during the bomb run, because that was the most dangerous time of a mission, except the ball turret gunner. The turret was way too tight to allow the gunner to wear a chute. To bail out of the plane, he first had to rotate the turret to position the ball turret door inside the fuselage, then squirm out of the turret, locate and clip on his chest chute pack, run to the door, and then jump.[7]

"After I snapped on my chute I ran to jump out the back door and there stood Hathaway. He made the mistake of standing there and looking out of the open doorway. He was frozen in place with fright. He was just standing there, and as I went by him and out the door, I tugged on him just enough that he lost his balance and out the door he went too."

Charlie experienced what it was like to jump out of a dying bomber. Rolling out of the bomber and into the slipstream turned him every which way for a time. But he soon slowed down to the normal falling speed of around 120 miles per hour. He recalled that he had no sensation of falling because there wasn't any reference point. At five miles up in the air he wasn't passing anything, and he didn't hear anything but the wind whistling by his ears.

"We were taught that if you had to bail out to let yourself free fall until you thought you were going to hit the ground, and then open your chute. To open any sooner, your chute might hit the propellers of the planes below you. So I kept free falling. I rolled over onto my back and everything. I was wearing a chest pack chute, and if I would have just pulled the ripcord, it would have taken my face off. I had to lay on my back and place an arm over my face, then pull the ripcord. The chute was spring-loaded. It felt like I was floating, sky diving, as I fell at 120 miles per hour. It didn't feel like I was falling. I practiced moving my arms and flipping around so that when it was time I would know how to flip over and onto my back to pull the ripcord. When I finally pulled the ripcord, it worked perfectly."

In training the men were instructed to free-fall until they were 5,000 feet, or one mile above the earth, and then to pull the parachute rip cord. The reason for the count and delay in pulling the ripcord was because when leaving the plane, the jumper was going forward at a very high speed. The jumping airman was moving forward at the same speed as the plane. Gradually the jumper slowed down to the normal rate that any given weight will fall through space. So, for a few seconds after exiting the plane, the jumper was going at a terrific speed but gradually slowing down. That is why they needed to count and wait to pull the rip cord.[8]

The USAAF had a standard operating procedure (SOP) for performing an emergency parachute jump from an aircraft. However, Charlie and the other crewmen never received any practical training. Exiting a B-17 while in flight was based on the location of each crew member. The bombardier and navigator exited through the front entrance door. The ball turret and waist gunners exited from the main entrance door. The tail gunner exited through a small emergency door in the tail section. The other four crew members, which included the radio operator, top turret gunner, pilot and copilot, exited through the bomb bay. The pilot had to maintain control of the plane and was to be last man out, otherwise the crew members might become pinned inside by centrifugal force if the bomber fell or spun out of control.[9]

Airmen jumping with the chest parachute were instructed that they would free fall for an additional number of feet after they pulled the ripcord. During that period the jumper would be still falling at terminal velocity. When the canopy, suspension lines, and raisers were fully extended, the canopy would start to fill with air, slowing down the rate of descent. After the parachute was fully deployed, the airman could expect to feel a very hard jolt or a violent opening shock. The jolt was even more severe at higher altitudes where the air was thinner and the descent speed higher.[10] Charlie described the violent opening shock as "the quickest damn stop I ever made!" But he was very relieved to see the beautiful white chute blossom out above him.

Having escaped the burning bomber, he looked around. "I saw Van Every. He was the last one out. His chute opened just as the plane blew up. The whole plane went to pieces. Then I started to count chutes. I counted all the chutes but one. I just couldn't find that one chute, no how."

"A German fighter plane tried to spill our chutes. He flew over us and dropped down, and the wind from his propeller could have collapsed a chute. My chute didn't collapse. He spun around and was coming back again when he suddenly turned again and left the area."

Because exiting the burning bomber was difficult, it delayed the escape of some of the crewmen by several seconds or more. This delay caused the men to be separated from each other by quite a distance once on the ground. Another reason most of them were separated while parachuting to earth was because each of them had remained under an open chute for a different length of time. Wind speed and direction also caused them to land apart from each other.

"As I was floating down I was still looking for the 10th chute, and I couldn't find it. At the same time I saw a wooded area down below and from up where I was it didn't seem to be too far away. So I pulled on the shroud lines to drift that way. I kept pulling, thinking I was getting somewhere, but I wasn't and that forest was miles away."

"I happened to look straight down and there was Finch, right below me. He was the 10th chute. If I would not have pulled my ripcord when I did, I would have went right through Finch's chute. He was right below me! I was maybe about 30 feet above him. I kept pulling on the shroud lines and moved away from him."

"Finch landed in the middle of a town, and I landed in the outskirts in somebody's back yard. Finch actually landed in the quiet little German village of Frieberg. Touching down 100 feet from the front door of what he soon learned was police headquarters. A man in civilian clothes was waiting for him, pointing a pistol that looked as big as a cannon right between his eyes. Rackiewicz got hung up on a telephone pole, about 10 feet off of the ground. I didn't think I would live to see the end of that day."

All 10 of the crew were captured and would spend the rest of the war in a German prison camp as *Kriegsgefangener*, a prisoner of war (POW), or, as they called themselves, *Kriegies*.[11] A German soldier told Charlie when he was captured, "For you the war is over." Well, it wasn't, because being captured was just the beginning of his longest and hardest mission. Some airmen from other bombers who were shot down that day weren't captured or killed and managed to evade the enemy and made it back to England. But not for Charlie's crew.

The chance of being captured was a real possibility for combat airmen. But Charlie really didn't expect the unfriendly welcome that met him on the ground. Accounts from American POWs who had safely escaped and evaded and made it back to England reported that German civilians had killed airmen when caught. Sometimes even wounded airmen were killed by angry civilians. Most airmen were abused by German civilians, and sometimes by military personnel as well.[12] For Charlie, the next few days would be some of the most frightening and perilous days of his entire military service.

Charlie landed safely but did not have a chance to evade capture. "I hit the ground and flipped backwards, hitting the base of my spine on a rock. I got right up and unbuckled my chute, but the people were right on me. Those people came carrying meat cleavers, guns, and God knows what. When I saw them, I thought, 'I've had it.'"

German civilians posed a greater danger to Charlie safely reaching a prison camp than German soldiers. He understood the hostility of the German civilians, but it was not a good feeling being surrounded by an incited mob. He heard some of them yell in perfect English, "Hang the bastard!" During this period of the war, Allied bombers really hammered the larger German cities and the combat airmen were warned to avoid German civilians if shot down. A large number of women and children had been killed by Allied bombers. German civilians did beat and hang American airmen.[13] He had good reason to be worried about being captured.

The civilians were infuriated because of the death of friends and relatives and the destruction of their homes by the bombers. Sometimes they formed vigilante mobs and lynched any airman they got their hands on.[14]

Because of this vengeance, it was better for Charlie, with no hope of escape, to fall into the hands of German soldiers. The German military generally didn't hurt helpless American airmen.

One horrible instance occurred when an American airman was attacked by civilians and his head split open by a sledge hammer. They shot and stomped on him and dragged his body across a field. Another airman was hanged from the top of a building by his parachute cords, and they left him to hang there all night. Another was tied to a motorcycle and dragged down a gravel road as a mob of civilians watched.[15]

Charlie thought he was going to be killed by a mob of angry civilians, and there was a good chance he would have been if not for some German soldiers. The mob that confronted him was armed with pitchforks, rakes, shovels, knives, clubs, and guns. One old man with a very old and large rifle pointed it at Charlie and pulled the trigger. *Click!* It misfired.

"If it hadn't been for three German soldiers, I'd be dead. Three German soldiers came running to me, and when they reached me, they turned their backs to me and stuck their rifles with bayonets outward, toward the civilians, and held them at bay. A kid had a gun pointing right at my side. The soldiers finally got the people under control."

Most ground combat troops captured by the Germans were caught as part of a larger group, such as during the Battle of the Bulge. But most airmen were captured alone because they parachuted to earth alone, and that makes it impossible to know how many combat airmen were beaten or killed by civilians. But there are many documented cases of the murder and brutal mistreatment of the hated *Terrorfliegers* (terror fliers), combat airmen.[16] The official records of the Nuremberg trials have many documented incidents of killings or beatings of unarmed American airmen in the custody of the German government.[17]

For Charlie, he never had a chance to evade capture by either civilians or the military. He was really hurting because he injured his lower back when he landed and could not even attempt to evade capture. Besides, they were on him so quickly that he never had a chance. Once he was in the custody of the German military, he was protected from the angry civilians.

Charlie, along with a few others from his crew, were now, luckily, in custody of the German military. "The German soldiers took us to a county jail. It was a stone building with bars on the windows, and they put us in there, with one guard on the door. The citizens were at the window with their knives and other weapons, waving them and hollering at us. We were concerned that the one guard could not hold them off and that they would get in and kill us."

He got sort of a strange visit while in the jail. "We were in there a couple of hours when a German fighter pilot entered the cell. I had a pack of cigarettes in the pocket of my coveralls, and I said to the other guys that we better smoke now before they take them from us. The German fighter pilot could speak English and he started talking to us. I handed him a pack of my cigarettes and he took two and gave the pack back to me." Charlie never asked the German fighter pilot, but he had a strong feeling that the pilot was one of the Germans that attacked their bomber earlier that day.

Charlie hoped for decent treatment from his German captors. As a signatory to the Geneva Convention, Germany had agreed to treat prisoners humanely.[18] When he was in the hands of the German military, they searched him, looking for weapons, and took everything of value, which wasn't much. He felt safer in the custody of the German military and was glad that they had saved him from the angry civilians.

Soon after being captured, Charlie and the other downed airmen were taken to the *Dulag Luft*. "They then came with a truck to haul us to Frankfurt, and as soon as we got on the truck, they took all of our cigarettes." They were being taken to the Luftwaffe interrogation center for Allied airmen at Oberursel, near Frankfurt. Luftwaffe police and interrogators were officially in charge of the captured airmen there, and they used tactics for extracting information that were rough but rarely barbaric.[19]

"Along the way the Germans stopped and picked up some dead American airmen and put the bodies on the truck with us. When we got to Frankfurt they made us get off the truck and held us there under guard. Two Germans climbed onto the truck and just tossed one of the American bodies off. Well, right then and there we let them know that if they didn't stop that, and dropped another body, there would be more dead people, and they knew it! So they quit that."

Charlie and the other downed airmen couldn't believe the devastation. For miles around Frankfurt, everything was flattened. Parts of the city and suburbs had been swept clean of every house and building. Entire city blocks lay wasted, nothing but ruins. In every direction there were enormous junk piles of twisted metal, brick, pipe, and broken concrete. The streets and utilities were in shambles. Most of the telephone poles were lying on the ground.

Moving deeper into the city, Charlie saw even more destruction as black smoke and ash filled the air. Buses and street cars were completely smashed. Scattered all over the place were lumber, stones, brick, gravel, metal and other debris. Swarms of slave laborers, young and old German civilians, and German soldiers worked to clear away the rubble.

He saw German soldiers repairing communication lines and miles of twisted railroad track in the marshaling yard. Frankfurt was completely destroyed, and he thought it would take years to rebuild the city. Charlie saw first-hand the destructive power of the bombers. Now he understood why the Germans hated him and the other bomber airmen so much. "Civilians spotting our uniforms shouted '*Luft Gangsters! Schweine! Luft Gangsters!*'"

Charlie and the other downed airmen were taken to Auswertestelle West. The facility was situated in Oberursel, about seven miles northwest of Frankfurt, and was the Luftwaffe's primary intelligence and evaluation center. It was also known as the *Durchgangslager,* or *Dulag Luft.* It was made up of three separate sections: the interrogation center at Oberursel, the hospital at Hohemark, and the transit camp at Wetzlar, which was 30 miles north of Frankfurt. Its objective was to gather information about the strength, disposition, and capabilities of the Allies.[20]

Charlie recalled that only critically injured airmen needing medical treatment were sent to a hospital. Captured airmen suffering from the shock of being shot down and captured received no medical attention, nor did most of the airmen with minor wounds. He was one of the many injured captured airmen who didn't receive any medical attention. "I hurt my back from rolling over that rock, but nobody else was hurt. We were really lucky."

Approximately 55 German military men stationed in the Dulag Luft conducted the interrogations. These men were chosen for the job because they had spent part of their lives in either the United States or Great Britain. The interrogators could speak English very well and were very knowledgeable about American culture.[21] They were also well educated. It was recognized as the greatest interrogation center in all of Europe, and American intelligence regarded it as the best German agency for getting accurate and critically important information from captured airmen.

As Charlie discovered, Dulag Luft was run by an efficient and highly trained staff that studied each prisoner in an attempt to discover his likes, dislikes, habits, and ability to resist. A method of interrogation was then determined and put into motion to quickly try and destroy his resistance.

If a prisoner looked fearful or appeared jumpy, he was threatened with punishment or even torture. Sometimes torture was carried out and prisoners were beaten up. The interrogators attempted to bribe many prisoners with clean clothes, better living conditions, food and cigarettes, but only if they answered important questions. Susceptible prisoners were fed lies of why they should talk and made to believe that resistance was futile. The prisoners had to spend many long and miserable hours of solitary confinement in a prison cell. The German interrogators overlooked little and carefully studied the results of each interview and devised new means to extract information.[22]

Dulag Luft was so successful that it was not restricted by most German authority regulations. It was accountable only to Berlin. The USAAF countered by training every combat airman on how to behave as a prisoner of war. They were instructed on the methods the Germans might use to gain information from prisoners. Name, rank, and serial number were the only bits of information the airmen should give to their captors.[23] Charlie and all combat airmen were trained until they knew exactly what to expect and what to do should they be captured. It was a court-martial offense and an act of treason to disclose any information as a prisoner of war, and patriotism and loyalty were stressed.

Their training warned against carrying any personal letters, documents, theater ticket stubs, photographs or laundry bills during missions, because those items could provide a lot of information to the enemy. Also stressed was the importance of destroying their plane, equipment and documents in enemy territory.

They also received instruction about their rights as a POW and how to resist interrogation. Charlie and the men were told that all captured airmen would be sent to the Dulag Luft for interrogation and that they could expect to be held there in solitary confinement for as long as one week. Some airmen would be confined there for up to 30 days while the enemy attempted to get technical or operational information out of them. An airman who was kept there for a long period of time was held there because he was useful to the enemy. Charlie was only there for a couple of days.

In their training they were told that upon arrival at the Dulag Luft, each man would be psychologically evaluated and an assessment made of his observed weaknesses. Aircrews were typically interrogated separately, usually beginning with the highest rank. But sometimes they would skip the officers and concentrate more thoroughly on the NCOs. The airmen were told that they would meet expert interrogators who spoke perfect English and had a lot of information about American organizations and equipment.

Charlie was also taught that the questioning techniques would vary with the type of personality a prisoner showed. He was advised that he would be exposed to different types of direct and indirect questioning methods. The Germans used one or more of 16 different interrogation techniques, which ranged from empathy for the prisoner's despair to appealing to his vanity and sense of self-importance.

He was given useful ideas to resist interrogation and to avoid being classified into a specific category. Charlie was instructed to maintain a strict and polite military bearing at all times. A good military bearing made psychological profiling hard, if not impossible. He was also instructed to be courteous, salute all ranking enemy personnel, and to stand at attention while being interrogated. Finally, he was cautioned to not try to outsmart the interrogator because he will catch one in lies.

Dulag Luft was built on flat ground and was not camouflaged or hidden. The camp was very large and covered approximately 500 acres. There were large, white painted rocks that covered the length of the front lawn and formed the words "Prisoner of War Camp." The same words were also painted in white letters across the roofs of many of the structures. The facility was vital to the Germans, and they knew the Allies would never bomb it as long as it was identified as a POW camp.[24]

Two parallel fences 10 feet apart formed the boundaries of the camp. These fences were 12 feet high and had barbed wire entangled between them. There were guards on both sides of the fencing, and watch towers were spread out around the camp at 100-yard intervals. Patrol dogs prowled the outer boundaries, and there were heavily armed pill boxes scattered on the outside of the fences.[25] Charlie recalled, "There were hundreds of guys of all kinds outside in a large barbed-wire enclosure—British, Australian, you name it, and they were all prisoners."

Upon arrival the officers and enlisted men were separated, and Charlie was ordered to quickly and silently undress. He handed the German guard his clothes and stood against a wall as they searched his clothes inside and out. Then they made him raise his hands over his head and bend forward. The guard roughly searched his entire body to make sure that he didn't have any hidden items. When the strip search and full-body cavity search were completed, one of the guards recorded Charlie's belongings and assigned him to a cell.

These searches, which always included a rectal exam, frequently found maps, mess hall vouchers, and tramcar tickets. The collection of this type of information provided a lot of data identifying the captured airman's unit of assignment. This information helped the Luftwaffe's assessment of the USAAF order of battle.[26]

Charlie was then photographed and fingerprinted for his individual

Kriegsgefangenenkartel. This card contained general information about him and a description of his physical features. The card also contained his assigned POW number and camp assignment. He then was placed in solitary confinement after finishing the preliminary in-processing.

He was put in one of the hundreds of cells which were located in one of the large 14 buildings at the evaluation center. Each cell in the building was intended for solitary confinement. The cell door was opened. It was very dark inside. A guard pushed him into the darkness and slammed the door behind him. He felt his way along the walls hoping to find a light switch, but there wasn't one. There weren't any windows, and the air reeked. He stood still for a few minutes and allowed his eyes to slowly adjust to the almost total darkness.

The cell was very small and had a low ceiling. The floor and walls were made of stone and the door was solid steel with no peep holes to see in or out. The cell had only a bench and nothing else. There was human feces on the floor. A previous prisoner had used the cell as a toilet and the stench was awful. Spider webs hung from the ceiling and corners. The dirty and foul-smelling cell was a real gut punch to his morale.

Charlie was weakened by the awful conditions at Dulag Luft. The prisoners were purposely kept in isolation and fed starvation rations. He recalled that he didn't receive anything to eat while he was there. Rodents roamed the filthy and damp cells and would go through a prisoner's clothing looking for something edible. Because of these horrible conditions, sometimes just the promise of a shower, a shave, and some decent food was more than enough to get a prisoner to talk, but he never did. Things were especially hard for the hundreds of airmen who arrived wounded and never received any medical treatment, a blatant violation of the Geneva Convention regarding prisoners of war.

Like most other prisoners, he was enticed, threatened and starved while he sat inside the gloomy cell and thought about his fate. It was all done on purpose to find any psychological weaknesses and increase the chances that he might divulge information to an interrogator. Charlie would eventually be taken to an interrogation room, where they conducted an interrogation.

The best interrogators in Germany were stationed at the Dulag Luft, and they usually got the information they wanted from a prisoner. Charlie expected the worst kind of treatment. He knew they would try to bribe him, starve him, and even torture him to get him to talk. In solitary confinement he was lonesome, hungry, dirty, and as miserable as could be. They offered him food, cigarettes, and nearly anything to talk. Lying to them only gave them an excuse for severe punishment. But he remained polite and to the point, and he told them he could not answer their questions.

The Luftwaffe interrogators at Dulag Luft were capable specialists who preferred methods more subtle than a beating. Fortunately, the Luftwaffe resisted Gestapo and SS pressure to be tougher on the captured airmen. The really talented interrogators were said to be able to "extract a confession of infidelity from a nun." The interrogator typically began by offering the airman chocolate and cigarettes and then swayed him into some light chat about American sports or movies. A conversation could be so pleasant that many airmen were unaware that an interrogation was being conducted. The interrogators sometimes amazed prisoners with the amount of intelligence they already had about the prisoner and his unit. They would assure a captured airman that he would not be telling them anything they didn't already know.[27]

Prisoners refusing to provide military or personal information were threatened. They were told that their families would not be notified that the airman was alive and safe unless he cooperated. Airmen captured without dog tags, which was the case with Charlie, were warned that they might be turned over to the Gestapo to be executed as spies. Fortunately, such threats were rarely carried out.

German military executions of captured combat airmen were rare. Some downed American airmen were sent to the Dachau concentration camp, primarily because they had no identification and had attempted to evade capture. But most airmen under German military control were placed in permanent prison camps.[28]

Charlie was taken to the office of a German officer. The office was a big, bare room that overlooked the prison building. It was furnished with a big desk and a couple of chairs, and the walls were lined with maps of Europe. "Two guards picked me up and took me into a building and into a German captain's office."

The interrogator politely informed Charlie that because he did not have identification tags (dog tags), he could be labeled as a spy and shot if he did not cooperate. The interrogator said, "We must identify you as a prisoner of war. If we are not convinced that you are a prisoner of war, you will be shot as a spy."

The interrogator asked Charlie to fill out a bogus Red Cross form. The form was designed to draw out sensitive military information with questions pertaining to his aircraft, destination, bomb load, and so on. "The German captain laid a paper down in front of me and I filled it in with only my name, rank, and serial number, and then put the pen down. The German officer could speak better English than me, and he told me that he had gone to college in Boston years ago." In perfect English, he then said to Charlie, "You know, you are a spy and here that means the death penalty. We shoot people like you. Now I'm going to give you a little time to think about it."

Charlie was determined to resist and not to divulge any information other than his name, rank, and serial number. "He waited a few minutes and then tore up the paper. He laid down another paper just like the first, and just like the first, I gave only my name, rank, and serial number, and laid the pen down. *Whack!* He slapped his gloves across my face! Then he started telling me what could happen to me. I didn't say anything. After a while he called the guards back in and told them to take me down to my cell and that he wanted to see me tomorrow morning before having me shot!"

"I was going to be shot as a spy because I didn't have any dog tags. I never wore them because the chain around my neck bothered me. They wanted my dog tags and I didn't have them. They were back in the barracks." Charlie had been told to make sure he always wore his dog tags, but he never did. The airmen had also been warned to not carry their .45 caliber semi-automatic pistols on combat missions, because the Germans were known to shoot captured airmen carrying firearms. He did not have a pistol when he was captured.

Back in a cell, Charlie pondered his fate. "The guards took me down and put me in a cell that was way underground. The hall floors were cobblestone, and because the Germans wore hobnails on the bottoms of their boots, I could hear them walking through the hallway. I sat in the pitch-black cell and could hear water dripping on the other side of the wall. This was one of their gimmicks that we were told they did to try and drive us crazy. It didn't drive me crazy because I knew what it was there for. The cell had only a bench to sit on, and I didn't sleep that night."

"In the morning I heard the cleats on the floor. Two German guards came for me. They got to my cell, opened the door, and off we went to see the captain again." His second experience with the interrogator began in a friendly manner, and he was even offered cigarettes and chocolate, which he refused, and the interrogator started off with some light chat about the war. The Luftwaffe interrogator even attempted to promote a sense of camaraderie with Charlie, stating that there was honor among airmen.

But Charlie wasn't falling for it, and it soon turned ugly. "Same thing with the paper. Name, rank and serial number, and I laid the pen down.

Then he gave me another crack across the face with his gloves and told the guards to take me down and shoot me! They grabbed me and I thought I was a goner. But they only took me down and released me into a compound."

"While I was in that compound, I got a chance to talk to a British guy who was actually a spy, and the Germans knew it. He told me that he had been beaten time after time and that he wouldn't be in here too much longer before they killed him."

If the first attempt didn't produce information, threats of violence typically followed. Largely, the interrogators at Dulag Luft did not use physical force with the prisoners, although some of their methods were abusive. They employed various psychological methods in addition to sophisticated techniques of questioning to produce information.[29] Occasionally, such as in Charlie's case, an interrogator who was frustrated by an airman's refusal to give more than name, rank, and serial number may have lost his temper and hit a prisoner. Usually this did not go beyond a slap on the face, and physical violence was not generally conducted.

One tactic the interrogators used was to pretend to be an advocate for the prisoner. The interrogator would tell the prisoner that he wanted to help him establish his identity as a member of the military and not as a spy or saboteur, who would be turned over to the Gestapo and executed. The prisoner was told that the best way to establish his identity was to provide detailed military information that only a member of the military would know. The interrogator would even offer rewards for cooperating.[30] Just like Charlie, if the captured airman refused to provide information other than name, rank, and serial number, the prisoner was thrown back into solitary confinement.

If Charlie would have played along with the game of having to prove his identity, the interrogator would have asked more questions. If he would have cooperated, he most likely would have been given some luxuries, such as a shower or something good to eat. If he would have showed promise, he would have been held there until he gave them all the information they considered important. He then would have been transferred to a specialist to focus on his technical knowledge. This process could take weeks. Charlie told them nothing and was out of there in no time.

Typically, after three to five days of examination and questioning, the airmen were transferred out. Charlie had dodged a firing squad and was on his way to a prison camp. "I was really glad when they took me out and put me on a train, because then I knew that they weren't going to shoot me. I think I was there [Dulag Luft] one day and overnight."

Charlie and the others were transported by train from the Dulag Luft interrogation center at Oberursel to the transit camp at Wetzlar. Arriving there, he was given his first chance to shower, shave, and discard old clothing for Red Cross–issued clothing. He was also given his first real food since capture. He received a Red Cross parcel having eight-ounce cans of corned beef, pork, and salmon in addition to biscuits, processed cheese, and condiments. He was also given a postcard and allowed to write a brief message to his family.

At the transit camp, Charlie and the other new arrivals were divided into groups of officers and NCOs in preparation for shipment to a permanent camp. From Wetzlar the prisoners were herded onto small box cars and sent deep into German-occupied territory. The majority of the prisoners were interned in four primary camps, officially designated as *Stammlager der Luftwaffe*, or usually referred to as Stalag Luft, followed by the camp's numerical designation. All four primary camps that were run by the Luftwaffe were located in eastern Germany to discourage escape. Stalag Luft I, near Barth on the north Baltic coast, held Allied air force officers; Stalag Luft III, near Sagan in central Germany, held both officers and enlisted airmen. The two other compounds, Stalag Luft IV, near Gross Tychow in northeast Germany, and Stalag Luft VI, located at Heydekrug in East Prussia, were used entirely for NCOs.[31] The *Wehrmacht* (army) and the *Kriegsmarine* (navy) ran their own prisoner of war camps.

If an airman was killed in action, those left behind could at least take some comfort knowing what had occurred and knowing the man was never going to return. Family members could grieve and move on with their lives, but the same could not be said for the families of the airmen listed as missing in action. Often when a bomber went down in combat nobody really knew if any of the men survived. The crew of the downed bomber was either dead, captured, or evading capture. Until higher headquarters knew for sure what had happened, they listed the crewmen of the downed bomber as missing in action.

Within a few days, when Charlie's fate was still not determined, his family received a telegram from the chaplain of the 447th Bombardment Group, which in part said:

> As chaplain of your son's unit I wish to offer you and the others of his family my sincerest sympathy. I know what anguish of mind you are suffering as you wonder whether or not he is safe. I wish to assure you that we share that feeling with you. You would, I know, like to hear something about the circumstances in which your son became a casualty, but I am not permitted to give such information. You will be notified by the Adjutant General when definite information is received as to what his present situation is. Please know that I am praying that you will have the consolation

of faith; that you may even now, in this heavy time of uncertainty, have much of that peace of mind which comes from the faith that God is still ruling, and from the willingness to place your son in His hands.

On May 25, 1944, Charlie's mother received the official secretary of war telegram, which said: "The Secretary of War desires me to express his deep regret, that your son has been reported missing in action since Twelve May over Germany. If further details or other information are received you will be promptly notified."

A couple of days later another communication arrived from the War Department:

> I know that added distress is caused by failure to receive more information or details. Therefore, I wish to assure you that at any time additional information is received it will be transmitted to you without delay, and, if in the meantime no additional information is received, I will again communicate with you at the expiration of three months. The term "missing in action" is used only to indicate that the whereabouts or status of an individual is not immediately known. It is not intended to convey the impression that the case is closed. I wish to emphasize that every effort is exerted continuously to clear up the status of our personnel. Under war conditions this is a difficult task. Experience has shown that many persons reported missing in action are subsequently reported as prisoners of war, but as this information is furnished by countries with which we are at war, the War Department is helpless to expedite such reports.

On June 30, 1944, Charlie's mother received the following communication from Headquarters, Army Air Forces, which said in part:

> Further information has been received indicating that Sergeant Eyer was a crew member of a B-17 bomber which departed England on a bombardment mission to Zwickau, Germany on May 12th. Full details are not available, but the report indicates that during this mission at about 12:10 p.m., in the vicinity of West Central Germany, our planes encountered enemy fighter craft and in the ensuing engagement your son's plane sustained damage. Subsequently, his Fortress left the formation and ten parachutes were seen to emerge from the disabled craft. Inasmuch as the crew members of accompanying planes were unable to make continuous observation of Sergeant Eyer's bomber, these facts constitute all the information presently available. The great anxiety caused you by failure to receive more details concerning your son's disappearance is fully realized. Please be assured that any additional information received will be conveyed immediately to you by The Adjutant General or this headquarters.

Finally, and many weeks later on October 12, 1944, Charlie's mother received the welcome news, under the circumstances, that her son was a prisoner of war in Germany. The letter read in part: "A cablegram has just been received from the International Red Cross, Geneva, Switzerland, reporting the transfer of your son to Stalag Luft 4, Germany. His prisoner of war number is 1226."

For crewmen missing in action, the standard procedure was to remove their belongings from their hut back at the base. In the 8th Air Force, where the casualty rate was extremely high, quartermaster personnel usually removed the possessions of missing crews within a day or two. For the airmen still living in that hut, seeing the photos and other possessions of their buddies could be upsetting. However, the other crewmen were not too upset to stop them from helping themselves to military equipment left behind. They knew their buddies would not have minded because they had also done it themselves.[32]

After some serious thought, and a shocking discovery at the stalag, Charlie knew why so many B-17s were shot down that terrible day. "The day we were shot down, we figured someone was telling the Germans. Later, in the prison camp, we found out that we had been flying with a German spy in the group. He was with one of the crews and gave information back to Germany. One day he walked into the compound in a German uniform, and he's lucky he had a German uniform on and that they had enough guards around him, or he would have been killed right on the spot. He had been relaying all our mission information to Germany."

CHAPTER 7

Stalag Luft IV

Charlie, along with many other prisoners, were pushed and shoved into a crowded and small boxcar. Rail targets were a high priority for Allied fighters and bombers, and this train had neither a red cross nor any other special markings properly identifying the train as one carrying prisoners of war (POW). This omission put the POWs in danger of being targeted and strafed during the five-day transit across Germany. The German guards seemed to enjoy letting the POWs sweat it out whenever there was an air raid.

The German boxcars were called "Forty & Eight." They were called that because of their capacity to carry 40 soldiers or eight horses and came into existence in France during the Great War, World War I. The boxcars were short and stubby, measuring only 8.5 by 20.5 feet. The Wehrmacht seized these boxcars to move German military units in Europe following the defeat of France in 1940. These were the same kind of boxcars that were used to move freight, POWs, and Jews, gypsies and other ethnic groups the Nazis considered subhuman to the many and widely dispersed concentration camps.[1]

The train ride to Stalag Luft IV was long and miserable. The boxcar was crammed full of POWs, and the doors were locked from the outside. The boxcar was too small for the 60 prisoners packed into it, and there was just not enough room to lie or sit down. Half of the group stood while the other half sat, and every few hours they switched positions. The hours went by very slowly, and Charlie became more uncomfortable with every passing moment. Everyone tried to hold their temper, but patience slowly went away as they all became increasingly irritated.

After five days, with the doors opened only twice a day, the conditions inside the boxcar became unbearable. The train trip was a completely inhumane act committed against the prisoners, especially since many of the men were sick. Charlie recalled, "We could have overpowered the one guard in the boxcar and taken his weapon, but where would we go? The door was locked from the outside. There was no chance of escape because we would never desert our wounded."

After a five-day journey with hardly any food or water, and no toilet facilities, they arrived at the small village of Kiefheide. The boxcar and the men were filthy and reeked of feces and urine. Charlie heard dogs barking as the boxcar door was opened, then he saw the vicious police dogs as they pulled on their leashes. He and the other POWs were shoved out of the boxcars and lined up on the road in formation, four abreast. There was a lot of commotion and loud shouting by German guards with weapons. He shuffled into formation with the others and tried to stay away from the snarling dogs.

When Charlie got out of the boxcar, he was very hungry, weak, stiff, tired, and somewhat frightened. He noticed that the guards they had for the train ride were now replaced by new guards dressed in the blue uniform of the Luftwaffe. The new guards conducted a head count, and when that and everything else was completed, started marching the POWs toward Stalag Luft IV, some two miles away. He and the other prisoners were marched through a pine forest, carrying nothing but their few possessions.

Charlie and the other prisoners walked along the road through a heavy forest for about 30 minutes and then all of a sudden they came out into a large clearing. Off in the distance he could see a large prison camp with a lot of wooden buildings. He also saw that it was completely surrounded by double barbed wire fences and guard towers, and he was somewhat shocked by the physical environment of the camp. It was a drab and dreary looking place sitting in the center of a silent and dark forest. He didn't know quite what to make of this ominous looking prison.

When the group approached the camp, a large locked gate was opened and Charlie and the others were led into the outer camp that contained the German administration/housing portion of the camp called the *Vorlager*.[2] He was told that they were in Stalag Luft IV,[3] a POW camp for enlisted airmen.

His first stop was in the vorlager to be deloused and processed. It had special facilities for the POWs, including a bathhouse, a storage building, and the cooler. It was a group of administrative and other auxiliary buildings located in front of the main prison camp. Also located within the vorlager were the camp's commander and his staff, some barracks for the several hundred guards and Russian prisoners of war, plus an infirmary for the POWs. There were also some smaller storage buildings which held clothing, mail, and International Red Cross food parcels sent to supplement the prisoners' scanty rations.[4]

There was a shower building located just outside the main fence near the Russian prisoner barracks, and Charlie and the other new arrivals were herded to that location. When they entered the building they were ordered to remove all of their clothing. German guards were positioned at each shower head and waited for the head guard's signal. Charlie and two other prisoners were shoved under a shower head and when the entire group was in position, the head guard told them they would have three minutes of hot water and then three minutes of cold water.

While he looked at his pocket watch, the head guard reached for an overhead faucet. At the same time, the other guards responded likewise and also grabbed their faucets. When the head guard shouted a command, they quickly and fully opened all spigots. The sudden blast of steaming hot water was more than Charlie could stand and he jumped back. Nobody could stand directly under the scalding hot water that shot from the shower heads. When the three minutes were up, the Germans quickly turned off the hot water faucets. Once again as the head guard looked at his watch, he shouted out an order, and just as expected, out came freezing cold water this time. From one extreme to the other, but Charlie and the other prisoners survived the ordeal and were a little cleaner.

Until he was liberated, that was the last shower Charlie would get. There weren't any communal showers inside the lagers. All he received to wash and get clean from that day until he departed the camp was one pan of hot water twice a month. "We were never able or allowed to wash our clothes. We were alive with bugs." In due course, all of the POWs contracted lice. They had no way to keep themselves clean, and lice and bedbugs infested the mattresses.

Immediately after their shower, Charlie and the rest of the newly arrived POWs were strip-searched, which included another rectal exam. They specifically looked for the small compasses issued to every airman as part of his escape kit. In addition to this personal humiliation, every article of his clothing was inspected for any items that could assist in an escape. He didn't have any restricted items on his person or in his clothing.

Before entering the lager he would be assigned to, Charlie had his photograph taken and was given a camp number. The number was stamped on a piece of tin which was also printed with the camp designation, Stalag

Luft IV. After being photographed, fingerprinted, and assigned a POW number, he was issued his bedding which was only two thin blankets. One was an American GI wool blanket and the other was a very thin German blanket which was made of very coarse horse hair. Some prisoners were issued eating utensils, but most didn't receive any of those items.

Stalag Luft IV was located approximately two and a half miles south of the railroad station and near the town of Gross Tychow, in the Pomerania sector of Germany, and about 15 miles south of the Baltic Sea. It was activated in April of 1944 but due to the pressures of the war was never fully completed. Stalag Luft IV officially opened, prior to completion, on May 14, 1944, with the arrival of 64 American POWs from the Dulag Luft.[5] Charlie was one of the very first prisoners to be held there.

There wasn't much food available for the entire month of May, and the first Red Cross parcels were not distributed in the camp until June 15, 1944.[6] The bulk of the POWs were American NCOs, but also include some 800 RAF (Royal Air Force) NCOs. From April 1944, the stream of prisoners into the camp was heavy until it was evacuated. Eventually, more than 10,000 POWs were interned there, a number far in excess for which the camp was designed. At one point Stalag Luft IV reached more than 13,000 POWs before the Germans began shipping out some of the wounded and sick to other camps.[7]

Stalag Luft IV was the camp where groups of American prisoners were bayonetted and attacked by police dogs. According to the International Red Cross, it was the worst of the luft camps, and the commandant was Lieutenant Colonel Otto Bombach. He was a die-hard Nazi who had lost his family in an Allied bombing raid. Ultimately, this new camp became the largest and most notorious of the four large camps administered by the Luftwaffe.[8]

Commandant Bombach was the person most of the POWs held responsible for their inhumane treatment. Many times Bombach let members of his staff mistreat and physically abuse the prisoners. Captain Walther Pickhardt and Sergeant Reinhard Fahnert were also hated for committing atrocities and mistreating prisoners. Following the war, prosecutors from the War Crimes Tribunal collected 58 volumes of testimony against Bombach, Pickhardt, and Fahnert for committing war crimes against prisoners of war, but all three men were set free and never even went to trial.[9]

The Germans had learned from their earlier prison camps. This camp was purposely located, designed, and built to eliminate as many escape and tunneling opportunities as possible. First, it was located as far north

7. Stalag Luft IV 113

and east in Germany as possible, which put it far away from the Allies. If Charlie would have escaped, he would have had a very long and hazardous trip to reach friendly territory. It was situated on sandy soil in the center of a very large cleared area in the middle of a forest. He would have had to dig a tunnel in sandy soil that would have required a lot of shoring up to prevent it from collapsing.

Hundreds of acres of trees had been cleared and the camp sat smack in the middle of that clearing. A tunnel would have had to stretch a long way just to get to the edge of the camp and even farther to reach the trees. Upon first entering the lager, Charlie noticed that the barracks floors were raised about 30 inches above the ground. This permitted the guards to see underneath the barracks and also allowed the dogs to get under there to sniff out any POWs attempting to escape.

Once inside the barracks, he discovered that the barracks floors were made of two layers of boards. The boards ran in one direction on the lower part of the floor, while the boards on top of those ran in the opposite direction. He knew it would be impossible to remove the upper boards over a small area and still get through the bottom layer because they ran in the opposite direction.

He also took notice of the two 10-foot-high barbed wire fences that completely surrounded the camp. The outer fence was reported to be electrified.[10] Between those two fences was rolled barbed wire (concertina) stacked four feet high. Charlie estimated that the distance of the cleared area from the outer fence to the edge of the forest was about 200 feet. A prisoner attempting to escape would have to cross that wide-open area in full view of the tower guards.

Looking around some more, he noticed the inner warning wire which was about 50 feet from the inner fence. It was a wooden fence about one foot high, and a POW who stepped over it would be shot on sight.[11] Located at close intervals around the camp were guard towers equipped with several strong search lights, sirens, machine guns, and trigger-happy guards. On the outside of the camp he saw guards on foot with police dogs patrolling the outer perimeter.

The camp was divided into four compounds, or lagers, and each was a separate unit. They were set up in a square and divided by a road from which a single gate lead into each lager. Twin barbed wire fences about 10 feet high, and running parallel about the same distance apart, surrounded each of the four compounds. Additional huts would be constructed between the barracks to house an additional six POWs each.[12]

The four separate compounds consisted of lagers A, B, C, and D.

Charlie was assigned to Lager B, in a room housing 24 men which had been built to accommodate only 18 prisoners. "Finch and Rakiewicz were assigned to my room. The other three enlisted guys ended up in other barracks. When we first got to the camp they put all the wounded guys in one barracks. Some guys had their ears burned off from their planes being on fire. Some guys had to jump through flames as they bailed out. Van Every had to jump out of the bomb bay and the fire was past there. He made it out without getting burned."

Charlie recalled that each lager had 10 barracks, a kitchen, an outside well hand pump, plus a latrine. The lager had a shed for storage of potatoes, carrots, and other food, which was never much of anything. The kitchen had a couple of large steam-type boilers used to cook potatoes, barley, carrots, cabbage and to make broth. The kitchen had only two or three large vats and no other utensils in which to cook food, so everything had to be mixed together and cooked like stew or mush.

He was housed in a small room inside a wooden barracks. The barracks was divided by a central hallway with rooms on both sides. The only entrance or exit from the rooms was through an interior door that opened up into the central hallway. The ventilation wasn't very good and many rooms didn't have a cast iron stove for heat. Charlie was lucky and was assigned to a room that had a heating stove. His room had a table, a few chairs, and eight two-tier beds (later triple-tier bunks were added). His bunk, like all the rest, was simply nothing more than wooden slats and a thin sack filled with either grass, straw, or wood shavings for a mattress.

Like the rest of the rooms, his room had only one window to let in natural sunlight and provide some ventilation. A single low-watt electric light bulb which hung from the ceiling in the center of the room provided very little light during the hours of darkness. As he recalled, the barracks shutters were closed about 5:00 p.m. each day. This was done to prevent the POWs from seeing what was going on outside of the barracks. Charlie and his roommates couldn't see when the German guards passed by as they checked the barracks. In the morning the guards removed the wooden braces that locked the doors at each end of the barracks. One of the prisoners then had to go outside and open the window shutters that were closed and barred shut the night before.

The small, single coal burning stove installed in Charlie's room provided the only warmth against the cold weather. Fuel for the small potbellied stove was coal briquettes. There were never enough of these briquettes to keep warm on the cold days, and in the winter Charlie wore every piece of clothing he possessed as he tried to stay warm. When the cooler temperatures arrived, the barracks windows were also closed during the day to prevent the little bit of heat they did have from escaping. But because the barracks was closed up so tightly, it allowed for practically no ventilation, and with the men overcrowded in the room, it was only a matter of time until the spread communicable diseases occurred.

The barracks had an indoor latrine, but Charlie and the others were only allowed to use it after lock-up hours. There wasn't any indoor plumbing. It was merely an enclosed pit under the barracks with an access door for ventilation and emptying. This so-called washroom had no running water and only a single toilet for use during the night. The latrine was emptied infrequently and it often overflowed.

During the day when the barracks were unlocked, Charlie and the others used the lager's common washroom and toilet. That latrine also consisted of a concrete lined pit for the sewage. He complained about how bad it stank, in addition to the toilet seats being very cold! Sometimes the pit overflowed with raw sewage and oozed away from the building and across the compound. He had only one source for toilet paper and that was from the Red Cross food parcels, because the Germans didn't provide any. He recalled that when a lot of men had diarrhea, it created a severe shortage of toilet paper which was a serious personal hygienic problem.

The sewage collection vessel was a metal tank about three feet in diameter and 10 feet long. It was mounted on a trailer and pulled by horses. On the upper rear part of the tank was a compression chamber. This contraption operated by vacuum and used highly explosive sewage gas. A large hose was put into the sewage pit with the other end connected to the tank. A German stood on the rear platform and worked a hand pump on the ignition chamber, which drew in sewage gas. After enough pumps, he struck a match, opened the chamber door, tossed in the match, slammed the door shut, and jumped off the vessel. The resulting explosion would blow the lid open and a column of flame about eight feet high shot upward. A recoil spring attached to the lid's base slammed it back down rapidly. This then formed a seal and stopped outside air from entering the tank. The vacuum created in the tank then sucked up the sewage from the pit and into the tank. The prisoners named this ingenious device the "Super Duper Shit Scooper."[13]

As soon as the guards opened the gate and led Charlie and the other prisoners into Lager B, some of the POWs already there asked them a lot of questions about the war, like where the new prisoners were from. A few days later Charlie was out there greeting new POWs just like everybody else, as he tried to learn about the progress of the war and other current events. The arrival of a large group of new prisoners was always a big deal and gave him the chance to find an old buddy or someone else he knew.

The prisoners already interned in the camp realized that the new arrivals were most likely real Americans. But they also knew that there could be German spies, or stooges, as Charlie called them, in these newly arriving groups who spoke perfect English and appeared to be American. German spies lived among the prisoners. The POWs in the camp eventually eliminated them all, and were very vigilant in not allowing another stooge into the camp. The identification process took a few hours, but until Charlie and each new man was positively identified as an American, the old prisoners would not speak to him.[14]

Just like the rest of the new arrivals, Charlie was encouraged to tell his story, which was motivated by more than just goodwill and comradeship on the part of the current camp POWs. Bringing out information from new arrivals was a necessary screening requirement conducted by the POW leadership within the camp. All new arrivals were asked a lot of questions and sometimes were put on display until someone positively identified them. He said that a new prisoner had to be identified by POW intelligence before they were accepted as legitimate.

Many of the stooges had lived in the United States. Most could correctly answer basic questions such as "Who is Babe Ruth?" or "How are the Phillies doing?" or something like that. Many were also familiar with a lot of localities within the United States. They would claim to be from one unit or another and were always full of information as to how and where they were captured. It was hard to spot these implanted spies, but the prisoners could always find someone among their group who came from that town or area, or had been in that unit, and they would thoroughly check into their stories.[15]

When the POWs found a man they believed wasn't a real American, they didn't throw him out, beat him, or single him out in any way. Doing any of those things would have blown the cover of their entire operation. What they did was simply to see that the suspected stooge never got any information. Eventually the Germans removed the spy because he was ineffective.[16]

Charlie and every new arrival to the camp was told about the penalties for intentionally or unintentionally breaking the strict camp rules. The most serious violation was to enter the restricted area between the warning wire and the interior fence around the lager. This restricted area was defined by the low wooden rail 50 feet from all four fence lines. Unless they first received permission from a tower guard to cross the warning wire, perhaps chasing after a loose ball, a prisoner who entered that restricted area was probably going to be shot. He was informed that the German guards were not required to fire a warning shot to halt any violation of camp rules. The guards had been instructed that if the occasion for the use of firearms was required, they must shoot to kill. During his stay in Stalag Luft IV, he witnessed the shooting and killing of prisoners for less serious infractions than crossing the warning wire.

He and the others used the warning wire around the lager as their walking exercise path guideline. Charlie also sat on the rear steps of his barracks and watched the prisoners walking past. By doing that he occasionally spotted someone that he knew from his old bomb group that had been captured recently. Sometimes a POW would see someone that they had gone through training with at one of the various schools. He quickly familiarized himself with the camp layout and started the process of determining what was expected of him and how best to get along and survive this new and very restrictive life behind the wire.

After being successfully screened, and warned about the very strict camp rules, he started to adjust to the new norms and expected behaviors of prison camp life. Many of the various attitudes and behaviors that he had to follow or adjust to evolved from the Geneva Convention standards of conduct.[17] But they were also based on what was considered to be acceptable among the prisoners and their dealings with the German guards. He found out just how great freedom is, because now he was in a situation where almost every decision was made for him by a man with a gun pointing at him.

Soon after becoming a prisoner, Charlie began to realize that probably the most important thing in his life was when and if he was going to get something to eat. Unlike food, there never was a shortage of water. If he wanted some drinking water, he had to take a pan or a cup outside to the well and draw the water by using a hand pump.

The Germans really didn't provide much food, and often the guards didn't have much food for themselves. To say the least, food was scarce in the camp. The prisoners occasionally got meat if a dead horse could be found nearby. It was not unusual for the prisoners to be served rancid meat or food infested with maggots.[18] On one occasion, Charlie watched as the Germans brought into the camp in open wagons, which were pulled by oxen or cows, raw meat that was covered with a green mold. Soon afterward he and the others noticed the finely chopped pieces of meat in the soup. Occasionally the Germans came up with something edible.

The camp sewage waste was used as fertilizer in the potato fields, and one day when the wagon came to remove the sewage from the latrine, Charlie noticed it was drawn by only one horse instead of the usual two. He soon realized they had some meat in their dehydrated vegetable soup the next few days. "A German horse died, and we got lucky. It provided meat for our soup for a couple of nights until we used up all of the horse. We were hoping that some more horses would die."

Charlie recalled that there were only two meals a day. The meals were either German-supplied food, Red Cross food, which wasn't very often, or sometimes both, when available. If it was German food in the morning, it usually included a little barley. In late afternoon, the meal might be potatoes with a little food from Red Cross parcels. The POWs tried making the food as appetizing as possible and invented many types of concoctions to make the food more palatable.

There was no breakfast as such, but every morning at about 7:30 the kitchen crew prepared either hot tea or ersatz coffee. They were both hard to get used to, but eventually Charlie decided they were better than nothing. Each room had a metal beverage container and the men took turns standing in line at the kitchen to get their room's ration. They then brought it back and the room leader made sure that everyone received an equal amount.

Charlie's basic diet was potatoes, cabbage, turnips and bread. In the entire time he was in the camp, he never saw apples, oranges, pears, plums, cherries, bananas, berries, corn, or eggs. But he and most of the men survived. Very rarely did he have any salt or sugar. When he got cabbage soup, he also received a little extra protein. The soup was usually full of bugs and worms. Many of the men picked them out, but Charlie just ate them, preferring not to look. Some prisoners actually enjoyed their texture and flavor.

Remembering the soup, Charlie said, "The soup had cabbage or barley as the main ingredients. The cabbage was sparse in the soup. I enjoyed the barley more because it filled me up and stayed with me longer. We had no seasoning." The best tasting food the POWs received was the barley cereal similar to cooked oatmeal. Nearly all the men agreed that the barley cereal was by far the best food they received. He ate almost every bit of food the Germans provided.

Meals were prepared in the lager's kitchen. Charlie recalled, "We ate in the barracks. One man from each room would go to the kitchen and they'd fill his bucket for the number of men assigned to his room. He brought that back and we divided it up. There was no mess hall."

Each room representative stood in line at the kitchen with a pail. When he returned to the room, the 20-plus hungry men crawled out of their bunks or got up from the floor and gathered around to get their fair share. Charlie said the portions had to be as equal as possible, or fights started if any favoritism was shown. The men in his room also shared the Red Cross food parcels when they received any. The Red Cross intended one parcel per man, per week, but that never happened in the camp, and sometimes as many as eight men had to share a parcel.[19]

The loaves of black bread also had to be divided into equal portions. The loaves were very uneven which made it hard for Charlie or someone else to cut up a loaf fairly, and no way to weigh the individual slices. For the evening meal a bucket of potatoes, or whatever else was cooked, was evenly spooned onto six plates, with four men to a plate. If there was an odd man left out, he received a little bit from each of the six plates. This was done to make the serving as equal as possible. He recalled many arguments as to who got more, but for the most part when it came to food, they all shared and shared alike.

On most days Charlie received a small portion of a loaf of a heavy grain black bread that contained a good amount of sawdust. Sometimes he even found pieces of wood inside. The bread also contained ground up leaves, oats, and just enough rye flour to make the whole thing stick together. It didn't taste too awful and was slightly moist. However, it would dry up like cracked clay if he tried to save it for too long.

The Germans brought unwrapped loaves of bread into camp stacked in an open wagon which was pulled by either oxen or cows. One of the best ways he discovered to make it almost edible was to cut it about a quarter inch thick and hold it against the side of the pot belly stove, which toasted it. Sometimes he was given a white margarine to spread on his bread. He and many of the prisoners thought the margarine was one of the better-tasting food items they received. Charlie usually had one piece of bread with some of the margarine and either the coffee or tea for breakfast.

Typically for Charlie, the later meal was either potato soup, cabbage soup, a dehydrated sauerkraut soup, or a dried greens soup. The boiled potatoes would have been good, but the cooks usually ruined them when they added a large turnip-like vegetable called kohlrabi. The strong turnip taste overpowered the potatoes, ruined the flavor, and made it hard to stomach, but it was either eat or go to bed hungry that night. He said the sauerkraut and greens soup smelled and tasted so bad that even though they were nearly starved, most couldn't eat it. Some of his roommates dumped it into the latrine, and many claimed that the soup odor was so powerful that it actually masked the smelly odors coming from the latrine, which was not easy to do.

The men helped those that were really sick by giving them a morsel of food from their own ration. Even though food was very scarce, Charlie never ate all he received and put some away for a rainy day. Because the prisoners were all NCOs, they were not required to do any physical labor by the Germans.[20] This was a good thing since rations were so low and the expenditure of a lot of calories would have been deadly.

The International Red Cross provided many thousands of food parcels for the prisoners of war, with the intention of distributing one parcel per man per week. That didn't happen. During Charlie's stay at Stalag Luft IV, he recalled receiving only two or three Red Cross parcels. When they received them, they were a gift from heaven. The POWs had to split a parcel among four men and survived by combining the German rations with the Red Cross parcels.[21]

"There were only a few times in the camp when we received Red Cross parcels. Four men had to share a parcel. There were two big warehouses right outside the camp, and the Red Cross parcels were all brought there. Truckloads came in. Wouldn't be long and you'd see the German trucks back up and load up with the Red Cross parcels and off they went. They were feeding their army with our food. I'm sure all the officers fed their families with those parcels."

Food was scarce and Charlie lost weight. The Red Cross provided parcels to the POW camps as a way to supplement the POWs' meager diet. Unfortunately, at Stalag Luft IV, the parcels were controlled by the camp commandant and the POW leaders were not allowed to be present when they arrived. The parcels were distributed and held back at the discretion of the camp authorities. To prevent hoarding and use during an escape, the guards punched holes in each of the cans, which resulted in much of the food spoiling before the prisoners could eat it.

Besides withholding their Red Cross food parcels, the Germans pilfered individual and bulk parcels of cigarettes sent to the POWs by the Red Cross. But the thing that really angered Charlie and the other prisoners was the Germans puncturing all canned goods included in the food parcels prior to issue. The Germans insisted that it was a necessary precaution to stop the hoarding of food which might be used in an escape. The prisoners complained about the abuse to the German authorities, but it didn't do any good.[22]

Each Red Cross food parcel included four packs of cigarettes, and bulk shipments of cigarettes were also supplied to all camps. For the prisoners who smoked, cigarettes were important and were the principal method of barter among the prisoners and sometimes with the guards. Although bulk shipments of cigarettes were sent to the camp on a regular basis, they were regularly pilfered or stolen by the German guards, whose own government ration of cigarettes was limited to only 60 cigarettes per month.[23] Using cigarettes for barter allowed Charlie to supplement his meager food rations, obtain articles of clothing, and buy small items to make his life more comfortable.

The Germans really didn't follow the Geneva codes and prisoners suffered and died as a result. They never provided enough food or clothing that met the standards of the Geneva agreements. A normal-sized American man during World War II required approximately 3,000 calories a day. At the very most, the Germans only provided for 1,500 to 1,900 calories a day.[24] The POWs were not truly starving, but they were always hungry. Charlie was always thinking about food and eating. "I'd write down recipes and meals in my journal that I would like to have—wishful thinking."

The senior medical officer at Stalag Luft IV was Captain Henry Wynsen, who wrote a report about the rations that the Germans issued. In his report, Wynsen stated: "Food consisted of daily rations of bread (approximately 20 ounces), margarine (2 ounces), and plain boiled potatoes or a soup mixture made of potatoes, other vegetables, or dehydrated sauerkraut. The POWs also received a meat allowance of ½ ounce." In the report he also estimated that the skimpy rations provided by the Germans, even when supplemented with Red Cross food parcels, provided each prisoner with no more than 1,200 calories daily. He also asserted that these dietary restrictions resulted in each prisoner losing 15 pounds, on average.[25]

Charlie said the Red Cross clothing supplies were the same story as the food parcels. Just like the food parcels, Red Cross clothing deliveries were also closely controlled by the Germans. He often saw German guards and workmen wearing American clothes and smoking American cigarettes, all the while his own clothing was in bad shape. "They took my flying clothes and gave me coveralls, etc., but no gloves."

Depending on the time of year, but typically soon after the last meal of the day, Charlie and all the POWs were locked up in their barracks for the night. During the spring and summer months with longer daylight, lock-up took place around 9:30 p.m. But by early autumn, he and the rest were required to stay inside their barracks starting at around 4:00 p.m. and until close to 7:00 a.m. the following morning. As soon as everyone was securely locked inside their barracks, vicious guard dogs were let loose inside the compound. The dogs roamed freely throughout the lager in search of any unauthorized activity by the prisoners. Charlie asserted that the dogs were bad enough, but even more dangerous were the German guards who would shoot to kill any POW who stepped out of their barracks after lock-up.

Because the Germans didn't provide them with enough eating implements, Charlie and the others had to make plates, pans, and other utensils out of the Red Cross food parcel tin cans. Using the empty cans, they cut off the bead where the side met the top and then used the rest of the can to produce a roll of pliable metal. They used kitchen knives, handles or whatever else they could find to hammer the rolls into flat sheets of metal around three inches wide and close to a foot long. They then placed the edges of the sheets on the edge of a table, and using a knife-handle as a hammer, pounded it to create a small standing edge along the entire edge of each metal sheet. Putting two of those together, so that the edge of one was inside the edge of another, they then hammered the two edges flat and created a good joint much like a standing seam is made on metal house roofs.[26]

They could create a single sheet of metal of almost any size. By crimping up the corners for a couple of inches, they could make a pan or plate. They did leak a bit, but cooking in them a couple of times, and not washing them all too well, which they couldn't do anyway because of lack of hot water, provided enough residue to seal the joints fairly well. Now they had useable pots, pans, and plates.

Stalag Luft IV was a non-commissioned officer's camp where most prisoners held the rank of sergeant. In accordance with the Geneva Convention, the Germans could not force the prisoners to work because they were NCOs. The NCOs of the Allied air forces were treated by the Germans with the same respect of rank extended to officers of other Western nations,[27] so Charlie had no work except for what he made for himself. Really his only work was cleaning up after himself and helping with KP (kitchen duty).

Charlie soon realized that it was pointless and meaningless to work because it didn't get him anywhere. He went to bed at night because there was nothing much else to do, not because he was tired. Except for meals, roll call, trips to the latrine, and sleeping, he and the others mostly just sat around. A lot of prisoners let themselves go, physically and mentally, but not Charlie. "I exercised some every day, but had to stay in B Lager. We laid in our bunks and thought about what we'd eat if we were back home. We spent hour after hour just thinking things up."

About the only daily structure he had were meals and roll call formations. On most days there weren't any organized activities at all. A major challenge for him was boredom and trying not to feel depressed and gloomy. To fight off those feelings, he tried to stay active in some of the hobbies and activities he had before being taken prisoner.

The POWs were helped in their efforts to engage in meaningful activity by the YMCA. The YMCA's mission was to provide for the physical, mental, and spiritual welfare of prisoners of war of all nationalities. When allowed by the Germans, the YMCA helped the prisoners by providing books, sports equipment, and religious things for worship services.[28]

Charlie kept himself occupied by playing cards, chess, checkers, and reading when he could get a book. He also walked laps around the inside of the compound. The POWs were able to talk and play games with other prisoners in their same lager, and plain old conversation in small groups were regular occurrences. The games they played were baseball, football, and volleyball. The YMCA also supplied some musical instruments and the POWs formed an orchestra and put on a couple of shows.

The POWs participated in a variety of activities during the long periods of confinement inside the barracks. Charlie recalled that some prisoners worked on small craft projects to either occupy their time or to make something valuable that could be used as barter. By far, for him and many of the prisoners, the most popular pastime was playing cards and games went on all the time. They made their own playing cards by using the cardboard cracker boxes from the Red Cross food parcels.

Charlie participated in most of the activities. "I learned to play chess and other games. We made up paper cards for card games. The guards gave us paper if we gave them cigarettes, and one guard would get us almost anything as long as we gave him cigarettes. That's how I got the paper for my journal, and I wrote it with a pencil. We had some guys that could draw, and I had them draw in my journal. I carefully kept that journal underneath my shirt during the march that was to come" (Appendix A).

He and all of the prisoners were very susceptible to disease and had to take care of themselves as best as they possibly could under the circumstances. One way of doing that was by getting plenty of sleep, and sometimes he slept 12 hours a day. That was a lot of sleep, but he had good reasons for sleeping that much. Sleep preserved his strength which helped to compensate for the lack of food. Sleep also made him less nervous and irritable and helped to control his hunger because he wasn't burning up as many calories.

As a combat airman, Charlie and the rest of his fellow prisoners had been trained to work as a team, and that training definitely helped them while in the prison camp. The pressure of living together in such cramped quarters for months with so many men could and sometimes did lead to friction, arguments, and physical fights. The men had no place to go to be alone for some peace and quiet. But the barracks in camp, just like the compartments of the bombers, were remarkably harmonious places. He and most of the prisoners, regardless of their different backgrounds, forgot about their differences and prejudices and worked together to survive the ordeal.

Because of their circumstances, the prisoners were forced to do things they had never dreamed or conceived of doing before. Almost every single day they had to sacrifice, endure, and work together in a common struggle to survive. One way Charlie found that he could contribute was by giving haircuts. "I gave the guys haircuts. I got a razor blade from a guard, and, using a comb, would hold the razor blade on the comb and then go around their heads. It was painful because eventually the razor dulled. My beard had grown straight out, all around, but it was good having a beard in the cold weather."

Some POWs took on leadership roles that were as important as any held within a chain of command outside of a prison camp. Some men provided religious and spiritual comfort to many prisoners as chaplains. Charlie recalled that the chaplains in his lager performed religious services in the utility room located in the lager's kitchen. The Germans reluctantly allowed it, but strictly limited the religious services. Services had to be attended by the guards who ensured that only the basic sacraments such as communion were performed. Prisoners were not allowed to give sermons.

"We had religious services. I sat for days and wrote songs that I remembered from church that we used for our religious services. Old hymns. We had services every Sunday and two guards were always inside with us to watch, but they never interfered. We had good turn-outs, but the Germans didn't like us being in large groups. The commandant approved as long as there were two guards present. Normally they would only allow four or five guys to walk around together in the compound."

Occasionally a prisoner's feeling of helplessness would drive him over the edge. The prisoners called it "barbed wire disease."[29] Its most noticeable symptom was a glum feeling of being hopelessly trapped. In its worst form it turned into a mental illness that left the prisoner unable to focus or even remember his name. Afflicted prisoners became listless and inattentive and spent entire days in their bunks just staring at the walls. Others fell from lethargy into a depression so deep and strong that they were unable to talk or communicate in any way. The uncertainty of their captivity aggravated the condition. Unlike inmates in a civilian prison, POWs never knew if and when they might be set free. That led some seriously ill prisoners to desire death over imprisonment.

For some POWs, imprisonment was more than they could stand. One day a prisoner decided to cross the warning wire and climbed the fence. He made it to the top of the fence before being shot. "A few days before Christmas a POW went crazy and started running toward the fence. The prisoner had been walking along the rail when he suddenly took off. The guards shot and killed him."

Throughout World War II, thousands of American ground combat troops pretended to be insane in order to be taken out of combat and sent to a field hospital and then back home. Nobody faked insanity in a stalag. Conditions in the camp hospital were as appalling as they were in the barracks, and the Germans refused to send home POWs suffering from mental disorders.[30] Charlie and the others could only count on their friends to help them stay sane.

"A guy in our barracks went berserk. He ran from one end of the barracks to the other, right into the door. It knocked him down and knocked him out for a while. Then he got up after he got his senses together and he ran the other way into the door. A couple of guys grabbed him and sat on him. He never did get straightened out. Some jumped the warning wire and were killed. If they were shot while on the fence, the Germans let them hang there for days."

He recalled that there were very, very few suicides in the camp. Most of the guys held up under the pressure, and like Charlie, more than a few actually benefited from the awful experience. He learned a lot about himself in those long months of confinement. He definitely learned how to get along with people under difficult conditions. He believed that the hardships he endured made him have a stronger appreciation for the things he had once taken for granted.

One thing that really helped his morale and attitude was receiving mail from home. Some mail for him got through, but sometimes some of it was not readable because it had been censored by the Germans. He was allowed to mail two letters and two cards a month. The amount of incoming mail was not restricted, but the German delivery system was very inconsistent (Appendix B).

The number of parcels a family could mail overseas was restricted by the United States. The shipment of packages was slow and many were lost and damaged. Sadly, few packages reached the POWs during the latter part of the war. Those parcels that did make it from home took forever to get there, were usually damaged, and often had been pilfered.[31]

If it wasn't lost or destroyed in transit, a letter sent from the camp took a minimum of six to eight weeks to reach the United States. The very slow delivery time was caused by a few things. All outgoing mail was first screened by a POW committee, then sent by rail through a German censorship office at Stalag Luft III before being forwarded to its final destination. Likewise, incoming mail sent to POWs was also routed through German censorship prior to delivery. This process became even slower after Allied air forces started attacking the German rail transportation system.[32]

Charlie and most of the prisoners passed around their letters from home and let everybody in their room read them. They all enjoyed reading a letter from any mother or girlfriend. Sometimes he, like the others, stayed in his bunk for hours re-reading the letter over and over. Some men posted some of the more interesting letters on the bulletin board for everyone to read. Many of the letters were very funny, but to some men it was just another thing that made them feel sad and lonely. Sadly, a lot of the prisoners never received any mail while interned.

Charlie and the other prisoners got their war information from three sources: new prisoners, Allied and German radio broadcasts, and secretly published camp newspapers.

News broadcasts from London were picked up by at least one radio hidden inside the camp.[33] Every day it was disassembled and the parts hidden to keep it from being discovered. If anyone would have been caught with any of the radio parts or the Germans discovered the names of those involved in obtaining messages, they would have been executed.

Radio receivers were not too hard to assemble because the POWs comprised a wide range of abilities and cleverness. Among the prisoners were many trained radio operators. The radio parts were smuggled into the camp hidden inside baseballs provided by the YMCA. The parts that were required for the assembly of a radio were hidden inside baseballs that were identified by their reverse stitching.[34]

Charlie and the POWs were fairly well informed in the camp and generally received news a few days after an event had taken place. He recalled that new information was usually brought to the lager by prisoners who had been at the infirmary in the *vorlager*. A selected prisoner would pretend to be very ill, and needing medical attention by the camp's Allied doctors, he would report for sick call. In the infirmary the latest news was spread among the prisoners, who then returned to their barracks after sick call and spread the word. He remembered that, usually, one prisoner moved from room to room giving the guys the latest news about the war and other important events. He was also certain that the Germans suspected that the POWs had a radio hidden somewhere in the camp, but they never could or did find it.

The news was encouraging in the fall of 1944. Both the Western Allies and the Russians were on Germany's borders and the skies were filled almost daily with Allied bombers. Every time a formation of them flew overhead, Charlie and the other POWs gathered outdoors and shouted roars of approval. But with winter approaching, the Western Allies offensive stalled along the Siegfried Line, and the mood in the camp turned gloomy.

In December word reached the camp of the massive German counteroffensive in the Ardennes, The Battle of the Bulge. A mood of despair crept through the prisoners, and the men began talking about the possibility of never being freed or seeing home again. For the next week or two, the spirits of the prisoners hit rock bottom as German forces continued their ferocious attack. In contrast, the German guards were jubilant, bragging, and Charlie remembered that they mocked the prisoners saying, "You *kriegies* are going to rebuild Berlin because you are the ones who destroyed it."

For Charlie, life inside the camp was not always boring and uneventful. One day a German soldier was high up on an electrical pole repairing a transformer or electrical wires. While he was working up on the pole someone carelessly flipped a switch and electrocuted him. Many POWs clapped and yelled when it happened, but the clapping and yelling didn't last long when the guards in the towers opened fire, hitting some prisoners. Many prisoners dropped down between the barracks and hugged the ground until the firing stopped. For some time after that, relations between the German guards and the prisoners was tense.

As Charlie remembered the event, "I was in the barracks and a guy was up on a pole when I heard a commotion. I was sitting at the window watching a German in uniform working up on a pole. All of a sudden I saw him shoot backwards, arms spread wide to each side, and he just hung there by his belt. Then he started turning black. It took a while until the Germans got the body down. A group of prisoners gathered and started clapping and laughing. A burst of machine gun fire stopped that. They shot into the ground but some of the guys got hit anyway. That settled that."

Another event Charlie recalled was the time on a hot July day when it started raining and the rain turned into an electrical storm. The thunder and lightning was severe, and a bolt of lightning hit a hut that housed six POWs. Several of the men in that hut were killed by the strike.

In September of 1944, an event occurred that showed just how tense things were within the camp between the prisoners and the German guards. German Luftwaffe pilots used the airspace over the camp and the lightly populated region to practice aerial combat maneuvers. The prisoners knew that the Germans conducted their training over the camp believing that their aerial performance would intimidate and demoralize the POWs.[35]

One day three German FW-190 fighters were performing maneuvers over the camp, flying just above a low cloud ceiling, as Charlie and most of the POWs watched. After several minutes of flying, most of which was hidden from view, all three fighters dived through the low cloud ceiling as they chased one another. But the last aircraft failed to pull out of its dive in time and crashed into the forest a short distance from the camp. The POWs heard the explosion and could see the smoke from the burning wreckage.

Suddenly the prisoners seized the moment and started cheering loudly, as they vented their hatred and anger at the Germans. The spontaneity and the strength of this uproar provoked an immediate and equally intense reaction from the Germans. The tower guards along the outer fence line quickly turned their machine guns toward the interior of the camp and started firing. Charlie heard and saw the rapid and continuous machine gun fire as they fired directly into the camp. By sheer luck the bullets passed over the heads of the stunned prisoners and didn't cause any casualties. Soon more guards rushed into the lagers and pushed the stunned prisoners back into their barracks.

In another deadly event, a prisoner jumped from a barracks window to the ground. This was not permitted, and only barracks doors were to be used for exiting and entering barracks. A German guard who was standing nearby ordered the POW to re-enter the barracks through the window. But suddenly the guard shot the prisoner, claiming the man had spit on him. The prisoner died 24 hours later.[36]

Occasionally the Germans fired their machine guns over the prisoners' heads to get their attention and to remind them who was in charge. Sometimes during daylight hours, the Germans ordered all POWs out of their barracks, and then test fired their machine guns over their heads. "Every so often we were forced to lay belly down in the compound. They test fired their guns from the towers, and instead of turning those guns outward, they turned them in toward us and shot into the ground around us. Some guys were hit. The commandant said it was an accident. That's how they worked on our nerves by keeping us fearful all the time. I kept reminding myself that I made it this far and that I'd make it all the way. Just stay cool."

Twice a day, every day, regardless of the weather, Charlie and all other prisoners had to fall out on the parade ground by the barracks and line up five deep to be counted. The commandant along with the POW camp leader stood in front of the formation, while armed guards stood in the rear of the formation, as they were counted by a couple of German NCOs.[37]

The commandant was a lieutenant colonel and was old compared to the prisoners. He always stood stiffly at attention in his black leather overcoat with his right hand over his heart, Napoleon style. According to Charlie, the prisoners called him "Commandant Rigor Mortis" because of the stiff way he stood at attention. The POWs utilized the roll calls and made them regular formations under their own leaders and their own commands. This helped a great deal to maintain prisoner self-respect, and it gave some military discipline to their day.

These mandatory formations were conducted in the morning and late afternoon to count the number of POWs assigned to each barracks. The purpose of these roll call formations was to keep accountability of the prisoners assigned to the lager and to spoil any possible escape. After the POWs were formed, one guard counted the front rank while another guard confirmed the number of aligned files and multiplied by five to determine the head count for each barracks.

If the prisoners cooperated, the entire process was completed within 10 to 15 minutes. However, roll call provided a rare opportunity for the POWs to passively rebel against their German captors by screwing up the count. This was just one of many forms of annoyance carried out by the POWs. Charlie called it "goon baiting." The POWs would intentionally leave one or two men in the barracks just to annoy the guards and screw up their head count. Every now and then, and just for fun, the POWs did this until the commandant ordered a search of all barracks.

One day the count was short by one prisoner. The men could tell that "Commandant Rigor Mortis" was clearly upset and he decided to make the count himself. He made the count and found all prisoners accounted for. He then ordered the guard who couldn't conduct the count accurately front and center and chewed him out. Charlie couldn't understand many of the words, but he knew it was a major ass-chewing. After calling the guard a few nasty names, the commandant dismissed the guard from his roll call duties. Sometime later the POWs learned that because the guard was not able to conduct a simple roll call, the commandant had him shipped to the Russian front.

Whenever the count didn't come out right, Charlie and the rest had to stand there until it was straightened out. During the hot summer it was not unusual for men to pass out from the heat before the guards were satisfied with the count. In winter, he thought he'd freeze before the torment was over. In the rain and during the winter this caused a lot of hardship particularly for the prisoners who were sick. Charlie recalled, "Sometimes when it was raining, the Germans kept us outside until our clothes were soaked. We had no spare dry clothes to put on."

Sometimes the POW camp leader assigned a couple of the prisoners to help them finish the count. Charlie said it was the responsibility of each room leader to make sure everyone was out of the barracks. Too many times after a couple of counts being incorrect, a search of the barracks found a prisoner still asleep in his bunk. Sometimes two or three POWs were missing at the same time, and the guards always chased them out of the barracks. They would stagger out onto the parade ground much to the dismay of the Germans and to a bunch of wet and cold prisoners.

The nights were long and he was never able to fall asleep easily, but he had made it through one more day. There was almost total darkness inside the barracks after lights out at 10:00 p.m. To find his way to the latrine, he had to feel his way along the bunks and hallway until he found it. Every now and then after lights out, and without warning, the guards came into the barracks with flashlights and conducted a spot check. "Night was the worst time, especially when it was cold. At least during the day I could go outside and walk around and get the blood circulating."

Guards manned the towers 24 hours a day, which had extra armed guards during formations. When any orders were given, they were passed to them by their own leaders, and normally not directly from the Germans. On occasion when Charlie had to speak to a guard, which was very, very rare, he addressed him as "mister" and did not use the guard's rank. The name *kriegie* given to the POWs was made up by the German guards. Behind the Germans backs, the prisoners call the guards goons.[38]

Another special type of guard inside the camp was called a ferret.[39] Their job was to roam around the lager, including inside of the barracks. They typically acted casual and friendly toward the prisoners, but were always on the alert for prime bits of information from conversations among the POWs. They also searched for anything suspicious and forbidden contraband the prisoners might have in their possession. A ferret reported his findings immediately up his chain of command.

A ferret was sort of like a detective. He was constantly searching for tunnels or other escape projects. The POWs considered them spies. Ferrets spoke good English and usually acted like a dimwit. Charlie and the other prisoners had nothing to worry about so long as they remained smarter than the ferrets.

According to Charlie, sometimes they played tricks on the ferrets. One trick they played was to gather in a group outside in the compound and pretend not to see him, as they talked loudly about a new airplane or weapon the Allies were developing. Then, when they had his attention and knew he was listening, they quickly feigned surprise and broke up the meeting. They hoped he would report the fake news back to his headquarters.

Tough treatment and the harsh killing of POWs underscored the tension that existed in the camp starting in the summer of 1944. The tide of the war had turned against Germany, and the Allied bombing campaign was slowly and surely destroying the country. The huge increase in bombing resulted in a substantial number of Allied airmen being shot down and captured. Because of that, the camp overflowed with many young and physically fit airmen. Charlie recalled that the German guards were mostly older than the prisoners, and many were disabled soldiers.

Germany struggled to find the needed manpower to feed the war machine. Many of the guards at Stalag Luft IV were disabled German veterans 40 to 60 years old.[40] The guards who were old men wanted the war to end. Charlie said that the older guards gave the impression that they would have rather been back in their home than in the camp. However, they also gave the impression that they would rather be stationed in the camp than on the Russian front. Some of the guards had been wounded on the Russian front, and Charlie discovered that they were easy to bribe with Red Cross food parcel items, especially cigarettes.

Some of the tension between the guards and prisoners was because of the differences in age and physical health. There was a shared fear by both groups of physical harm. Both groups had different forms of power that threatened the other. Charlie and the POWs hated and resented the guards' arbitrary rules, in addition to the enforced starvation and the unnecessary use of deadly force to maintain order. The prisoners despised the rigid, obsessive camp rules and only passively obeyed, which angered the guards. The Germans were afraid that the more numerous prisoners would riot and threaten their lives. Charlie strongly believed that one of the reasons the prisoners were underfed was to keep them in a physically weakened state, which reduced the threat of violence and escape.

To keep things lively and interesting with the guards, the POWs pounded on the barrack's floor after the guards had closed the doors and the windows were shuttered. They used a wooden slat from one of the bunks and hit the floor with it, and they called out in a loud whisper, "Hey, Joe, get out of the tunnel." They did this when the guards were just outside of the barracks making their inspection of the grounds. Within minutes the front door of the barracks was thrown open, and guards armed with automatic weapons stormed into the barracks and chased the prisoners out. They then carried out a search for a tunnel, and, of course, there wasn't one.[41]

The guards, using metal rods, regularly checked under the barracks for any tunnels. Many times in the middle of the night they woke up the POWs and conducted an unannounced inspection. The guards tore open mattresses, ripped up the wooden floors, and generally ransacked each barracks room. Sometimes they allowed the guard dogs to chew up the prisoners' possessions, and sometimes they just blatantly stole items from the POWs. Charlie recalled, "The Germans pulled surprise inspections, and we never knew when they were coming. They went through everything in the room."

The International Committee of the Red Cross, an independent humanitarian agency headquartered in Geneva, Switzerland, also conducted inspections of prisoners of war camps. When inspections were scheduled, the Germans always quickly made some improvements to camp conditions. But these improvements never lasted longer than the visit of the inspectors.[42]

The guards carried automatic weapons as they patrolled outside the camp perimeter throughout the night. Pulling on their leashes and patrolling with them were snarling guard dogs. These guard dogs had been trained to hate Allied uniforms and were so unpredictably vicious that every now and then one would turn on its master.[43] At night the dogs were released inside the compound and roamed freely throughout the lagers and underneath the elevated barracks.

The POWs hated the guard dogs, and Charlie recalled how they annoyed them whenever possible. The dogs were easily riled as they stalked underneath the barracks where they could be seen and heard through the cracks in the flooring. The prisoners formed two separate groups and positioned themselves at opposite ends of the long barracks hallway. One group stomped on the floor, which attracted the attention of the dog, which barked and barked and barked. Once the dog was really stirred up, the first group of prisoners stopped their stomping, and the second group at the other end of the barracks started stomping, which caused the dog to run to the other end of the barracks to investigate the new noise. The prisoners kept this up, going back and forth, until the dog was completely exhausted from too much activity. Charlie and the other prisoners laughed and laughed as they listened to the frantic efforts of the guards attempting to call off their dogs amidst all the barking and jeers coming from the men inside the barracks.

The men were starving and hatched a plan to get one of the guard dogs for food. "Every night they left dogs [German Shepherds or Alsatians] loose in the compound. The dogs could run underneath the barracks, which were up on stilts. We got the idea to kill one of these dogs. I examined the barracks door, which were panel doors. I suggested that if we could take out the lower panel and put it back in without being noticed, we could remove the panel and with a piece of meat from a Red Cross parcel, get a dog to stick his head inside. And when the dog sticks his head in, *wham*! Hit it with a club and suffocate the dog so it can't bark, and then pull it in."

"The day before, we talked to the guy in the kitchen, because he would have to get rid of that dog immediately! He said we should put the dog under somebody's coat and have four or five others walk with that guy to the kitchen, so the guards couldn't see a bulging coat. We can butcher the dog in a hurry and it will be in your soup tonight, the cook said. We can get rid of the hide and head and all that without a problem."

"We pulled it off! We left the dead dog lay in the hallway until morning. If a guard would have come in, I guess we would have tried to convince him that it died of natural causes. They were now missing a dog and they couldn't figure out what happened to it. The cooks cut the meat up real fine in the kitchen. The guards searched every barracks, but they never searched the kitchen. That night we had dog with our soup."

The first rule of being captured was to escape if possible, and that duty was recognized by the Geneva Conventions.[44] The subject of escape was discussed from time to time, and some plans were devised but never executed, according to Charlie. The POWs had the courage and determination to escape, but the many obstacles were just too much to overcome.

Chances of escaping Stalag Luft IV weren't too good, and Charlie and most of the men knew it. He realized that to have any chance of making it across Germany, he'd have to be wearing either civilian clothes or an enemy uniform. Getting caught wearing either of those would ensure instant execution by the Gestapo. Probably less than 2 percent of American prisoners attempted to escape German camps and an unknown number made it to freedom.[45]

"I don't know of anyone who tried to escape. We were too weak to escape. Many mornings when I sat up in my bunk everything started to spin. I was very weak from lack of food and in no shape to attempt an escape."

With the many thousands of prisoners in the camp, a revolt could have certainly caused big trouble for the Germans. But Charlie and the others knew that many prisoners would have been shot and killed. The only weapons the POWs possessed were homemade clubs and knives, which were no match against machine guns and rifles.

Some of the guards were sadistic and cruel beasts, and the most notorious of the guards was Sergeant Hans Schmidt. The POWs called him "Big Stoop." He was a very large, slow-moving man, about six feet, six inches tall and weighing close to 300 pounds.[46] His age was between 40 and 45 years old, and he had a square chin and a long scar on the left side of his face.

Big Stoop was well known in the camp for his large size, extremely bad temper, and likelihood to randomly hit prisoners for little or no reason at all. According to Charlie, he would sneak up behind a prisoner and slap their ears with his unusually large hands, which sometimes ruptured their eardrums and brought most men to their knees in pain.

It was not uncommon for him to confiscate letters and photographs of wives or girlfriends and make disgusting gestures and offensive remarks to provoke a passionate reaction. Understandably, the POWs intensely hated Schmidt. "Big Stoop" was a mocking reference to an uncivilized cartoon character featured in *Terry and the Pirates*.[47]

Prisoners were occasionally beaten upon arrival at the camp and the few personal possessions they had were confiscated. Many times it was Big Stoop who dished out the abuse after being encouraged by Captain Pickhardt. Big Stoop regularly slammed prisoners against walls, tossed them over tables, and severely beat them with his fists or a stick. During searches of the barracks, he commonly shoved around and slapped prisoners. He also overturned bunks and furniture, and if he found any food in a room, flung it onto the floor or over the blankets.[48]

With his eyes looking down, and swinging a thick leather belt, Big Stoop regularly patrolled the compounds. One day the men watched helplessly as he beat a prisoner without mercy with the belt. The buckle of the belt made scalp wounds so deep that the prisoner's skull was showing.[49]

The POWs consider Big Stoop a beast, not human. Charlie said that many prisoners would have killed him if they would have had a chance. According to Charlie, he may have been decapitated at the end of the war by some POWs taking their revenge. "He was taken care of when we were liberated."

One prisoner provided a very shocking account of Big Stoop's treatment of the POWs in a sworn deposition provided to the Judge Advocate General's Department after the war. According to the testimony of Staff Sergeant Athel Arnew, he had arrived at Stalag Luft IV with a new group of POWs on September 23, 1944. After a strip search and the confiscation of their Red Cross food parcels, the prisoners were ordered to dress. A prisoner next to Arnew placed his foot on a bench to tie his shoe, which thoroughly angered Big Stoop. The prisoner didn't understand Big Stoop's ranting or instructions. Big Stoop suddenly charged the unaware prisoner and hit him with a rather large stick which was more than three and a half feet long. Big Stoop violently hit the prisoner on the back and neck with the stick, in addition to punching him with his fist. The prisoner was beaten to his knees and tried to crawl away, but Big Stoop followed him and kicked him in the back and sides with his hobnailed boots.[50]

The commandant, Lieutenant Colonel Otto Bombach, was also a very mean and vile man. He thoroughly enjoyed harassing the prisoners and made them suffer at every opportunity. His harsh treatment of the POWs was demonstrated one day after a bread ration was stolen from the guards. When Bombach was told about the theft, he ordered the prisoners of that lager to fall out in formation. He told the men that he would make them stand out in the inclement weather until the guilty prisoner confessed. When no one stepped forward, punishment was threatened. Only after 10 POWs were pulled out of the formation for what might have resulted in them being shot was the guilty prisoner forced to step forward by the other prisoners. That prisoner was never seen again.[51]

Charlie's and most of the others prisoners' health was fair. Their most common problems were skin issues resulting from poor sanitary conditions. He recalled that there weren't any showers or delousing facilities within the lagers, so fleas, lice, scabies, and bed bugs were widespread. The Germans didn't provide any insecticide or delousing powder to control the infestations.

The camp's infirmary was staffed by two American doctors, two British doctors, a British dentist, and 14 additional medical personnel, all of whom were POWs. The medical facilities were wanting, and the infirmary had only 132 beds for more than 10,000 prisoners.[52] The equipment was out of date and the number of trained personnel inadequate. There was a small operating room for minor procedures, but serious cases had to be sent elsewhere. POWs who were seriously wounded were sent to a German hospital, where they received better care. Few prisoners received any follow-up care.

The infirmary doctors identified three separate groups of men who needed medical care. The first group, 15 to 20 percent of the camp population, was made up of men who were wounded, burned, or maimed in aerial combat. Another group, which represented more than 50 percent of all prisoners, suffered from gastritis, diarrhea, and diphtheria, plus a variety of skin diseases. They also noticed that more than a few prisoners suffered from psychological disorders ranging from irritability to outright insanity.[53]

In November and December 1944, temperatures dropped to an average of 35 degrees Fahrenheit. Stiff winds off the Baltic Sea, to the north of the camp, further pushed the temperature below freezing. These conditions created a risk of frostbite and other exposed flesh injuries. Charlie and the POWs lacked adequate clothing to keep them warm in these cold weather conditions, so they stayed inside the barracks for longer periods of time to protect themselves from the cold, severe winter.[54]

When it was really cold, the prisoners doubled up and shared blankets. Except for his shoes, Charlie went to bed fully dressed in an attempt to keep warm enough to sleep. Some prisoners had no choice but to sleep on the floor because of overcrowding and a shortage of bunks in the camp. It was so cold inside the barracks that a man sleeping on the floor would find his blanket frozen to the floor in the morning.

The only warmth generated in the prisoners' barracks, besides body heat from the overcrowding, was from the single coal burning stove. The stove was fueled by a very limited daily ration of poor-quality peat bricks made of compressed coal dust. Charlie recalled that the weather became even colder in late December 1944 and January 1945 and the daytime temperatures were below freezing for weeks.

Soon after the first snowfall occurred, the prisoners engaged in a huge snowball battle. It took place during roll call formation and the men had a blast pelting the men on the other side of the parade ground and being pelted in return. The air was thick with flying snowballs, and several guards were hit. The commandant was furious as the guards tried desperately to put an end to the wintry battle.

The POWs received Red Cross parcels prior to Christmas that contained real American Christmas food. This included turkey, plum pudding, coffee, chocolate, raisins, butter, wheat biscuits and many other items. They were even given an extra Red Cross parcel and lived high on the hog for a few days.

Since Christmas Eve was very special, the commandant gave permission for the camp lights to remain on until 1:00 the following morning. The prisoners were allowed to be outside all Christmas Eve because 10 men agreed to be held as hostages.[55] There wasn't any trouble. The Germans even opened the gates to all four lagers so that the prisoners could visit buddies interned in the other compounds.

When the clock struck midnight, the POWs gathered in the center of the parade field and sang Christmas carols for 30 minutes. The weather was extremely cold with the temperature well below freezing, and as the snow fell with no wind, the beautiful Christmas carols could be heard throughout the camp. The entire camp was lit up by the powerful tower searchlights, while outside the fence the guards with rifles and dogs continued their patrol of the outer perimeter. At the close of the Christmas carols, the American and British leaders addressed the prisoners and offered words of inspiration. Before the prisoners quietly returned to their barracks, they sang "God Bless America" and "God Save the King" as a salute to the approximately 800 British airmen kept in D lager.[56]

For Charlie, Christmas of 1944 was something to remember. There was a Swiss gramophone (record player) that made the rounds of the camp. It included wonderful recordings such as Bing Crosby's "Silent Night" and "White Christmas". The American prisoners also enjoyed listening to the Russian prisoners assembled along the outside of the camp fences as they sang some beautiful Russian Christmas carols.

The commandant was even treating the prisoners nicely during Christmas. He allowed the prisoners to pile snow up against the sides of the barracks to block the icy winds from blowing under the barracks flooring. But he made the POWs promise not to take advantage of his kindness by digging escape tunnels, which could have been hidden by the snow piles.

Charlie recalled that by January 1945, the camp population had greatly overflowed the capacity for which the camp was built to house. Rooms now housed 24 men, and the prisoners were forced to sleep two men to a bunk. The weather turned even colder, and the POWs were given less fuel for their stoves to heat their uninsulated and drafty barracks. Even worse, their food rations was also reduced.

Upon assignment to a barracks, the prisoners elected representatives as allowed by the Geneva Convention. The main responsibility of the room and barracks leaders was to maintain order and discipline within the camp and to be a representative for prisoners to the German authorities. These positions required the leaders to settle petty interpersonal conflicts and to assign minor housekeeping duties and other tasks. The POWs cooperated since they really didn't have any other options. The prisoners in each barracks then elected a group representative. These individuals assumed the same responsibilities as room leaders, but functioned at a higher level within the leadership hierarchy.[57]

Sometime in January Charlie recalled that the POW camp leaders told him and the others that because the Russian army was only a few miles east of the camp, they would probably be leaving the camp soon on a forced march. They also informed the men that the prisoners in the poorest health were going to be moved out of the camp via train. A train ride while locked in boxcars travelling across Germany was no picnic because there was always the threat of being bombed or strafed by our own air force. Each room leader was required to submit names of those he believed were in the worst physical shape and could not make a forced march, and approximately 1,500 men were picked for the train ride.

On selecting those to take the train, Charlie said, "Northrup was voted our room commander. Then he was voted out and they voted Finch in. When the time to prepare for the march arrived, Finch was the room commander. Northrup couldn't march because he was still learning how to walk from his injuries. Finch put Northrup's name on the list to go by train. He got mad at Finch because he wanted to go on the march. But there is no way he [Northrup] could make the march."

Word spread that the camp would soon be evacuated. "I could hear the Russian guns off in the distance. The Germans decided to move us out of there to keep us out of the hands of the Russians, and I'm glad they did because the Russians were not nice people."

Charlie could hear the Russian guns in the east and he was hopeful that liberation might be close at hand. Liberation, however, was not the plan of the German military. In mid–January of 1945, the sick and crippled POWs were shipped out by railcar to camps deeper inside Germany. Charlie and the remaining prisoners were told to prepare for a three- or four-day march to a better camp. On February 5 an announcement was made that the camp would not be evacuated, but that message was soon followed by another announcement telling the prisoners they would be moving out in the morning.

The prisoners were going to have to be moved a long way, so they prepared for a march. The weather was terrible, and they were in poor health, to say the least. They were going to be evacuated in the midst of a tremendous battle, and Charlie believed that a march like this would undoubtedly cause many casualties. Three Russian armies launched an all-out attack along the 400-mile front of the German-Polish border, and a terrific battle was raging between Russian and German forces.[58]

Charlie and the other prisoners could tell that the German guards were afraid of the Russians, and as the Russians came closer, it increased the guards' anxiety and fear. The guards were becoming extremely nervous and he knew he and the others had to carry out all orders promptly and not irritate the guards. The heavily armed guards had been ordered to shoot any man who broke ranks or who intentionally disobeyed orders. No questions asked! Any prisoner attempting to escape would be shot on the spot, and that could endanger the lives of the rest of the prisoners. The guards had orders to shoot any prisoner who fell out from exhaustion and who could not continue the march. The prisoners believed that they would be safe if they stuck together as a unit.

On February 6, 1945, approximately 6,500 POWs departed Stalag Luft IV on a forced march that would last as long as 86 days for some. Most prisoners would walk hundreds and hundreds of miles during the coldest winter in years.[59]

CHAPTER 8

The March

This was a march of great suffering. For 80 days Charlie marched long distances in harsh weather on starvation rations. He lived in filth and slept in open fields and barns. Clothing, medical care and sanitary facilities were either non-existent or completely inadequate. Many POWs suffered from malnutrition, exposure, trench foot, exhaustion, dysentery, tuberculosis, and other diseases. The almost three-month-long march took place during the worst winter in northern Germany in many decades.

In early January 1945, more than 6,000,000 soldiers of the Red Army were deployed along a front line that stretched from the Baltic Sea to the Adriatic Sea. Opposing this tremendous force were 1,500,000 German soldiers assigned to the Eastern Front who couldn't stop the Russian assault.[1] As the Red Army closed in, Charlie took notice that the actions of many German guards clearly became more tense, arbitrary, and harsh. Incidents of guards shooting into the lagers and the barracks now occurred more frequently.

Knowing of the Russian advance stirred Charlie's hopes for liberation but also created some uneasiness and insecurity. For many prisoners, thinking about an evacuation and departure from the relative safety and security of the camp was upsetting. He and many others realized that an evacuation was going to require a forced march of some length in the middle of a severe winter and under harsh conditions.

In January 1945, the disabled prisoners were evacuated by rail, and the prisoners remaining in A and B lagers were moved to the other two compounds. The largest transfer moved about 500 prisoners still confined in B-Lager to another lager.[2] The move to another compound did not make Charlie happy because he had spent eight months in one barracks and felt comfortable there. But the move to another lager and a new barracks was nothing compared to the hell he was about to experience on the forced march.

He and the remaining POWs had to be relocated into the other lagers to allow the Germans to house many thousands of Allied POWs that arrived from other camps further east. The arrival and sight of these thin and wasted English, French, and Polish POWs, some without anything on their feet, and hardly able to walk, shocked many of the Stalag Luft IV prisoners.[3]

They had been on the march for a few weeks and were in very bad shape. Seeing how physically bad off these new arrivals were was all the proof Charlie needed to convince himself that things on the Eastern Front weren't going well for the Germans. With the arrival of these prisoners, a lot of speculation began as to when Stalag Luft IV would have to be evacuated. He had heard rumors that the camp wouldn't be evacuated, but from what he was seeing and hearing, that didn't seem likely.

Because of the increasing likelihood of an evacuation, Charlie and the other POWs started repairing their clothing that was ripped, torn, or otherwise in bad shape. To protect their face and head, some prisoners converted their scarves into ski masks, which covered the entire face except for the eyes and mouth. They also improvised and turned long-sleeve shirts into knapsacks in order to carry their small amount of personal possessions. Some of the prisoners who had been physically inactive started walking the lager fence lines as they tried to condition their feet and increase their stamina.

In the meantime, the Red Army crossed into Pomerania. On February 1, 1945, advancing Russian forces captured the town of Ratzebuhr [sic], which was only 32 miles southwest of Stalag Luft IV.[4] At night Charlie could see flashes of bright light coming through the barracks' wooden blackout shutters. The flashes of light were followed by the boom of artillery fire. The sounds of the artillery helped the prisoners monitor the advance of the Russians as they speculated about being liberated.

Finally, on February 5, 1945, all the endless rumors and speculation stopped when the prisoners were notified that they would be leaving the camp the following morning. Charlie and the other prisoners were told that they would have to march for three days, rest for a day, and then march two more days to reach a new camp. This notification started a mad, last-minute rush as the anxious prisoners packed and organized their improvised knapsacks with clothing and the small amount of food they had hoarded. Charlie had to judge the value and usefulness of his personal possessions, and he selected only those items that he thought might be useful on a march of unknown length.

On February 6, 1945, Charlie and the other POWs under German control walked out of Stalag Luft IV, fleeing the approaching Russians. This march would later be known as the infamous "Death March" when thousands of American and Allied POWs marched throughout the winter of northern Germany.[5] These men would be lost to the world for months. Not even the Red Cross would be able to track them. They would travel mostly by foot, but sometimes by rail, through the spreading turmoil of a dying Germany. They would see both the suffering they caused with their bombs and the ruthless enemy they risked their lives to defeat. What Charlie would see and experience would be hard to believe for anyone who had not been part of the terrible ordeal.

Charlie's group were not the only prisoners to be moved. Allied POWs from other camps were on forced marches in other parts of Germany. The Red Cross tried to monitor these marches, but because of the chaos, it was unable to find out how many prisoners were moving, their current locations, or where they were headed. Red Cross representatives did inform the Allied powers that sources inside Germany indicated that the POWs were in grave danger.[6]

The thousands of American POWs in Stalag Luft IV were split into two columns and started marching westward along a narrow stretch of land near the Baltic Sea, which was just north of the main Russian push toward Berlin. The guards told the prisoners it would be a three-day hike to their next destination. That was a lie, and many of the prisoners were still walking aimlessly down roads when the Germans finally surrendered in early May. Exactly how many men died on this brutal march is unknown. For certain, many perished in what was for the American airmen the European equivalent of the Bataan Death March of April 1942 in the Philippines.[7]

When many Americans hear the phrase "death march," they think of Bataan. When Japanese troops overran the Philippines in 1942, they forced thousands of American and Filipino soldiers to march across 60 miles of the Bataan Peninsula in tropical heat with little or no food and water. Hundreds of Americans and thousands of Filipinos died in the march that came to be known as the Bataan Death March, one of the greatest atrocities ever committed against American military forces.

But there was another death march perpetrated upon American POWs during World War II, a march hundreds of miles long that lasted nearly three months, a march undertaken during a brutal German winter and filled with sickness, death, and cruelty. Though this march involved thousands of American military men, it has been all but forgotten by Americans today.

8. The March

The winter of 1944-1945 was extremely cold and one of the worst to hit northern Europe in a very long time, with temperatures as low as −30 Fahrenheit.[8] The POWs marched through rain, ice, and snow, along muddy and rough roads without any concern for their safety or well-being. This march was made without proper clothing or shoes to protect them from the cold, and the weather and cold temperatures would significantly affect the prisoners until April.

The prisoners walked approximately 140 miles in the first eight days. Marching into one of the worst European blizzards in recent memory, Charlie and the others were temporarily blinded by the blowing snow. With his head down, shoulders hunched against the wind, he sometimes dozed off as they walked. As the snow continued to fall, his pack got heavier. He soon became bone tired, and his feet were worn out from plodding through the deep snow. Each advancing mile became slower and more difficult. When a prisoner staggered and fell from exhaustion and exposure, his friends pulled him back to his feet.

On the first day the POWs were marched out of the camp amidst much haste and confusion. The prisoners were awakened early in the morning and told to be ready to move within the hour. Soon the prisoners gathered on the compound's parade field fully dressed in their overcoats and carrying makeshift knapsacks or blanket bedrolls.

According to Charlie, after they assembled on the parade field, they were marched out of the compound in sequence by their barracks number. From the compound he and the others next went to the *vorlager*. There each prisoner received a small portion of black bread and one Red Cross food parcel to feed himself with for the anticipated short march. He and the others were offered a second parcel, but like himself, most men had neither the strength nor ability to carry an additional 10 pounds of weight.

Walking out of the camp, he said they passed by a huge store of canned food from the Red Cross parcels which had been withheld from the POWs. Carrying all of his belongings, which was mostly clothing and a blanket for the cold nights, Charlie was very limited in his ability to carry more. On that first day of the march, he and the other prisoners ate most of the canned food, which made some of them very sick, further aggravating the problems they already had with dysentery and colds.

The prisoners then meandered in unorganized bunches to the one road that led out of the compound where they were met by agitated guards shouting commands. Under an overcast sky, Charlie and the other prisoners were pushed into a column four wide, which he estimated was more than a mile and a half long. Although the POWs could walk on their own, the physical and mental fitness of most in the column was not very good. Most of the men had lost a considerable amount of their body weight since being confined, and that weight loss adversely affected their stamina to make a long and arduous march.

More than 70 percent of the prisoners had been wounded or suffered from some form of physical condition or psychological disorder. Most of the ailing and disabled POWs had been evacuated several days earlier when nearly 3,000 POWs were transported by rail to other internment camps. Still, hundreds of other debilitated prisoners were now forced to depart the camp on foot.[9]

Approximately 8,000 prisoners marched out of Stalag Luft IV on February 6, 1945. Charlie said, "I was in the first group of 2,000 men. When we left on February 6, 1945, the snow was chest deep. The roads had been plowed so that they could empty the camp. Finch and Rakiewicz were with me. Finch would later be separated from our group and end up in a camp that was taken over by the Russians."

"When we left the camp, there were guards maybe 50 feet apart on both sides of the column, and they had dogs. We had those guards for some time, but then some of them started disappearing. They, and us, started becoming less and less."

Initially the POWs were guarded by members of the Luftwaffe, including guards from Stalag Luft IV. The notorious Big Stoop accompanied some groups and was just as violent on the march as he had been in the camp. "The guards," Charlie said, "were all guys that had been wounded on the Russian front or wherever they had been fighting. They were mostly elderly guys from 35 to 50." By the end of the march, many of the Luftwaffe guards were replaced by members of the *Volksstrum* (home guard).[10]

On the first morning the POWs were marched across the snow-covered countryside in a northwest direction toward Belgard and away from the unrelenting approach of the Russians.[11] "The guards told us that if we marched fast enough that first day that there would be a train waiting for us, plus some hot food. We started marching at a good pace but never got to any train. They told us that just to get us moving faster. They made an excuse that the next day it would be there. But we knew better and now didn't walk as fast. Then they started marching us longer, sometimes until after dark."

Charlie remembered that at the very start of the march, some of the POWs were very excited and had dreams of being freed. Some were joyful and thought that being on the road was better than being trapped in the camp. A few prisoners thought about escaping from the column and wait-

8. The March

ing in the woods for the Red Army that was right on their heels. For many prisoners, the evacuation of the camp and the loss of physical safety and emotional security that the camp had provided made them very nervous. For the most part, Charlie and the other POWs were constantly in fear during the march.

The guards kept the column mostly on back roads and away from any large towns, but small towns could not be avoided. The prisoners were told to remove all insignia from their clothing so that they could not be identified as American airmen. Nevertheless, the villagers often recognized the men as *terrorfliegers* and reacted angrily.[12] Stragglers were sometimes left behind in towns, and Charlie heard the rumors being spread that they were killed by hostile civilians. The thought and threat of death were ever present.

After a few hours of marching Charlie was physically exhausted by the bulky items he was carrying. His feet were numbed by the hard march over sometimes icy, sometimes muddy, and generally bad roads. His muscles were very tired and strained from carrying the bulky Red Cross food parcel.

Before departing the camp, when they had been offered Red Cross food parcels, their greed and hunger blinded their judgment. Each Red Cross food parcel weighed 10 to 11 pounds and that extra weight would have to be carried. Some prisoners moved the contents of their parcel to their knapsack. Others tried carrying individual cans in their overcoat pockets or inside their bedrolls. The difficulty in performing this task caused many POWs to throw away cans of food, soap, and toilet paper because they thought some items were expendable.

One item Charlie and most prisoners quickly discarded were the canned prunes because many of the men had dysentery. Personal possessions, along with essential clothing too difficult to carry, were also tossed to the side of the road by prisoners who feared that if they fell out of the column they would be shot. In no time, a collection of discarded items littered both sides of the road, making the route look like that of a defeated army in full retreat.

Toilet paper was very important and thought to be an essential item for personal hygiene, especially for anyone with dysentery, but it was bulky, not a very good bartering item, and not edible. Most prisoners believed that they would only need one roll of toilet paper for a three-day march and they soon discarded any surplus. The men threw the extra rolls of toilet paper to German women along the route. Charlie recalled that the women were very happy and really appreciated the toilet paper gift. It would only be later that he and the others realized the error of giving away such an important item.

Charlie and the other prisoners were forced to sleep outside on the first night of the march, and only a recent warming of the temperature prevented them from freezing to death. A blizzard on January 27 and 28 had covered the region in deep snow and pushed nighttime temperatures below zero.[13] Fortunately for the prisoners, the unusually warm temperatures in early February had melted some of the snow and broken up the ice on the rivers.

Very early the next morning they received a little hot water for coffee and were soon formed up to continue their march towards the west. The physical demands of the march now began to affect the group integrity of the column. Many men struggled hard to keep up with prisoners from their assigned barracks and those whom they had a connection. By mid-morning, the elongated column of prisoners had split into many fragments of a few hundred men each.

By the afternoon of the second day, Charlie and many prisoners started to believe that they might not make it to the evening's halt. He was really worn out, and the march was an absolute torment. They halted for the night near the small village of Stalzenburg.[14] There the prisoners were split up into groups and put into small barns in and around the town. This was about 15 miles from where they had started from that morning. The men had only been on the road for two days, yet many of them were already exhausted.

For the first few days of the march, Charlie and most POWs tried staying close to their roommates and other men that they knew. But the daily demands of the march caused some to become separated from their barracks unit. This separation increased their worry and produced a growing sense of loneliness and gloom within the column. At times a prisoner was only separated from his buddies and roommates for a day or two, but sometimes the separation was permanent.

The cohesiveness in Charlie's group was adversely affected for many reasons, but the leading cause was physical stamina. Many POWs struggled to maintain their place in the column and to stay close to their roommates and their buddies. The integrity of the group was further reduced toward the end of each day when the healthier and more physically fit men sped to the head of the column, hoping to get into a barn for the night. Getting there before the others provided those men with a better chance of finding a better sleeping spot, a chance to forage for food, or to get a position in the front of the line for something to eat. Prisoners who trailed behind often found themselves put in a different barn at the end of the day and then assigned to march with a different and unknown bunch of men the next morning.

According to Charlie, in the beginning it was mostly every man for himself. Some POWs survived the march by being selfish, and they hoarded and hid food and firewood. However, because the men had been thoroughly trained to function as a team, he and many men started to align themselves with others and formed small groups to improve their chance of survival. The POWs named these informal unions of two-, three-, or sometimes four-man groups "combines."[15]

They united with each other on the basis of compatible personalities, physical strength, and survival skills. There was an unspoken agreement that each member would provide whatever physical and emotional support necessary to sustain the other combine members while on the march. This buddy-system arrangement was important for their survival, and the men of a combine looked out for each other in all aspects. The main reason for a buddy more than anything else was to help each other if someone became ill. This buddy system helped to keep Charlie alive.

Charlie's combine buddy was a prisoner named Sam. Together they hunted for food and firewood and shared everything, including their body heat. "It was hard to buddy up with anybody because if they went out and got stuff, they wouldn't share. Whatever they found, they ate. Sam and I shared. We were buddies. We never let the others know when we had found food, and we ate a lot of the stuff while we were marching. Everybody was doing the same thing." Charlie and Sam had only a single thin wool blanket each, and to keep warm at night, they paired up and combined both blankets for added warmth.

"They gave each of us a blanket and half of a tent. You buddied up with someone [in order to combine the two tent halves to form one tent for two men]. I buddied up with Sam from New York. If we were put in a field, then we'd put the tent up. One night when it was close to spring with cold nights and sleet during the day, and after marching all day, we were soaked and freezing. They put us in a field that night. I said to Sam, 'Let's put up our tent on this little grade.' We crawled in and we were so tired we instantly fell asleep. We woke up in the morning and we're not in our tent. We had slid out! We had laid in the rain and sleet all night."

When the guards allowed a rest, the POWs sat down on one side of the road while the guards watched them from the other side. Charlie dumped his pack and flopped down on the snow. Eating while sitting in the snow was cold, but after many hours of nonstop marching he was too tired to care. All of the prisoners were too hungry, tired, and cold to worry about getting colder. It was at this time that he realized this march was going to be the greatest ordeal of his life.

Not all POW groups travelled along the same roads or at the same pace. It was more like a mass of humanity that zigzagged its way mostly in a southwest direction from the Baltic Sea. The result was a diverging, converging living river of men that flowed slowly but predictably west and later south. Charlie said, "We marched zig-zag and sometimes marched with civilians. Thousands and thousands of people were marching. There was no end to them, and they had nowhere to go."

On the march it seemed that there were more chances to escape than there had been back in the camp. But now an escape attempt was significantly riskier because of their depleted physical strength and stamina. Serious thought of escape, much less an actual attempt, required a lot of courage or an extremely strong sense of desperation. One item someone planning an escape would need was a map, and with that Charlie thought he might possibly be of assistance.

"The Germans had a guy with a bicycle and he would go by us, and whatever he was carrying, he always took up front to the head guard. Every once in a while, you'd see him coming, and one day I thought, 'I'm going to find out what he has.' He had a flat carrier rack on the back of the bike and had a large rubber band holding maps on the bike. I walked along the outside of the formation and kept looking back. Here he came, peddling down through, and I just waited for him. As he went by me, I just reached out, grabbed a roll and pulled and had a whole wad. I quickly got back into the formation and hid. The guys knew what I did, and I said to them, 'If anyone stops us looking for these maps, we have to pass them back and forth and spread out.' Well, the Germans came through the column and the maps were going all over, from one to another, hiding them and passing them around. They didn't search us. The guy on the bike felt it when I pulled them off his bike, but he never saw who did it. When we got into a barn that night we took a look at them. They didn't do us much good so we left them in the barn." According to Charlie, this event took place early in the march.

There were four things the prisoners had to consider for an escape attempt. First, they had no idea where they were; second, they had very little food; third, there was safety in numbers; and fourth, it was just a bad idea. Charlie said the German guards generally considered the prisoners excess baggage and just needed an excuse such as an attempted escape to get rid of as many POWs as they could.

8. The March

Charlie estimated that there was approximately one guard for every 75 to 100 prisoners. "The guards were far apart and they'd allow the column to get strung way out. Sometimes I didn't even see a guard. The Germans did that on purpose. In the wooded areas, guys who made a break for it ran right into German machine guns. The Germans had it all preplanned."

"Two guys were planning an escape, and whoever had some food gave it to them so they had some stuff to keep them going. They broke and made a run for it. When they did it, the guards were pretty far apart. They ran right into a machine gun. The next day a guard came and threw the two caps down. *Comrades! Todt!* We then realized that if we wanted to get out of this alive, we had to stay together and not try anything stupid." During the latter part of the March, prisoners who attempted to escape and were caught or freely returned to the column were openly beaten as a warning to the other men.

The POWs soon settled into a daily routine of walking, sleeping, freezing, and starving. They were usually awakened about 5:00 a.m. and then maybe had something for breakfast. Next they were put in columns of three or four and it was follow the leader to the next stop, as guard dogs stalked the edges of the column. Charlie recalled, "They basically marched us from sun up to sun down. We marched through mountains that had been picked clean, not even a weed."

Charlie recalled that February 13, 1945, was a hard march of more than 30 miles in the rain, snow, and sleet before the column arrived at a small town. Everything he had was frozen from the wet, cold weather. He noticed that a lot of prisoners had dropped out. Some had been picked up by a wagon to get medical care, but other men who had been left on the side of the road were never seen or heard from again. According to Charlie, it now had been eight days and well over a 100, or perhaps 150, miles since they departed Stalag Luft IV. It was obvious to him that an end to this march was not in sight, and the final destination was still unknown.

The disorganized POW columns were part of the greatest panic migration in European history. There were more than seven million people, most of them from the eastern regions of Germany, moving toward the center of Germany. By the end of January, approximately 50,000 refugees were moving into Berlin every day.[16]

Charlie noticed that most of the German refugees were women and children. Most of the fit men had been drafted into the German armed forces. They had to flee on foot during one of the worst winters in recent history, and the refugees could only move a few miles a day on the snow-packed roads. Many died from the extreme cold or starved because of the unrelenting and bitter weather which forced temperatures below zero for many weeks.

Because of the extremely nasty weather, the refugees had to abandon their possessions and had no choice but to leave their dead, including young children, on the roadside as they fled Russian tanks who ran over and crushed the slow-moving German civilians on purpose. As many as 2.2 million Germans from Eastern Europe were unaccounted for at the end of the war and are believed to have died during this huge forced migration.[17]

As the column marched along, Charlie passed through silent and abandoned towns where refugees lined the roads in horse- and cattle-drawn carts, waiting to move out. Some days the POW column was temporarily halted by the thousands of civilians moving in one direction. He recalled that the German refugees usually moved from the center of the road when they encountered a POW column. It was hard for him to believe, but the civilians actually moved slower than the prisoners. To him it appeared that many of the civilians were bitter and dejected. The civilian refugees were in fact prisoners too, for the SS troops moved them along at the point of a bayonet.

He noticed that some were in wagons, but most were walking. Each civilian carried several bundles, and many tried to carry more than they could handle. Young boys helped old men. Mothers carried their babies. Even young children carried bundles and food. Most were inadequately dressed and were half frozen from the bitter cold. Babies screamed and mothers cried as the column slowly plodded along.

He saw small children as they peeked out from under huge piles of household possessions. Their faces were red from the bitter cold. Moving past the POWs on the road were huge hay wagons pulled by starving horses, and Charlie could plainly see their bones showing through their skin. Stern-looking old men rode up front, and without emotion watched as the children begged the POWs for some food. But there wasn't enough to share.

Charlie and the other prisoners silently watched as German army soldiers and SS troops pushed and shoved the refugees into an endless line of walkers. The SS troops had set fire to buildings and homes. All civilians were being evacuated, and nothing was to be left behind for the Russians. He knew that German civilians who resisted were shot on the spot and left to die on the road. He and the other prisoners heard the screams and

8. The March

shots. The SS troops were particularly cruel and never argued. Shooting was quicker and ended arguments.

Sometimes, a rough-looking German army unit passed them on the road. Charlie noticed that these Wehrmacht units were headed in the opposite direction, eastward, toward the Russian front. "We saw great big formations of kids around 12 years old, marching towards the Eastern front. We figured they were going to fight the Russians." He noticed that these were not the goose-stepping fanatics seen earlier in the war. They were very young and appeared to be extremely frightened, and they too begged the American POWs for food. There was none to be shared.

Conditions were very confused, and sometimes the POWs were placed in harm's way. "We were going to go through a town, but SS troops were in the town and it was being bombed by the Americans. A German messenger on a bicycle arrived and spoke to the leader of our group. The first group [POWs] that went into that town were pretty near wiped out. Our group was held up outside that town. After the messenger, they changed our route and took us around that town. Then we ended up with 1,000 men instead of 2,000. We didn't know what was going on."

Charlie and the prisoners also witnessed another awful sight. This time it was thousands of Russian POWs being marched deeper into Germany. The sight of these prisoners was very upsetting because the Russians lacked any warm clothing, looked starved, and were treated very brutally. The Russians looked very bad, to say the least. Some had no shoes, and it looked like they had rags wrapped around their feet as they walked in the snow. The sight made him realize that there was much more brutality than he had experienced so far. This sight caused a lot of uneasiness among the men about their future treatment. He had compassion for the Russians, but at the same time, he hoped that he would not be treated so cruelly.

On one occasion Charlie's group was subjected to brutality at the hands of some SS troops. "We marched past a hospital that was full of amputees. There were SS troops there and they wanted to put on a show. We had to walk past this huge hospital, and they had all these guys in wheelchairs sitting along the road, four, five, and six deep. This was a set-up. We marched right past them, and as we marched by, the SS troops grabbed some of our men, pulled them out of the ranks, and beat them right there in front of the guys in the wheelchairs. This was to show that we were responsible for their injuries. If our guys were not killed, and if they couldn't walk after the beating, they were just left there. They probably shot them. I had a hand on my shoulder, but I didn't get caught by the SS troopers."

A major problem, and a dangerous one, was straggling. At the very start large numbers of POWs fell behind. Blisters became infected and many men collapsed. Some dragged themselves along in spite of the extreme suffering. Many men walked with large abscesses on their feet and frostbite on their hands and feet. Many others marched with fevers as high as 105 degrees Fahrenheit. Many men suffered relentlessly from dysentery cramping, lost control of their bowels, and soiled themselves. Wherever the column went, it left a trail of bloody bowel movements and discarded underwear.[18]

Within hours of leaving the camp, Charlie recalled that the column formation dramatically fell apart as weaker and less physically fit prisoners fell to the rear of the now drawn-out column. These first stragglers were prisoners who developed blisters, had aching feet or joints, or had tired muscles. Some of these problems were caused because they didn't have adequate shoes.

The prisoners with blisters, aching feet and joints, and tired muscles suffered, but they didn't cause much concern because they would most likely toughen up. The medics made up a slogan: "Keep on marching and your blisters will turn into calluses and your aches into hard muscles."[19]

As prisoners in the column began to weaken and fall back, self-appointed medical personnel and a few other considerate individuals fell to the rear of the column and helped anyone in need. These medics provided inspiration and gave whatever help they could. Often those giving assistance willingly remained behind with the men who dropped out of the column. They wanted to protect these men from being terrorized by the German guards. These unselfish and brave men were frequently stuck with a bayonet or smacked with a rifle butt-stock.

Before long, straggling became serious, as blisters became infected and abscess developed and had to be opened. Charlie developed quite a blister. "At the beginning we marched for two days. I was wearing high-top German shoes with cleats. By the end of the second day I had a blister, and it was really sore. That night I grabbed some snow before I went into the barn and took my shoe and sock off and held some snow against the blister. I rubbed it and cleaned it to keep it from getting infected, I hoped. I was really worried about that. My socks had more holes than cloth, and they were rotting away on my feet. I decided the next morning when they got us up to not put that shoe on because there were snow banks all along the way. I thought I would just walk in one stocking foot, not knowing if it would freeze or not. I walked that whole day with just the stocking on. Every time they gave us a break, I sat down and rubbed snow on it to keep

8. The March

it clean. I did that for two days, and then I put my shoe back on, and I could walk all right. Every time I got a chance, I'd take my shoe off and rub snow on it, and eventually the blister healed and I could keep my shoe on. I didn't have any more trouble with blisters after that."

One day a POW dropped out of the column and nobody stopped to help him. A few minutes later, as the group marched on, Charlie heard a gunshot and looked at the other prisoners with surprise. The prisoners were shocked when the guard returned by himself. This incident reminded him that the Germans really were the enemy and would kill a prisoner without caring. This became all the more obvious when this scenario would be repeated many more times during the last month of the march.

The number of stragglers increased every day until it became impossible to help them all. The Germans allowed the POWs to organize a "slow party" which was made up of sick men who were allowed to continue at their own pace. Also, the guards gave the column a few farm wagons to transport the sick. Uncomfortable and cold as the wagons were, every morning there was a long line of prisoners waiting to get on them. Unfortunately, there was only room for the sick.[20]

Charlie recalled that the "sick wagons" were large farm wagons pulled by horses. The sick wagons provided relief and lifesaving opportunities for hundreds of prisoners who were very weak or ill. But getting a place on a wagon was a mixed blessing. The sick prisoners on a wagon were exposed to cold weather, and some men developed serious frostbite as a result of long periods of physical inactivity.

Valentine's Day, February 14, 1945, started as most days did with a skimpy breakfast before marching again in the gray, miserable conditions of freezing rain and relentless cold. All day long Charlie and the POWs marched over slippery, icy roads, as the freezing rain later changed to snow.

He said that they were forced to swiftly march many miles, making this day one of the worst days so far. Most of the men had intense dysentery and were not allowed to stop to relieve themselves. When they marched through a town the men slowed down a bit, dropped their trousers, and just went right there. The Russian army was only a couple of dozen miles behind them at this point, and the men weren't even allowed to stop for a drink of water. Without taking notice, some prisoners scooped up handfuls of snow to quench their thirst, only to find the snow full of urine and bloody feces.

The POWs marched for two hours and then were given a five-minute rest. Charlie and the prisoners were supposed to finish their toilet needs during the short halt. Because of the extreme cold, frozen fingers, and button-down flys on their pants, it usually took them the entire five minutes just to urinate. To accomplish this normally simple task, he helped Sam by unbuttoning his fly for him, and then Sam returned the favor.

By the afternoon, Charlie had estimated that they had marched as far as, if not further than, any previous day. Yet now, the column did not halt, and the pace of the march showed no signs of slowing down anytime soon to find shelter for the night. While walking the pain was absolutely agonizing, but he knew that if he dropped out, he might be shot. His body and legs felt only numbness and pain. He willed his mind and directed each step, and finally the long march came to an end.

Day had turned into night when the march finally halted late that evening. After covering more than 20 miles, Charlie's group was moved into a large clearing in a pine forest. Even though there were many barns in the immediate area, the prisoners were forced to sleep outside, and many didn't have anything to protect themselves from the elements. They were not even allowed to build fires to keep warm or to cook, and they had to camp in complete darkness.

Charlie recalled, "Swinemunde was the place we slept in a field. It was snowing and freezing, and Sam and I put our tent up." In the Swinemunde area the bitter Baltic sub-zero winter froze the POWs. Charlie and Sam were completely exhausted from the long march, and after they put up their little tent, they crawled inside, huddled together, and covered themselves with their two thin blankets and some pine branches.

The ground was wet from the precipitation of the day. There were recently cut pine branches scattered on the ground, and the prisoners gathered the boughs to serve as insulation from the wet ground and set up their sleeping area. The field where the men had to sleep was not only wet from days of rain and snow, it was also contaminated with the feces of dysenteric men who had stayed there before.

There were many stragglers and sick men who could hardly walk. The stragglers and sick men who could barely keep up arrived at the bivouac site late and were unable to find a decent place to lay down. Nevertheless, they were forced to bed down for the night in those impossible conditions and without anything to eat. Charlie knew there were hundreds of sick prisoners that night, but the Germans made no effort to provide shelter.

During the night the snow stopped, but then a cold, driving rain began. Somehow Charlie managed to sleep for a few hours. Some prisoners were certain they would not still be alive in the morning and said their good-byes to their buddies before they fell asleep. For many men, it was the worst night of their life, even worse than being shot down.

8. The March

The next morning, Charlie and the other cold and numb men who managed to have slept at all woke up and discovered that the rain had stopped and several inches of snow had fallen on them overnight. Depressed and hungry, they were rapidly put into column and forced to move out without any food or water, and at the same pace and just as far as the day before.

On February 16, 1945, the International Red Cross estimated that more than 6,000 POWs from Stalag Luft IV crossed over the Usedom Peninsula into central Germany. That number suggested that many hundreds of prisoners were no longer part of the column. Many of these men had straggled when they became too sick or disabled to continue and were left along the road. Some of these prisoners might have been placed in military hospitals, died from exhaustion, illness, or possibly killed. Some had been taken into Russian custody, and many of the Allied POWs picked up by the Red Army were never returned at the end of the war.[21]

Not only did the Red Cross not know where the POWs were at any given time, Charlie and the other prisoners didn't know their location most days, how the war was progressing, or any events occurring in the world. "While we were marching, we lost all contact with the outside world. The only thing we found out, toward the end of the march, was when Roosevelt died. A guard told us. He had a hard time telling us until we understood what he was getting at. *Todt!*"

Their next bivouac was near Anklam, 90 miles north of Berlin.[22] There they used some of the small barns and other buildings in the area as temporary hospitals. This was the POWs' first real period of rest since they departed Stalag Luft IV two weeks earlier. This brief pause in the march allowed the German authorities the chance to account for all their prisoners. While there, the prisoners received a small ration of soup and bread. Later, Red Cross parcels were distributed on the basis of one package for every four men. The halt provided a much-needed opportunity for Charlie to conserve his strength and care for his sore feet.

The temporary halt near Anklam also allowed the medical personnel to look after the many ailing POWs staying in the barns in the surrounding area. The medical personnel lacked sufficient medications and only possessed a small supply of bandages, tape, aspirin, and salves. These items came from medical parcels sent by the Red Cross and allowed them to treat infected blisters, abscesses, frostbite, and, in some cases, gangrene.[23] Many prisoners complained of aching joints and had severe dysentery. Most of the men suffered from moderate to severe malnutrition and had lost more weight.

Following the brief period of rest, the large gathering of POWs quartered near Anklam were divided into three separate columns and marched to different internment camps deeper inside Germany. Two groups of approximately 1,500 prisoners each headed north toward Stalag Luft I at Berth on the Baltic coast. The second group moved south toward Stalag VIIA at Moosberg. The third and largest group, and the one Charlie was part of, comprised of roughly 3,000 POWs, continued to move westward across northern Germany toward Fallingbostel and Stalag XIB.[24]

"We walked by a concentration camp for kids. As we got closer to them we could see their ribs. Their stomachs were extended because they were starving. It was a big camp full of thousands of kids. I didn't see any adults. Just kids. Their arms had only skin covering the bones. We didn't look much better but at least we had clothing on. Most looked like they wearing only diapers or something resembling a diaper, and this was winter!"

Still they marched deeper into the Third Reich. Temperatures were well below zero, and the POWs' clothing did not keep them very warm. On February 22, 1945, after marching 10 miles on some bad roads, they arrived at the village of Tarnow.[25] There the prisoners each received some potatoes, a small portion of soup, and part of a Red Cross food parcel. The following day, the group continued their march and walked about five miles before doubling back.

Now it started to rain heavily, and the column was hurried to the nearest barns. Charlie, like a lot of prisoners, had severe diarrhea and was passing blood through his bowels. Some prisoners who were even worse off were coughing and spitting up blood. A few men from the group slipped away to a nearby village to trade for food and were caught. The German guards beat them with rifles and clubs, and some were shot at, but fortunately nobody was seriously injured.

"They kept us away from towns. One time they took us through a town and there was a bakery on the street we were on, and we could smell it. Well, when the column got to the bakery some of the guys busted in, but the guards didn't shoot. They got some stuff, but I didn't get any because I was already past the bakery when that happened. We were now down to 150 guys."

Charlie and the rest stole food whenever they had a chance to do so, even though they might have been killed if they were caught. He and the others took advantage of every opportunity to get something to eat. He ate anything he could beg or steal. Sometimes he could find some potatoes, cabbages, sugar beets, and different kinds of grain. These items weren't always available, but when they were, he and Sam took what they could. If they were really lucky, they might find some eggs in a chicken's nest or perhaps even milk a cow. But eggs and milk were seldom found.

In his words, "the starvation was the worst part." Food was completely insufficient, and when finally liberated, Charlie was showing many signs of starvation. If the march would have lasted much longer, the starvation would have begun to cause death in his group. The food consisted of what the guards could obtain for the POWs. The food was generally limited to small rations of potatoes, a rare small portion of watery soup, bread and sporadic varied items from Red Cross parcels. They received bread more than any other item.

The prisoners added to the meager rations by exchanging cigarettes and other Red Cross items with the German civilians. The men also added to this by scrounging, stealing vegetables stored in mounds in the fields and even foraging for edible wild plants. They went to sleep hungry, awoke that way and stayed hungry during the day. The insufficient rations made Charlie dizzy, and every time he bent over, he would almost pass out.

The starvation caused him to take chances that may have gotten him killed. "There was a big field there, with a large row of kohlrabies. One guy hollered, 'Let's go!' We ran, and the German guards held back the dogs. We went into that field and took as much as we could carry. We got our stuff, got back in line, and off we went again. The guards didn't do anything to us."

If the prisoners saw a mound in a field along the roadside, they would break from the column and run to the mound. They had only their hands to dig, and they would take as many potatoes, or whatever was in the mound, as they could carry. Sometimes the entire group of prisoners rushed into a field. Sometimes they ate the potatoes raw as they marched, and sometimes they cooked them when they stopped for the night.

"Once in a while, after marching one or two days, they'd set up these big kettles with barley soup. Usually only one kettle. The guards dipped a little bit out into your cup, and after everybody was fed, they'd let us go back for seconds. We scraped the side of the kettle with a spoon to get what we could. Some days we didn't get fed at all."

"When we got to a farm we always checked to see if they had chickens. The Germans would have a guard at one barn door and that was the only place you were allowed to go in and out, if you had to go to the bathroom. To confuse the guards, one guy would go, then two guys would go, then three guys would go. After a while he didn't know how many were out. That gave whoever got out first a chance to sneak around and get eggs or whatever could be found. In their fields they always had rows of kohlrabies which were covered with straw and dirt piled over top. You could always see the end where the people had been taking stuff out of. We'd go to that end and take whatever was there. We filled our shirts full and then went back to the barn and divide them up. Sam and I were always together, and I always made sure he had plenty if I went. If Sam went, he would see that I got some."

According to Dr. Leslie Caplan, a captured flight surgeon who was on the march, the rural areas through which they passed did not seem to have a food shortage.[26] The German guards just didn't provide much food. The prisoners stole what they could, often from the pigs on the farms where they slept. If a piece of meat was gotten from a chicken, rabbit, dog, or even rat, it was typically undercooked and sometimes just eaten raw. A roaring fire would bring not only the attention of other POWs, but the guards too, and being caught with stolen food could result in execution. Some prisoners were so hungry they simply resorted to eating grass. They'd boil it, but it was hard to get down because it was so bitter, so they mostly just drank the juice.

On one occasion the guards crowded the POWs into a barn and slammed the door closed. It was pitch dark inside and the prisoners had to find a place to lay down. They had marched late into the night which disrupted the distribution of the day's rations. In the center of the poorly-lit barn, which was covered with livestock manure, the guards just dumped a pile of raw potatoes on the ground. A wild rush took place as the prisoners grabbed what they could, and in doing so they smashed many of the potatoes into the filth of the dirt floor. The prisoners closest to the potatoes managed to get some while others realized that it was useless to even try.

"One night they put us in a barn with steers in it, and it was full of manure. Not much straw, and it was wet. They forced us in and we had to lay down. After we were in the barn the German guards told the farmer to cook potatoes for us. There were little openings, not windows, just small ventilation openings in the exterior walls of the barn. When they brought the boiled potatoes, they just threw them into the barn through the holes. Well some guys got a lot and some guys didn't get any, but I got three potatoes. They had landed in the manure, and I picked them up and rubbed them on my overcoat and ate them. Sam also got some potatoes."

More than a few times, Charlie even ate cattle and hog feed. He wasn't sure how much nutrition value it had, but it was filling. One night, "we were put in the top part of a barn, and the cattle were down below. I dropped down through a hay hole to where the cattle were. It was dark, and I felt my way around and happened to bump into something. It was a feed bin. I opened it up and filled my shirt pockets full. The grain tasted like coconut, and it was made from kohlrabies that had some stuff on it, and it was made as feed for the cattle. It tasted good. Because I was so hungry I made a mistake and just started eating and eating. After I was full, I laid down and fell asleep, and sometime during the night I woke up in severe pain. I tried to move but I couldn't because I was bloated. My stomach was huge, and I couldn't even bend my neck to get up. I knew I had to get up, and tried a couple of times to get up, but I couldn't even roll. All of a sudden, the gas from the grain blew my mouth wide open and the air rushed out, and my stomach went down. When it let go, it was just like a big balloon when you let the air out. I gave some to Sam and warned him not to eat a whole lot of it and told him what happened to me."

Charlie recalled some very hungry prisoners stealing from pigs the feed that was thrown to them and grazing like cattle on grass along the side of the road. A handful of stolen grain, eaten while marching, often provided Charlie with a mid-day snack. The catching of a chicken caused great excitement, but most of the meat eaten by the men was a farmer's cat or dog. Some starving men ate uncooked rats.

"One day they put us in a barn while it was still daylight. The barnyard had a stone wall all around it where they would let out the cattle. They marched us into that and let us stay outside. While we're sitting there relaxing a cat climbed over the wall. A couple of guys grabbed whatever they could find, and one guy had a pretty good-sized stick in his hand. The cat jumped down into the barnyard, which was a big mistake. The cat ran and the guys kicked it and tried to grab it. One guy dove at the cat just as another guy swung a stick and he broke the guy's neck. One less prisoner. The cat got away. We were down and out after that. They intended to eat that cat, and I would have helped eat it if they would have caught it. We would have eaten anything."

Most days Charlie's main focus was food and how to lessen his hunger. It was the number one thing on his mind, and it tested his resourcefulness and character. Eventually the malnutrition made him less alert and he had a hard time understanding things. He was completely fixated with thoughts about food, even though he seldom talked about it.

Even the guards were hungry most of the time. A prisoner stole a German guard's ration of bread. They wanted it back, and the guards took every tenth prisoner of the 200 in the group to a barn. There the 20 chosen men were lined up against a stone wall and were to be shot if the ration of bread was not returned immediately. The bread was given back and the execution was called off.[27]

"The German guards got more food than us. They were fed at the farmhouses. But when we slept in the fields, they didn't get any. The people on the farms had to make them full meals."

Disease and illness were largely caused by dirty water and affected nearly every prisoner. Their water was usually from dirty surface water or questionable well water. Often there was so little water provided that the men drank whatever they could. They ate dirty snow and drank from ditches that had been used as latrines. Some disease and illness could have been prevented if the guards would have allowed the prisoners to boil water for purification. They also weren't allowed to bring drinking cups with them when they departed Stalag Luft IV. As the march progressed, the men were able to obtain tin cans to use as cups. Many days they went without a drink of water.[28]

In spring, when the bitter cold and freezing rain were finally behind them, they encountered a new problem. The weather had warmed enough that they now marched with their overcoats slung over their shoulders, and the new problem was thirst. At least when there was snow on the ground, Charlie could quench his thirst as he walked by scooping up a handful of snow. But without any snow, he and the others had to mostly endure a waterless march. He could get water at a barn in the morning, but without anything to carry it in, he was unable to drink until they arrived at another barn in the evening. Sometimes as they passed small streams, he and some of the POWs would break from the column and drink water from the stream. When they could find some, Charlie and the others ate the charcoal from old cook fires to help relieve their dysentery.

The Red Cross parcels they had received when they were near Anklam assisted the POWs in trading with local civilians, even though such activity was strictly forbidden. Regardless of that prohibition, many prisoners risked the consequences and bribed their guards for them to turn a blind eye as they traded soap, chocolate, and cigarettes. Some men were so hungry that they traded away their watches and rings or anything they had of value for food of any kind.[29]

Although Charlie was starving, there was plenty of food in the rural areas they marched through. Their small supplies of coffee, chocolate, and cigarettes were luxury items wanted badly by the Germans civilians. If a prisoner was really lucky, he could trade for eggs and bread, and a good trader could get most anything. Some German women gave many things for a chocolate bar.

Charlie knew that the guards had orders to shoot prisoners who traded with civilians, but they rarely fired on the POWs for that reason. A successful tactic was to bribe a guard with cigarettes and chocolate bars. Many guards just looked the other way while the prisoners traded with civilians. If the prisoners disliked a guard, but the guard had traded with them previously, they might threaten to squeal on him. Sometimes doing that made the guard give the prisoners even better things, including items that were strictly forbidden.

It is understandable that the POWs initially feared German civilians. These fears were further aggravated when on some occasions the guards went ahead of the column into a village or town and announced that the *terrorfliegers* were coming, which sometimes provoked a hostile reception. Yet, in rural settings, Charlie soon learned that not all contact with civilians was hostile or negative. Many civilians were quite willing, given the opportunity, to trade with him, and traded bread and other foodstuffs for sundries like soap and toilet paper.

Charlie said the small German towns appeared clean and orderly, but gloomy and unfriendly. There was a general appearance of desolation. There were plenty of women and small children in every town, but not many men. After a column passed through a town, the streets were littered with trash. The roads wound through boundless, carefully-tended pine forests. They were dark green forests intermixed with small plowed fields and the occasional small farmhouse and town.

Whenever available, the POWs slept in barns, but it was not unusual for them to have to stand all night or sleep outside due to lack of space inside. Usually there was some straw for Charlie to lie on, but many times he had to make do on a filthy and damp floor. Way too often the guards made certain areas of a barn off limits, which caused available shelter to go unused. Most of the farmers protested when their cattle had to be removed to make space for a lousy bunch of dirty prisoners. Charlie remembered, "In March there was a lot of rain and snow, and a lot of times we ended up out in fields, and we had to sleep outside no matter what the weather was doing. Luckily, some nights we got into barns and we were glad we did because we weren't getting wet."

Charlie and all of the prisoners were infested with lice, and sometimes they had to bed down with the farm animals or near the animals. Sometimes the prisoners who needed shelter for the night were denied access to the barn because the farmer complained that the POWs were too lice-ridden to sleep with his livestock. It was apparent to him that the welfare of the livestock was more important than his welfare.

The guards didn't sleep with the prisoners, and typically stayed in a nearby farmhouse. The barns used to house the POWs were primitive and dirty, and most were dirtied with standing puddles of urine and piles of manure on the floor. However, the barns provided much needed relief from the wet, cold weather outside. Charlie was always grateful for any chance to sleep in a barn, especially one that had enough hay or straw to provide bedding.

The guards assigned quarters inside the barn. Outside of the barn German women usually had large fires burning, and they boiled water in large vats to cook whatever food was available. The farm women usually wanted to trade potatoes, onions, and bread for cigarettes, chocolate, and soap. In the good barns, the straw was piled high and it was warm inside. Charlie always wanted to sleep in the straw or hay. When they did, he and Sam dug out a bed large enough for them both, packed it down, and unrolled their blankets.

Most farms had root cellars filled with potatoes, and the German guards often demanded they be used to feed the prisoners. When the group stopped for the night, prisoners who were still capable of carrying out additional duties at the end of the day helped cook the evening meal while the rest of the POWs eagerly waited, hoping to get something to eat. Some nights they didn't get fed at all. If they arrived too late after sundown, the guards just shoved the prisoners into a barn and slammed the doors shut. Charlie and Sam, along with every other man in their group, then had to find a place to lay down in the pitch black of the barn.

The barns lacked many of the things needed for decent housing. One necessity was light. Germany was under constant bombardment by the British RAF at night and any light acted as a beacon. Lighting a match in the barn got a POW in serious trouble with both the guards and the other prisoners. According to Charlie, because they had no lanterns or flashlights, when it was necessary for a man to go outside to relieve himself, a signaling system was used to get a prisoner out of the barn and back in again without stepping on anyone.

When a prisoner reached the door to go outside, he put on his shoes. When returning, he removed his shoes and crawled with the shoelaces tied together and the shoes hung around his neck. The prisoners arranged their sleeping in squares or rectangles making movement through the barn less perilous. A constant whispering chatter was their dead reckoning system for returning to their combine. It sounded like this: "Hey, Charlie. Here, Sam. Hey, Charlie. Here, Sam." This went on until the man finally returned to his spot, after pissing off every prisoner he passed along the way.

8. The March

Charlie recalled that they followed a specific procedure when leaving the barn to defecate. First it was very important that the prisoner attracted a guard's attention and requested permission to *Scheissen*. Once permission was granted by the guard, the prisoner moved to the right or left, keeping the side of the barn within arm's reach. At some point he turned his rear to the barn, backed up one step and squatted. The purpose of doing it this way was to prevent him from stepping in another's feces and then returning to the barn and dragging a trail of stinking shit throughout the barn.

One night, thousands of miles from home, Charlie bumped into another man from his hometown of Hamburg. "We marched for a full day and around 4:00 p.m. we came to a barn that was full of prisoners on the outside. We were put in that barn for the night. While we were outside and waiting to get into the barn, I was listening to a guy, and his voice sounded familiar, but I couldn't get a good look at him. He sounded like a guy I knew, Bill Dalious. He was a friend from Hamburg. We used to go to Rip's Corner and sit together drinking Cokes and eating hotdogs. Bill was drafted into the Army after I went in the service."

"I followed him into the barn. He crawled back and laid down, and I followed him and laid down right next to him. I looked at him and I was sure it was Bill. I nudged him and quietly said, 'Hey, do you know where Rip Trexler's restaurant is in Hamburg?' Bill said, 'Are you Charlie Eyer?' I said, 'yes.' He didn't recognize me at all. He said, 'I thought I saw you in a bunch marching.' Bill hadn't been a prisoner long and had been captured during the Battle of the Bulge. We had a good talk. Later we came back on a troop ship together."

Every prisoner was 20 or more pounds underweight when the march started, and their resistance to illness was very low. Most doctors would have advised not to move these men in freezing weather or march them in the snow for long hours at a time. Doing so could mean sudden and certain death for many of them.[30]

From a medical viewpoint the march was dreadful. Sanitation was primitive, and the predictable result was disease, suffering, and death. Charlie said that during the march, the column passed Allied prison camps, but they were too crowded to take in the entire group. Sometimes they did leave the most seriously ill men.

Soon after the march began, the first case of diphtheria, which is a highly contagious disease, appeared among the POWs. Pneumonia and tuberculosis came next. But the one illness that overwhelmed and threatened the health of every prisoner was dysentery. Dysentery is an infection of the lower intestinal track caused by living in filthy, crowded conditions and by drinking unsafe, contaminated water. Within days of leaving the camp this sickness became widespread and affected almost everyone in the column to varying degrees of severity. The main symptom of dysentery is the loss of bowel control.[31] Charlie suffered from dysentery the entire march.

This was made worse by the guards expecting that the prisoners not relieve themselves until the column halted for a five-minute break every few hours. All during the torturous march, Charlie and the others shuffled along the roads which were lined with dysenteric men relieving themselves. The sad sight of a prisoner defecating right on a village street was not unusual and provoked little or no response from the German civilians.

Like the rest, Charlie couldn't stop the urge to relieve himself, even when he was hit with a rifle butt or threatened to be shot for leaving the column. But sometimes the threats and physical abuse worked. Often while marching along, when he could not hold it any longer, his bowels suddenly released and the feces ran down the inside of his pants legs. He was embarrassed by the accidental discharges and it was a major hygienic problem because he didn't have any toilet paper, soap, or water to wash either himself or his clothing. If he was lucky, he found some water or snow to at least rinse off his filthy hands.

After a long and hard day of marching, Charlie and the other prisoners were packed into a barn. They were so crammed into the barn that at night it was almost impossible to get outside quickly to relieve themselves. Sometimes Charlie soiled his pants with bloody, reeking feces before he could get out of the barn. Latrines, which weren't dug very often, were only hastily-dug slit trenches. They placed a small log longways over the slit at a tapering height so that the taller men could use the higher end and the shorter men could use the lower end. When his dysentery was really bad, Charlie was actually glad when they didn't get much food because it helped to slow down his severe diarrhea.

The physical burdens of the march, in which hungry, poorly clothed, and physically exhausted men struggled in miserable weather, weakened the immune system and the health of many of the POWs. Charlie and most of the prisoners were infested with diseased fleas and lice from sleeping in barns on straw or hay used for livestock. The parasites were relentless, and the almost constant itching drove him crazy.

Charlie said everybody had lice. His main concern was removing the eggs. The tiny eggs were usually found in the seams of his shirts or underwear and were neatly laid in a straight row of a dozen or two. He had only two effective ways to get rid of the eggs. One was to pick the eggs out individually and crush them between his fingernails. The other was to burn them out with a match. But he had to be very careful when doing that because he could end up destroying the seams and the stitching of his already ragged clothing.

The barns offered shelter and some warmth from the bitter cold, but it also stimulated the nightly journey of the bothersome lice. The lice never stayed in one place to feed and always moved around seeking a better spot. Charlie constantly pinched and squeezed trying to kill the little bastards, but he always lost the battle. Sometimes he had so many lice living in his eyebrows and eyelids that he could barely close his eyes.

Charlie's health was understandably a major concern to him. His survival was tested every day and the terrible treatment by the guards did not help his chances. The cold caused frostbite in some men and, in some cases, gangrene and amputation. He watched other men as they collapsed from hunger, weakness, fear, or pain. He needed some rest. While he and many other prisoners stood for hours in the cold and miserable weather to get a drink of water or something to eat, the sick rested inside the barn in the straw and ate whatever rations were available and brought to them. He, like many other POWs, tried to give the extremely sick men extra food when possible.

The Germans provided almost no drugs needed to treat the prisoners. The POW medical personnel had some Red Cross medical parcels, which only provided them with a small amount of bandages, tape, aspirin, lice powder, and salves. So they improvised. As an example, they used heated bricks as hot water bottles. For dysentery cases, they made charcoal and let the patients chew it and swallow the powder. Sulfa pills were given only to the most serious cases and those with pneumonia. The medical personnel didn't have any stethoscopes. To listen to a man's lungs or heart, they had to remove his shirt, scrape off the lice, and place their ear directly on his chest.[32]

The medical personnel did most of their work in the barns. Things were very hard on them because they had marched all day also and then often worked while the column rested. On the days of rest, they walked extra miles to provide medical care to the scattered groups of prisoners.

Non-medical prisoners volunteered to assist the medical personnel with non-medical tasks. They dug latrines when shovels were available. They prepared and distributed food and boiled water. They carried from the sick wagon to the barn those patients with infected feet who were unable stand and those who were too weak to walk. For the seriously ill prisoners that also had dysentery, the volunteers carried them to and from the latrine throughout the night. Whenever the Germans could not or would not provide horses to pull the sick wagon, teams of 12 prisoners volunteered to pull the wagon and alternated when a group tired.

March 1, 1945, was three weeks after the evacuation of Stalag Luft IV. At this point in the march their strength and stamina were greatly reduced by the many days of snowstorms, fierce winds, and cold temperatures. The inclement weather engulfed the prisoners as they moved in the direction of Fallingbostel. On the following day they marched another 20 miles through heavy snow and strong winds.[33]

A month after the march began, Charlie took a good look at his fellow prisoners and saw himself in them. They were all distraught, starving, bearded, and filthy skeletons that no longer looked like civilized young men. He and the rest shuffled along like beaten down dogs, and just like an animal, he urinated and defecated in the open, with nothing to wipe or clean himself with.

"One time a woman came out of a house and to the edge of the road. Her son was a prisoner in the U.S. She wanted to know how they were treating the prisoners in the U.S. I told her that she had no worry. I said they're treated well. She said it is terrible the way they are treating you."

By the middle of March 1945, Charlie had marched approximately 250 miles across northern Germany.[34] His attitude was very poor, and in spite of the guards' demands, he and the rest could only walk slowly. He didn't talk very much, and neither did the others as they struggled to keep up with the column. Being fed by the Germans was getting even more infrequent, and what they were given now was mostly rotten root vegetables, stuff that normally was only fed to livestock. He and the other men were now reduced to digging through garbage for anything to eat.

"One day they got us up real early, at daylight. We marched the whole day, and it rained and rained and was cold. That day we marched into the night. We were on a muddy dirt road, and I was walking right behind a guard who had a stick that he used as a cane. So I stepped on it, which tore it out of his hand. He stopped and picked it up without saying a word. I wanted him to turn around and shoot me. That's how I felt. Let's end this. But he picked the stick up and went on. I waited a while and then stepped on it a second time. I was thinking, 'Now turn around and shoot me!' He stopped, picked up the stick and continued on. I waited a while and then stepped on it again. This time he picked it up, turned around, and in plain English said that he didn't want to make this march any more than me, but if he doesn't, they will shoot him on the spot. Then I felt better. I figured that if he had to make this march, then so did I."

Charlie noticed that now the German guards were almost as bad off as the POWs. Most were older men who struggled carrying large packs. He didn't feel sorry for them and laughed at them when they grumbled about the cold and nasty weather. He and the other prisoners stumbled along almost like blind men. There no longer was any semblance of organization in the column. The guards also trudged along miserably and really didn't pay much attention to the prisoners. But he did notice that guard dogs still stalked the column, and guards carrying machine guns still covered the group.

On March 28, they reached a town just west of the Elbe River. There the prisoners were loaded into boxcars and transported to Stalag XIB in Fallingbostel, some 30 miles away. Stalag XIB was a collection prison for tens of thousands of prisoners from many countries.[35] Like the rest, Charlie was ready to get back into a camp where he hoped there was adequate food and shelter.

When the POWs neared the new camp, Charlie could smell burning wood and coal, which brought about memories of warmth and comfort. He and the other exhausted prisoners, after having survived many hardships during the past many weeks, hoped they would receive shelter and rations in this camp. But they were sadly disappointed. When they moved into this permanent camp, they were met by thousands of other prisoners already confined in the crowded camp who wanted nothing more than to get out of the awful conditions.

After moving inside the camp, Charlie soon saw that his hope for a permanent shelter and decent food was not to be, because neither were available. He and the rest of his group were placed in large open tents, with very little straw to insulate them from the damp ground. Later that evening, he and the other new arrivals received only a tiny amount of soup and some ersatz coffee. This wasn't any better than what they had been fed while on the march.

However, their stay here definitely helped the extremely exhausted and ill prisoners to survive. More than food, those men desperately needed rest and medical care. Many could hardly walk without someone helping them, and some men who were seriously ill were admitted to the camp's hospital. The camp's hospital was overcrowded with an estimated 600 patients, many of whom were dying from starvation at the rate of 10 a day.[36]

Charlie was disgusted by the appalling conditions in the camp. He was also stunned by the incredible number of prisoners, in particular the tens of thousands of men from many different nations. This camp was run by the harsher Wehrmacht, not the Luftwaffe. The conditions in this camp were not the same as those he had experienced back in Stalag Luft IV. Here there wasn't any order, comradeship, or even an inclination to help and share with each other. These circumstances, along with living in tents and the lack of food, didn't give him any cause to feel better.

The newly arrived POWs had to assume a more rational and self-serving attitude if they were to survive in this setting. Now they had to live with Russians, Poles, Serbs, Greeks, Czechs, and Italian prisoners, each with a different cultural background. Living amid the throng of POWs, in extremely dirty conditions, was going to make surviving at Stalag XIB very difficult.[37]

They weren't given any Red Cross food parcels, which meant that Charlie would have to rely only on the unreliable rations provided by the Germans. If he thought that was bad, what was even worse was when they were told that food was only available for the prisoners who were considered permanently assigned to the camp. Transient prisoners like himself would not receive any more rations while there. Fortunately, Charlie's group would only be there a day or two.

After being there for a day or two, Charlie's group of POWs from Luft Stalag IV was awakened very early in the morning. They were quickly assembled and marched to the rail station at Ebstorf.[38] The guards repeatedly prodded the prisoners to move faster, promising that there would be food at their next stop. He was not surprised or disappointed when the promised food failed to appear. Later in the day he and the rest did receive some bread.

Some POWs were loaded into boxcars at Ebstorf, but Charlie and the other prisoners not loaded on the train at that location were marched another five miles south to Uelzen.[39] There they were put in waiting boxcars with other prisoners who had arrived earlier that morning. As usual, way too many prisoners were crammed into each boxcar.

Charlie recalled that the boxcar he was put in had been used to haul cattle, and the inside was filthy and smelled just awful. Inside the boxcar they didn't have any water and very little ventilation, and the dysentery completely overwhelmed the prisoners. They used toilet boxes but those soon overflowed. With nowhere else to go, he and the other men had no choice but to urinate and defecate right on the boxcar floor. Except for a few cracks of light, the boxcar was dark. After dark he saw a glow in the sky to the west and heard the rumble of artillery.

8. The March

With the boxcars overloaded, and the doors closed and locked, conditions inside the boxcar became incredibly disgusting. The prisoners could not lie down, so they took turns standing or sitting on the hard floor. Charlie, crammed together with the other men, had to sit with his knees drawn up tightly under his chin. The men rotated between standing and sitting every four hours until the horrible trip was over. He recalled that some men passed out from lack of food and water. Others were so ill they vomited or lost control of their bowels and there was no way for them to clean themselves. Some men were so miserable they broke down and cried. According to Charlie, this was the most degrading experience of the entire forced march.

Later that night, the train pulled out under the cover of darkness and proceeded to travel south on a two-day trip to Stalag XIA at Altengrabow.[40] Charlie recalled that it was nearly impossible to move about the boxcar without stepping on, hitting, or falling on another POW. It was also impossible to sleep. The boxcar rocked back and forth as it slowly moved down the tracks. Charlie was exhausted from the lack of sleep and the many hours of standing. By dawn he had become totally worn out and was very hungry and thirsty. The smell continued to get worse and worse, and it made even the strongest men sick to his stomach. Charlie's nerves, like many of the other men, were on edge.

Thirst caused the greatest suffering, and of all of the hardships, not having any water was absolutely the worst. The POWs were given little or no water while locked in the boxcars, even though there was water available in the rail yard. Charlie's tongue swelled, and his throat felt as if it were closing. He was so dry that he could hardly talk or swallow. His lips were dry and his eyes burned. Without some water it would even be impossible for him to eat, if he ever got some food.

Some prisoners in his boxcar went crazy and started screaming and crying. He and some other men eventually, and with great difficulty, calmed them down. Nerves were eventually strained to the breaking point, and some prisoners started behaving like animals. They were being treated like animals, and he realized that if these horrible conditions and treatment went on much longer, they might all start acting like animals.

The mental torment the POWs experienced while packed in these boxcars was made even worse by the substantial Allied aerial activity in the area. Charlie and the other prisoners knew there was a good chance that the train might be strafed by Allied fighters while they were trapped in the unmarked boxcars. He believed the Germans purposely wanted to attract and encourage attacks from the air. This train ride was the worst experience of his life, and some prisoners died inside the boxcars. Fortunately for Charlie he survived the trip and arrived at another camp.

They arrived in Altengrabow, which is between Magdeberg and Berlin. There he and the others stayed for about 10 days in a big wire compound which was called "Gooks Gulch." This was a very strange POW camp. Approximately 8,000 POWs were crowded into circus tents, 500 to 600 men to a tent. Some were in smaller tents of 100 prisoners each. Together in this enclosure were Sikhs, Hindus, Gurkhas, Senegalese, Nepalese, French, Scottish, English, Poles, Americans, and a few others. The place looked and smelled like a circus. As usual, food and sanitation were major problems, and international relations weren't very good either.[41]

At night Charlie watched the RAF bombing around Magdeberg and Berlin. When the big block-buster bombs exploded, they shook him awake as he slept on the ground. During the daytime it was the USAAF who bombed targets nearby. There were air raids and sirens sounding almost every hour. He also saw P-47s and P-38s fly overhead, strafing German convoys and railroads in the area.

Charlie loved hearing and seeing Allied planes overhead. But as he watched them flying by, he realized that those airmen were free men and would soon be back at their own bases, with good food, a warm bed, a decent bath, and a future. At that moment, for him, a hot meal of any kind was more desirable and needed than any other basic comfort or need.

After approximately 10 days at Gooks Gulch, Charlie and some of the other Stalag Luft IV POWs were on the road once again and marching westward. His column of POWs was soon spotted by a friendly fighter plane, and when the pilot recognized the column as POWs, he waved by rocking his wings and then flew off. Sometimes columns were not recognized and were strafed by friendly fighters, which resulted in POWs being hit and killed.

Charlie experienced one of those mistaken strafing attacks by Allied fighters. "We were marching with German civilians and they had horses and wagons. Some were pushing carts. Some were carrying everything. They didn't know which way to go to keep away from the Russians. One day they're going one way and the next day they're coming back. Then they'd go another way. Many days we marched with them, and one day as we marched with them, here came some of our fighters. I heard machine guns firing and looked up and saw it was fighters. There was a deep ditch on both sides of the road and everybody jumped into them and laid there. They mowed down some people. I don't know how many were killed."

"After everything quieted down, there was a creek there and the guards said that if anybody wanted to go down there and wash they could because they were going to hold up there for a while. I hadn't washed in almost a year, so I went down to the creek and thought about just washing my shirt to get the bugs out. I took my shirt off and when I looked at myself and saw how skinny I was, I just shook my head and said no, it wasn't worth cleaning. So I buttoned up my shirt and went back up, sat down, and waited. I was starting to look like those kids I had seen at the concentration camp." Charlie weighed 147 pounds when he was shot down, and he weighed only 87 pounds when he was finally liberated. An adult man, 5'7" tall, weighing only 87 pounds!

At the creek, when he stared into the water, Charlie saw his face. He saw a dirty, starving, unshaven skeleton. He never truly knew before what it was like to be really dirty. His skin was all dry and flaky from not being cleaned. His hair was filthy, and it would take a lot of water to ever get his hands clean again. When he opened his shirt, he saw how skinny he had become. His clothes were full of what looked like talcum powder. It was actually a huge amount of dead skin, and who knows what else. His skin was worn thin, and there was nothing between it and the bones. He really was in bad shape, as were most of the others. He was more than thin. He was emaciated, nothing but skin and bones. Time seemed to be running out for Charlie, and it occurred to him at that moment that he might die.

Each day presented a new trial and a different experience. Charlie's gut told him that liberation was just a matter of time. There were certain signs, including a more relaxed attitude of the guards, which gave him the impression that Germany's defeat was certain. But this was just a feeling, and he still had to find a way to survive until that day. The only certain thing that had changed was the weather, which had improved. The daily marches were now shorter, which meant that the halts at the barns were longer, which provided more time for the sick to rest.

One day the prisoners received news that Hitler had given the order to kill all POWs.[42] The prisoners were nervous and frightful that the guards might open fire on them, and after they had survived so long on the horrible march. The Germans guards soon figured out that it was probably not a good idea to kill the POWs, and they ignored the order, but they never told Charlie and the other prisoners that they weren't going to kill them.

It was clear that something was happening as they moved along. It seemed that there were fewer guards than before. "At the end we were down to about 150 prisoners, 10 guards, and no dogs. The guards were getting more lenient and letting us alone more."

The Americans were now only a few miles away. Charlie could clearly hear artillery in the distance and knew the day of reckoning was at hand. The POWs didn't have any information but something felt different. When they entered a small village, he saw white sheets hanging from the windows. A surge of knowing passed through him, and he felt it would soon be over.

Most German military personnel were not fanatical Nazis. The guards knew that Germany was on the verge of total defeat, and most wanted the war to end. Today they were the guards, but tomorrow they might be the prisoners. The guards still displayed their authority, but most of them were actually afraid to harm or anger the POWs because they feared retaliation. Charlie believed that if Germany would have been winning the war, many of the POWs would have been shot.

In late April 1945 the sense of liberty was in the air. U.S. Army single-engine reconnaissance planes were seen tracking the POW column.[43] Charlie said the guards informed the prisoners that they were nearing American ground units. Then, on the morning of April 25, 1945, the prisoners were marched through a German defensive position. The Wehrmacht had tanks and anti-tank guns dug into the hills facing to the west and the Elbe River.

"We were marching along and saw all of this military equipment off in a woods. Could this be the German front line? We saw kids around 12 years old, all in uniform and carrying rifles, going towards the front. Then an American recon plane flew over. We took our coats off and waved them. The plane dipped its wings and we knew that he had seen us. He flew around over top of us for at least an hour or an hour and a half. Then he dipped his wings once more and disappeared. Next thing we knew, here comes another one and does the same until he leaves."

"Then we got to a barn and they put us in. We were actually between the two front lines. There was a three-day truce. There was no shooting. Our spokesman for the 150 guys in our group passed the word around that the Germans were going to vote that night and that he had to go to that meeting in the farmhouse. They were going to vote on whether they should turn us over and surrender or take us in another direction. He said when we went into the barn tonight, to get anything we could find, sticks, anything as a weapon. Because when he came out of that meeting the guards would be with him. He said if he started whistling, that means we were going to overtake the guards. So be prepared and have something ready. If he whistled, they planned on taking us somewhere else. If you don't hear anything, don't do anything."

8. The March

"So he came back to the barn and he wasn't whistling. He told us that they were going to surrender us tomorrow. We didn't trust the Germans, but we hoped it was true. Bright and early the next morning they started us marching. We went for miles and finally got to a little town. Just a few houses, all with white bed sheets hanging out. The whole town had surrendered and all the people had left."

"We marched hour after hour, not knowing where we were going. Finally we saw two guys way down the road, but we couldn't make out who or what they were. As we got closer, it was a German soldier and an American soldier [he recalled the American soldier as being an MP, military police officer], standing side by side. The American told us that three miles down the road we'd see two more guys, a German and an American. After we passed them, we'd have another mile or two and we'd be free." It was a larger-than-life moment, and tears began to flow down Charlie's face.

The no-man's land between the two front lines was a narrow passage. Charlie watched as the German guards piled their arms in quiet surrender. When the guards surrendered, Big Stoop took off down the road. Some of the prisoners went after him, and according to what Charlie was told later, and believed, decapitated him.

Now a newfound energy strengthened Charlie's frail legs. "Boy, now we walked! We walked so fast that the guards were dragging behind. We came to a bridge over a river. It was a temporary swinging bridge. There were officers of all ranks standing on the bridge and they shook everybody's hand as we came onto the bridge, welcoming us back and thanking us for what we did. Then we crossed over the bridge and we were free!"

The forced march was over for Charlie on day number 80, as he crossed the Mulde River at Bitterfeld, Germany, and into U.S. lines. The freed POWs were met by Patton's 104th Infantry Division (Timberwolves) on April 26, 1945. Charlie had walked for 80 days and nearly 750 miles. It was over! He was going home!

Charlie had endured unbelievable hardship which affected him for the rest of his life. The exact distance covered will never been known, but I estimate the total for the route he took to be nearly 750 miles. Worst of all, several hundred American soldiers, perhaps more than a thousand, died on this pointless march to nowhere. There is no way to measure the misery Charlie and the other POWs suffered on the march.

The march would be given several names, including the Death March, the Black Death March, the Black March, the Shoe Leather Express, the Bread March, and simply the March.[44] It is recorded as part of the history of World War II, but many people, including myself, would never have known anything about it if not for Charlie and those who lived through it and were willing to tell us about their experience. Through them it will live forever. Though often overlooked by history, the death march across Germany ranks as one of the most outrageous cruelties committed against American fighting men.

Charlie had survived the most horrible experience of his life and gained knowledge that was priceless. He made some great discoveries, perhaps the most important discoveries of his life. One was the proof that the human body can take much more punishment than he had previously thought was possible. If the desire and will to live are strong enough, a man can withstand incredible hardships and survive. Also, when encouraged and challenged by his buddies, a man can do the impossible.

Chapter 9

Liberation

Near the end now, the panicked German guards, who absolutely feared the advancing Russians, pushed the tired POWs all day. The prisoners marched until three o'clock the next morning and had walked nearly 18 miles before halting. There, the prisoners bivouacked for three days before being moved another nine miles to Bitterfeld.[1]

It all happened on April 26, 1945, "one of the happiest days of my life." Charlie and his group of POWs were in a small village nine miles from Bitterfeld when they got the order to march toward the American lines. They thought the Germans were handing them another lie. But this time the Germans were telling the truth. The guards offered no opposition to this change in the fortunes of war. Without ceremony or emotion they voluntarily stacked their weapons. Then the Germans formed ranks to concede the sudden, yet long-expected change of roles between the guards and their prisoners. Charlie's physical condition that morning was nothing more than skin and bones. He guessed that he could not have survived another week of the march.

This nine-mile march was the fastest one that Charlie made. The sheer happiness on his face and the others had to be clearly obvious to everyone. Some men laughed, some cried, and many had a bewildered look on their face. Is it too good to be true? Walking along, he tossed away some of his possessions to the side of the road. He and the others almost tore apart the first American soldier they saw. Charlie without doubt must have appeared wretched to the American soldier. He was filthy, had a full beard that stuck straight out from his face, long, unkempt hair, and a body full of lice.

To Charlie's surprise, American soldiers of the 104th Infantry Division greeted them on their arrival at Bitterfeld.[2] There, as tears of joy streamed across his cheeks, he walked into the American lines across a bomb-damaged bridge. That night, the small portions of K-rations and C-rations he ate tasted almost as good as Mom's homemade pot-pie. After a few bites, he headed to the shower room and clean clothes. He stood in the shower for a long time, used a lot of soap and just let the water run over his emaciated body. It was good to be alive!

"We got on the other side of the river where we were liberated, and the first thing we got were K-rations. They gave everybody K-rations, which was the worst thing they could have done. But that was all they had to give us initially. They didn't have any other type of food to give us. The first thing I did was to smoke a cigarette. I knew we shouldn't eat the K-rations, not in the condition we were in. But the guys sat down and ate and ate and ate. Then the diarrhea and throwing up started. Oh, were they sick. I ate a little bit of cheese and nothing else, and I was all right. I didn't get sick. They put us in a beautiful building with tile floors and a lot of rooms. The next morning they came with trucks to take us to Camp Lucky Strike."

There were a few brief moments of joyous celebration, but mostly Charlie was just completely exhausted and had little interest in or thought of anything but sleep. Almost completely physically and emotionally drained, days passed before he entirely appreciated his change in status from prisoner to free man. "It still didn't feel real. It took some time to realize I wasn't dreaming. That lasted for a long time, and sometimes I wondered if I really went through it. It had been real!"

Liberation had finally come when he reached a friendly unit. Charlie knew freedom was getting closer each day and he believed that was the important thing that sustained him and kept him going during his almost three-month-long trek. The cavalry had finally arrived and saved the day! He was very glad that America had the will, and its military had the initiative, the guts, and the ability, to defeat the enemy and win the war.

On May 8, 1945, Hitler was dead and Germany crushed, and the German military surrendered unconditionally to the Allies. The war, which lasted from 1939 to 1945, killed an estimated 55 million people, including five million Germans. But it was the Russians who had lost the most. They suffered losses in excess of 26 million dead. It has been estimated that the Red Army alone lost somewhere around eight million soldiers. Nobody really knows how many others were killed, wounded, or displaced throughout Europe.[3]

Within this churning mass of people, and traveling through many villages and the carnage of a ruined Germany, tens of thousands of former POWs were moved to designated airfields. From these airfields, some were airlifted to medical clearing stations in Belgium and France. To quickly and efficiently move the former POWs, a vast airlift of B-17 heavy bombers and C-47 transports flew from air bases in England to various assembly points in Germany and transported thousands of POWs.[4]

Near Le Havre, France, was Recovered Allied Military Personnel (RAMP) camp, Camp Lucky Strike, an American army base. It was several square miles of land and a city within itself. Following the capture of the French port of Le Havre, numerous "cigarette camps" were set up as staging areas for new soldiers arriving in the European Theater of Operations.[5] It had originally been a German airstrip. Several such camps existed in the area and were named after popular cigarette brands (Old Gold, Twenty Grand, Chesterfield) as a means of security. Later on, several of these camps were selected specifically for American POWs being evacuated from Germany. Camp Lucky Strike was the most notable facility, and the one where Charlie would spend some time recuperating.

The camp was comprised of 12,000 tents and housed as many as 100,000 men at a time. It was a city unto itself with theaters, hospitals, a PX, and gift shops. There were food tents everywhere. However, because the prisoners had been surviving on a starvation diet, they were advised not to eat too much too fast. The medical staff gave Charlie and the former POWs specific instructions on what and how to eat.[6]

Charlie said, "The camp [Lucky Strike] was set up but it wasn't really finished yet. When we got there they just let us go into the mess hall and eat. Then we had problems, sick people. A woman officer, a dietician, finally arrived, and she immediately stopped everything. She knew what we had been through and knew we couldn't be fed like that. She had cards made and each person got a card. When I went in for breakfast, they punched my card, same at lunch time and evening meals."

The former POWs were told to eat only as much as they were given in the chow line and not to come back for seconds. They were also encouraged to take the vitamin pills they were given. Charlie and the rest were also told to go to the specified tents for eggnog or cocoa between meals if hungry, but not to drink more than one cup, and not to overeat.

"They had one tent where they had iced eggnog in great big garbage cans. She said we should drink whenever we were hungry. Drink eggnog and drink more eggnog, because that we could easily digest. We didn't get sick from it. I wore a path to the eggnog tent. Down and back, down and back. I even went down after dark and drank a couple of cups."

The men were also told to stay away from candy, peanuts, doughnuts, hotdogs, pork, rich gravy, liquor, spicy foods, and anything else that would make them sick. Just imagine having been starved for a year and then being told not to eat too much! It was awful for Charlie and the other liberated prisoners. He had a soft diet for several days, because his stomach had shrunk and needed to be slowly stretched. He was warned that overeating or eating solid foods could be very harmful.

"Each time I went to eat, my card was punched. They only gave me a small amount of food, and no seconds. That was working all right, but a couple of days later the Red Cross moved in. They set up with coffee and donuts, all you want. Well, guys started falling over dead! They died from overeating donuts and coffee. The camp soon shut down the Red Cross and sent them away. I got into a routine that I could live with. I didn't go in for breakfast. I went in at lunchtime and in the evening, and I didn't eat that much. I told them to cut back on what they gave me. I was doing all right and so were most of the guys after the dietician talked to us. We listened to her about eating too much, and slowly things started getting better."

There was a long row of buildings at the end of the base where Charlie remembered he went for delousing. After he had bathed and powdered, he moved down the hall to the clothing department. Without regard for size or proper fit, he was issued a whole wardrobe within minutes and eventually departed through the other end of the building. "We got new army-issue clothing. They had showers, and I got a haircut and shaved. I received no medical care at Lucky Strike." On another day he recalled processing through some kind of intelligence center where he filled out a bunch of forms and answered hundreds of questions asked by an intelligence officer.

Charlie was gaining about a pound a day and feeling much better. The average POW had lost from 35 to 45 pounds, which was on average nearly 25 percent of their normal body weight.[7] "I gained weight and by the time I left there I had put on a lot of weight. I couldn't see my ribs anymore."

Approximately 20 percent of all men who were liberated from German internment camps required immediate hospitalization for malnutrition. Others suffering from other conditions were hospitalized when they returned to the United States.[8] While at Camp Lucky Strike, Charlie and the other liberated men rested and were not required to do any physical labor. "There were German POWs that the Americans had captured. Those prisoners did any physical labor for us, like moving cots, etc. They were in much better shape than we were because they were taken care of."

Weeks passed by before the U.S. Army sent notification to Charlie's

9. Liberation

family to inform them he was alive and well. "I had not contacted any family members while at Camp Lucky Strike. They knew I was alive, but that was all" (Appendix C). He stayed at Camp Lucky Strike for approximately three weeks, healing, resting, reading, eating, and sleeping. Most of the stay was like moving slowly through a dense fog for him. It seemed as though he was stoned, as his mind and body continued healing.

Eisenhower, Supreme Allied Commander, visited the camp. Many of the men went to see him and had an opportunity to talk with him. Some expressed a bit of dissatisfaction (Appendix D).

"Eisenhower came to talk to the group. I had just been in the mess hall for lunch. Leaving the mess hall, I glanced down the road and saw this car coming with flags on it, and it had to be a general. I didn't know he was coming. So I stayed where I was, and when the car went past me, I saluted. My brother Raymond was driving him. I didn't go to listen to his speech, and I missed seeing Raymond." Charlie learned later that his brother, Master Sergeant Raymond Eyer, who was the Car-master for the 121st Quartermaster Car Company (Pennsylvania National Guard), was Ike's chauffeur that day.

That day, May 23, 1945, General Eisenhower spoke to the thousands of former American POWs at Camp Lucky Strike. Eisenhower stressed the importance of the USAAF and thanked the men for what they did to win the war. He also said he was personally going to do everything to get them home quickly. Ike went on to say, "Speaking for everyone in America I want to express our gratitude to you all in helping to defeat Germany. You men carried the ball for us and we will not forget it." His comments were well received and acknowledged the fact that the USAAF had been hitting German-occupied Europe two years before the U.S. Army landed any ground troops in France.[9]

I'm sure Eisenhower was sincere, but the liberated POWs returned from Europe with little recognition or consideration of their status by the American public aside from their families. Many people stigmatized these servicemen for having been captured. High ranking officers refused to approve the creation of a specific medal designed for service members held as prisoners of war. Sadly, these senior officers, along with a large portion of the American public, were ignorant of or uninterested in what the POWs had faced.

The country and the government did not recognize or acknowledge how much these men suffered or the deep and lasting impact of their experiences. The thousands of liberated POWs in Camp Lucky Strike and the other camps in May and June of 1945 could not have imagined they would be forgotten. Charlie was too overjoyed and hopeful to believe that America would not care about him or what he had survived.

In May 1945, more than 100,000 American POWs started to make their way home. The U.S. government later acknowledged that 130,201 U.S. service personnel, 32,730 of whom were combat aircrew members of the USAAF, had been captured during the war and held as POWs. Tens of thousands of American service personnel from World War II are still listed as missing in action (MIA). Most likely, many other American servicemen who perished on the forced marches across Europe or were detained by the Russians during the closing months of the war are included in the number of U.S. personnel listed as MIA.

"I think I was at Camp Lucky Strike for about three or four weeks. When I left the camp, they took me by truck straight to Le Havre, France. There I got on the boat to come home [June 3, 1945]. It was a large troop ship, filled with mostly ex–POWs. I knew when I went up the gangplank that I was in for more trouble—seasick."

Charlie walked up the gangplank to the main deck of a large passenger ship and took a look around for himself. The sailors and officers of the ship's crew sincerely and pleasantly greeted him and the others. There were doctors and nurses onboard to take care of them. There was plenty of food and he could eat like a king if so desired. Movies were shown twice a day. He was required to exercise every morning, but most of the time he just did as he pleased. The crew did everything they possibly could to provide the men a good time and a nice journey home.

"It took five days to get to New York City, and I was sick every day, but I didn't throw up after the first day. I hadn't eaten anything for fear of throwing up. Little by little I could eat more. The smell of fish being cooked made me sick. I was bunked in the forward part of the ship and it was a long way to the head [latrine]. By the time I got to the head, I wasn't sick anymore."

"I went to the galley and asked the navy guy in charge if he could give me a job, something to do because I was seasick. He said he would find something for me to do. So he put me on the potato masher. The vats were enormous. I had to crawl up on a step ladder and used a bucket with holes in it to scoop up the cooked potatoes. Then, turning around on the step ladder, I dumped them into the masher vat next to it. I got dizzy from turning around back and forth. I thought I might fall in because those potatoes were heavy and I still wasn't that strong. Then I had to open large packages of butter and throw them in along with bags of salt and pepper as the immense masher churned."

9. Liberation

Finally, on the fifth day, Charlie and the other returning servicemen lined the side of the troopship to see the Statue of Liberty as they sailed into New York Harbor. For him, that grand old lady stood for everything that was good and right about America. "We got into New York City harbor late on the fifth day. There were no empty berths for our ship, so we had to lay overnight until a berth opened up. At least in the harbor the water was calm. The next morning we tied up at the dock. Trucks picked us up and took me to a camp in New Jersey. There I got a physical examination, but it wasn't much of one."

"In the camp, the first thing we got was a delousing. I went through it seven times before I didn't itch anymore. The bugs in my eyelids were finally dead. We had to strip down and throw our clothing onto a heap, and from there they took them outside and burned them. We went to the next room, until the room was full of men. There were these things in the ceiling where a powder came down and blew around so the powder got all over us. I held my breath. It only took a minute. Then it was into a shower for 15 minutes. Then into the next room where I got all new clothes and shoes and everything. I finally got a decent uniform. The next day, if you had any itching, you did it again."

Finally the day arrived when Charlie could return home. "I got dressed and they trucked me to Philadelphia to catch a train to go home. That was where I met this guy from Fleetwood. He asked me how I was getting home, and I said by bus. He said I should go with him to Allentown on an open-air trolley. I said that sounded good. This guy said they were having a big party for him when he got home, and that I could go along with him, and that it would be fun. I still hadn't called anybody at home. It was a pleasant trolley ride, and his cousins picked us up in Allentown. We went to his place and they had anything you wanted to eat and drink. We partied all night and the next morning he drove me home."

Before departing Fleetwood, "I called Milt Starr and told him I was coming home and to tell Mom that I was on my way and would be home shortly. He delivered the message, and Mom and Pop were waiting on the porch when I got home."

Arriving home, Charlie and Mom and Pop were all overwhelmed with emotion upon this long-awaited reunion. All had longed for this day, and it was understandable that his parents greeted their son with admiration. He, however, did not think of himself as special. "Les [his brother] was in a hospital in Washington, D.C., when I got home. Raymond came home after I did. It was hard to realize what I had seen and went through, and then it stopped. I took a long time to get over it."

Charlie was not debriefed or given any kind of medical or psychological care at the time of his discharge. "I never received any kind of counseling and ended up with malaria and a back injury." He was given an extended leave of absence and then quickly mustered out of the service. "I was in the service for three years, two months, and 21 days."

Like most ex–POWs at that time, he was left on his own to deal with horrible memories, nervousness, and even some harmful behaviors. But he still was thrilled to finally be home and he did his best to relax and appreciate being with his family and friends.

"I just couldn't quite get things together. I kept thinking was this all real, and what's going on? It was so fast, even though it was weeks. Often I would think, did I dream this? You know, you get shot at like that, and that many times, and it does something to you. It's a strain on you. And then all of a sudden, it's all over, and I can't quite get it together. It took a long time to do it."

Many former POWs displayed a noticeable underlying tension and irritability that was obvious to their family. He was not the same guy they knew prior to going off to war. Traumatic events are connected to feelings of tension, anxiety, outrage, and anger. Some former POWs acted as if they were ashamed of something. Many families were surprised, if not shocked, to learn that he now drank, a lot! Studies done long after the war found that many of the former POWs still had nightmares, flashbacks, and extreme reactions to traumatic events that had occurred more than 50 years ago.[10]

Charlie returned home with terrible memories that would haunt him for many years to come. Many like him suffered from PTSD for the rest of their lives. He wanted a new beginning. But for now, he focused on what he wanted to do with the rest of his life, and not on the mental torment created by the war.

Chapter 10

Postwar

A large number of former POWs found they could only hang around the house for a limited amount of time before they headed to a local drinking establishment. The never-ending thoughts of combat and imprisonment, plus too much emotional stimulation, made them short-tempered during the day and prevented a good night's rest. Being miserable slowed down these men from making a speedy change from the hell experienced as a POW to the peaceful and safe environment of home and family.[1]

The experience of war had shredded many veteran's lives, leaving many feeling lonely and detached. Many former POWs turned to booze to drown out painful memories. Bars and clubs provided less intense social interaction and were visited more and more. Veterans preferred to hang out and drink with other men who had experienced the horrors of war. The alcohol dulled the unsettling memories of the war and helped to ease uncomfortable moments with family and friends.[2]

"Adjusting to home life was not fun. Certain noises would cause flashbacks. I remember my son Kevin was in the living room, and he was playing with a large cardboard box. The whooshing noise the box made sounded just like flak exploding and flying by the airplane. It caused me to fly off the handle. I had to control myself. Loud noises would make me grit my teeth, and I had to realize that it was okay."

Family and friends, with good intentions, sometimes made things worse for him when they failed to understand his feelings and what he had gone through. Sometimes the family just didn't know how to react to disturbing accounts of his ordeal. Such reactions sent a clear impression that family and friends couldn't handle his disturbing facts or images.

Just as difficult for Charlie, and most returning combat veterans, was the struggle to reconcile what had been experienced during the war with long-held beliefs and attitudes about themselves. Many of the veterans were troubled by the differences between how they ideally saw themselves and their actual conduct during the war. Many were confused by the way they felt about their war experiences, and it would take some of them years to come to grips with their feelings.[3] "It took the better part of five years until I felt it was over."

Some lost their belief in God and sense of a moral order. Others had survivor's guilt. They believed that they were not worthy of surviving while others, who they supposed were better men than themselves, had died. This was especially true for airmen who had escaped from a burning or dying airplane when his buddies did not get out.[4]

"I received no recognition from the military when I got back. To get a Pennsylvania POW license plate, I had to write to St. Louis to get verification that I had been a POW. I have the Air Medal and for every five missions I got an oak leaf cluster. For 25 missions I got a silver oak leaf cluster, and for 50 missions I got two silver, plus another oak leaf cluster for the last nine missions. Mike Werley [unit administrator for the Hamburg National Guard Armory] got in touch with the Department of Defense and got all the medals I should have gotten. Campaign medals, etc. I never bothered with that stuff. I was just glad to be alive."

Charlie's mother received a letter from the Adjutant General's Office of the War Department on January 23, 1945, while he was still a POW, and it read in part:

> I have the honor to inform you that, by direction of the President, the Air Medal, one Silver and four Bronze Oak Leaf Clusters, representing nine additional awards of the Air Medal, have been awarded to your son, Staff Sergeant Charles M. Eyer, Air Corps. The citation is as follows:
> "For meritorious achievement while participating in forty sorties against the enemy; while participating in heavy bombardment missions over enemy occupied Continental Europe and for meritorious achievement in aerial flight while participating in sustained operational activities against the enemy from 27 August 1943 to 6 September 1943. The courage, coolness and skill displayed by this Enlisted Man upon these occasions reflect great credit upon himself and the Armed Forces of the United States."

Health problems caused by malnutrition, gastrointestinal diseases, skin diseases, malaria, and a back injury, all caused by his military service, affected Charlie for years. "My back injury from the parachute landing bothered me, and it was painful. In the POW camp it developed into a cyst and one day it opened up and felt better after it had drained. The only time it bothered me after coming home was while driving a car. The bouncing over the roads would trigger the pain. I got away with it until I started riding horses. Then I had the cyst removed, but still had trouble with my back for years, even after seeing a few doctors. I had some bad days with the malaria." Decades after he returned from the war, he would still get the shakes from the malaria every time the weather suddenly turned cold.

In the fall of 1948, he met and began dating Catherine Budden. Many of their dates consisted of her attending parades as Charlie played in the American Legion Drum and Bugle Corps. They married on March 18, 1949, and moved to their home outside of Orwigsburg, Pennsylvania, in 1950. Daughter Joellyn (Susie) was born in 1952, and son Kevin was born in 1958. He loved his children, grandchildren Jason, Sharon, David, Marnie, and great-grand-children Cole, Michael, and Megan.

Charlie's love for his family was great, but he especially loved small children and babies. Many of his birthdays were spent with the family gathered at Knoebels Amusement Resort, where he really enjoyed riding the carousel. Playing miniature golf was also a favorite pastime, and he often intentionally made wild shots and fooled around on the course just to make the kids laugh. He did all kinds of silly things to make the children laugh and made almost any situation funny.

Charlie loved the long drive to his daughter's farm in Bloomsburg, Pennsylvania, which he and Catherine visited often. He loved when his children and grandchildren visited him, and every summer he planned his vacation time around their schedules. He always liked when the children helped paint the fences and the bridge on his property, and he would let the children ride the tractor while he mowed and help pick the cherries and plums from his trees. After the work was finished, he'd load everyone up in the old station wagon and take them swimming or out for ice cream or maybe miniature golfing.

During the 1950s, Charlie became an electrician and worked for a period of time for Cal Bagenstose. He was an electrician on two very large construction projects, the Hamburg Field House and the Roadside America building in Shartlesville. He also enjoyed helping his neighbors whenever he could and was known as the neighborhood electrician. In his later years he enjoyed working around the house, and especially anything that involved using his tractor.

Charlie was employed for 33 years as the maintenance repairman for the Hamburg Armory of the Pennsylvania Army National Guard. He started working there on September 24, 1958, and retired in 1991. He was highly respected, but even more, he was loved by the officers and soldiers assigned to the Hamburg unit, and to honor him, they gave him a large retirement party on April 20, 1991. Over the many years of his employment for the armory, he had received numerous awards, citations, and accolades for the excellent performance of his duties. At the end of the day, every day, without fail and with a chuckle, he'd always say to the full-time troops stationed at the armory, "Let's get out of this fire trap."

The one thing Charlie was most well-known for at the armory and beyond was his boiler room office. Down in the lower part of the armory was the boiler room, and in that boiler room Charlie had his "office." Inside the room was an old red wooden desk, a matching red wooden swivel chair, another cushier chair, hassock, and folding chairs standing in the corner if needed. There was always a pot of hot coffee on his desk, and the boiler room was always very toasty warm during the colder months.

In his boiler room office, Charlie hosted everyone from young privates to seasoned generals. Many young NCOs and officers visited his boiler room office and sought out and received his wise counsel and advice. Typically, when a young soldier came to him with a trivial military problem, his standard response was "Don't worry about that. That's just chickenshit."

One day he had a special visitor, Major General Richard Scott, USAF, Adjutant General of Pennsylvania. General Scott was visiting the armory for some unknown reason, and whatever it was, he never got around to it. Charlie invited the general into his boiler room office for a cup of coffee, which was gladly accepted. When General Scott saw the B-17 Flying Fortress model that hung over the desk, he asked Charlie if he was a veteran, to which Charlie replied that indeed he was and had been a gunner. General Scott had been a fighter pilot during World War II, flew out of England, and was also shot down and taken prisoner in 1944. He had been interned in Stalag Luft III. Well, the general never did get to do what he had come to Hamburg for because the two of them spent most of the day drinking coffee and talking about the war and their common experiences.

Charlie absolutely loved his job at the armory. At lunchtime, he and one or more of the soldiers stationed at the armory usually ate lunch at Joe Wisser's restaurant. When Charlie drove through Hamburg with his windows down, nearly everyone he passed would yell and wave, "Hey, Charlie!" He loved his hometown and had more friends than most people, and two of his best friends were John Bachman and Bill Keller.

Charlie loved to hunt and fish. He bought the kids their first fishing rods and taught them how to fish, and best of all, how to dig bait worms out of the manure pile near the barn. Charlie enjoyed hunting with his son Kevin and brothers Skip and Raymond, plus other friends, and rarely missed a chance to be out in the fields or in the forest. He was a crack shot because of his extensive firearms training in the military, especially when it came to bringing down pheasants on the wing with his shotgun. He also loved playing solitaire and would spend many relaxing hours as he turned over card after card after card.

Horses were also very important in his life. He first fell in love with horses as a teenager when he rode some at local riding stables. After the war he owned his own horses, and Charlie's love of riding them is the primary reason for the family's love of horses today. There were always a couple of horses around to ride, and he especially loved riding along the mountain trails near his home. He also loved dogs and could usually be found with one by his side when he was outside working on his property.

Beginning in January of 1998, he and his children began work on a series of video tapes about his military service and war experiences. The final tapes where he talked about being shot down, his POW experience, and the death march were extremely difficult for him to get through and to tell his family about. Sometimes the interview would go late into the night as they recorded many of the really horrible events he had survived. At those times it seemed that he couldn't stop himself from telling his family everything, but then at other times, he just couldn't say the words to describe the horrors and torment. The video project was completed four years later in January of 2002, when Charlie was 80 years of age. We are humbled and forever grateful for his willingness and courage to share his story.

They also videotaped him as he spoke to both civilians and veterans alike, and for a considerable amount of time, under the wing of a B-17 at the annual World War II event at the Reading airport in 1999. Kneeling under a wing of a B-17, he spoke to anyone interested in hearing all about the bomber and flying combat missions. While he was crouched under the wing a man approached, stood silently and listened for a few minutes, and then asked if Charlie had been a POW. He replied yes and told the man that he had been held in Stalag Luft IV. This man had also been shot down and had been in the same camp, but in a different compound, and they chatted for a while and shared their common experiences. Small world. He was the last surviving member of the first bomber (Shanker Ali) crew. Captain Van Every called Charlie several times after the war to check up on him, and long after the war he attended a few reunions with both crews.

Charlie willingly went through hell and faced the possibility of a horrible death to keep his nation safe and free. When the killing and destruction stopped, and the war ended, he returned home to the liberty bought and paid for with the lives of his buddies. He loved his family and country even more because of the price paid, and his desire was to live the American dream.

On Thanksgiving Day of 2003, Charlie fell ill and was taken to the Lehigh Valley Hospital. A week later he was transferred to a hospice inpatient unit. His loving family brought him home in December of 2003, where Charles Milton Eyer, age 82, passed away on January 3, 2004.

Charlie greatly loved his country, his family, his friends, and his God, and I am glad he was my friend. In contrast to how the horror of war changed him, he transformed that pain into a love which he freely shared with everybody.

"It took years, and I was never the same. I don't care how old you get, you're never the same."

Epilogue

Many young American men died in aerial combat during World War II. It was a horrendous exchange, hoping that each life lost might bring the war closer to an end, but nobody knew if that would turn out to be true or not. What we know today, many years after the war ended, is that the casualty toll for the USAAF in Europe was horrendous. Many of those missing were never heard from again, and the loss rate of bomber crews stands near the top of the list for all combat arms.

On Memorial Day, Charlie always attended the local services in his hometown of Hamburg, Pennsylvania. In the quiet cemetery he silently stood as he listened to the speakers and ministers, watched as the firing detail fired their salute to the dead, and listened to the bugler blowing Taps. He was giving his silent tribute to the thousands of servicemen and women who never returned. I am positive at those times Charlie remembered the many, many takeoffs and landings that had been made, and the reason for it all.

Charlie discovered that he couldn't forget the days when death was all around him. Just like many young men who survived combat, he could never really leave the war behind. It affected him and changed the way he lived the rest of his life. But rather than letting himself be stuck in the past, he focused on what he hoped would be a brighter future.

When Charlie returned home after the war, he found that in America, life had gone on without him. He had to focus his energy on adjusting to the postwar nation. It was up to him to adapt himself to fit back into society and not the other way around. He had little other choice but to find a way to fit into the America that awaited him. His only desire was to enjoy life again after years of sacrifice and hardship.

But try as he might to focus on his new life, sometimes Charlie had difficulty forgetting his terrifying experiences. He had to fight jumpiness caused by his combat experiences. A shout, a car backfire, or a sudden and loud noise could set him off and sometimes kept him on edge for quite some time. As time went by the uneasiness gradually lessened, but the terrible memories never did. For a short period of time he turned to alcohol in a vain attempt to blot out the terrible nightmares of combat, the prison camp, and the march.

But Charlie also learned that the war was responsible for many positive developments in his life. After surviving the hell of war and imprisonment, he eventually came to feel that no person or situation could be as alarming or threatening to him as what he lived through during the war.

After a few years he found contentment and the happiness just to be alive. He didn't worry about folks having more money or more fun than he did. Just having his family and friends around him was good enough. If the war had taught him anything, it taught him to appreciate the simple things in life. His military experience and his countless brushes with death made Charlie see that life is very fragile. The memories of war and the injuries were everlasting for him. At first Charlie struggled with his memories of the war, even as he went on with the business of living his life. For Charlie, the war had left memories that had remained hidden for decades but never really disappeared.

There are two types of combat veterans, those who want to remember their wartime experiences and those who just want to forget. Many did forget for decades after the war. To them, the war was only pain, misery, and death. They chose to forget the war and focused on their peaceful civilian lives. Long after the war, when these men reached middle age or old age, some wished to take a look at what they had gone through.

As they aged, and when many retired from their occupations, they got together again at reunions. They talked about their days in the service. They missed and honored their fallen buddies, but always tried to keep things on the light and funny side. There were some very humorous things that happened, though perhaps they didn't think of them as funny during the war. They now wanted to keep the memories alive and to pass along the message to young folks about the horrors of war and the sacrifices of military service.

Many men would eventually re-examine their wartime service, but not just to educate younger generations or reminisce with buddies. In the end they revisited these experiences because their memories never really went away. Whether they realized it or not, many had tucked away their wartime memories in their subconscious. The memories had always been there, just waiting for the day to come when they would be dealt with again.

Charlie wanted to forget the war when he returned home so that he could go on with the rest of his life. After many years he finally realized that the painful wartime memories could no longer hurt him. Time had healed many of the wounds. Like many, he came to realize that people tend to hang on to the good memories and try to forget the bad ones. The good memories always brought a smile to his face and helped him to make peace with the bad memories.

Charlie found pride not just in his postwar achievements, but eventually also in what he had done so many years earlier as a young combat airman. Beyond the pride he showed when looking back at his service, he also became reflective of those days past. In so doing, he expressed the core of what a combat airman had been all about: pride, sacrifice, fear, humor, fellowship, and suffering.

The destroyed cities of Europe have been rebuilt. The old airstrip at Rattlesden, England, is overgrown with weeds, and the old buildings are falling down. But if you listen close you can still hear the voices of young airmen and the roar of bomber engines. Sadly, most of those young, brave men have passed away now. They saved the world and then returned home to raise their families and to live the American dream.

During the war, Charlie became more than an ordinary and common guy. If he had never accomplished anything else for the rest of his life, he could claim one thing. He had clearly answered the question that many men ask themselves. He had faced the supreme test of looking death in the face and finding that he was not wanting. He discovered that he had the courage and the will to do those things that needed to be done in mortal combat. That alone marks him apart from most men. Yes, Charlie Eyer was the bravest man I have ever known.

Appendices

A. POW Journal

The following items are just a small portion of what Charlie recorded in his POW journal while he was held in Stalag Luft IV. It contains many more pages of items such as these, including menus and pencil drawings of the stalag, B-17s, and miscellaneous animals. During the march, Charlie protected his journal by keeping it next to his chest, and it survived in remarkably good condition.

A Gunner's Wish

I wish to be a pilot,
And you along with me;
But if we all were pilots,
Where would the Airforce be?
A pilot is just a chauffeur,
It is his job to fly the plane;
It is we who do the fighting,
Although we do not get the fame.
It takes guts to be a gunner,
To set out in the tail;
When the ME's are coming and the bullets begin to hail,
We'll be the best damned gunners, Jerry ever met.

A Prisoner's Prayer

Grant thy grace, O merciful Lord,
Both to me and to my comrades;
That we may never cease to trust in thee,

Staff Sergeant Charles Eyer's prisoner of war journal cover page, 1944–1945.

Who alone art able to help us.
Give us courageous hearts and a patient spirt,
And hasten the day when we may see,
Our homes and our native land once more,
Give us grace to trust fully in righteousness,
Of the Lord, THY SON.
AMEN

Thanks for the Memory

Thanks for the memory
Of flights to Germany
Across the cold North Sea
With blazing guns
We fight the Huns
For air supremacy
How lucky we were.
Thanks for the memory
Of M.E. 109's
Of flak guns on the Rhine
They did their bit and we were hit
And ended our good time
We hate them so much.
We drifted out of formation
We jumped and what a sensation
And now to sweat out the duration
Our job was done
We had our fun
Thanks for the memory.

A Gunner's Day

A gunner's day is never done,
Up at dawn before the sun,
With the roar of engines in his head,
Wishing he could have stayed in bed.
Chow at four, fried eggs, and such,
Won't have time to eat too much,
Briefing at five, the crew is all there,
Anxious to be up in the air.
See to your chute, ammunition and guns,
For you know boys, it's not for fun,
Jerry will be there, up in the blue,

Waiting for someone, maybe you.
Take off at six or maybe six thirty,
Hoping no one has a gun that is dirty,
Form with the group at 12,000 feet,
See that formation, they really look neat.
Put on your mask the air is getting thin,
Off to battle with a grin,
We're over the water now test your guns,
Enemy coast, here comes the fun.
Flak at six, flak at twelve,
Watch out boys, there giving us hell,
Here comes fighters, coming in low,
They may be ours don't shoot till you know.
P-51's and P-38's,
Our escort is here, their never late,
They're fighting fools, each man and his ship,
There is never a Jerry they couldn't whip.
The air is cold, just fifty below,
Turn up your heat, so you don't freeze a toe,
A sharp lookout Boys, the target is near,
We don't care to meet the enemy here.
There is our target, plenty of flak,
Bombs away! Boys, now we turn back,
Coming out of the sun, there's enemy ships,
Aim true boys, we've still got more trips.
There goes one down, another one too,
Our fighters are busy, to see none get through,
There is flame in the sky as another goes down,
The pilot bails out, he is safe on the ground.
They're on our tail, the guns start to roar,
There's blood on your guns, you shoot as before,
Your ship has been hit, but still flies thru the air,
You think of your loved ones, our whisper a prayer.
Smoke from the target leaps high in the sky,
We'll show these damned Jerries we know how to fly,
The fighters have left us, the few that were left,
Our fighters got some, we got the rest.
We've been up six hours, two hours to go,
Tho we're doing 200, it seems very slow,
England at last, the tail gunners learn,
We think of our buddies who will not return.

We fly over the field, the crew gives a sigh,
We've finished another, to do or to die,
Wheels touch the ground, with a scream and a bump,
Our ship brought us back over the hump.
We're tired and dirty, thirsty and sore,
The sun has gone down an hour before,
First clean your guns, do it good boys,
For that gun is life, us, mine or yours.
A sandwich and coffee, your chute to turn in,
Go to the briefing room, turn in the gin,
Two meals a day, both in the night,
Gets on your nerves, but still ready to fight.
The Mess Hall is warm, in cold of night,
You sit down to eat, talk between bites,
You talk of the fighters, theirs and ours too,
And of the boys that didn't get through.
Of ship going down, exploding in air,
The bullets that missed your head by a hair,
Your ship full of holes; guess Joe is in bed,
He has a flak fragment lodged in his head.
Then head for your sack at nine or ten,
A letter from home, another from "Lynne,"
I love you she wrote, then you know you've won,
And a gunner's day is never done.

P.O.W. Menu

- BREAKFAST

German Tea or Coffee? Jam
Or Cottage Cheese (once a week)
¼ loaf bread & 1/18 lb. Butter (per day)

- DINNER

Cabbage Soup or Pea & Bean
Soup or Barley Soup (with meat)
Carrot Soup & Dehydrated Greens
(No choice of soup)

- SUPPER

German Tea or Coffee, Boiled
Potatoes & Salt

- LUXURIES

Cream Cheese—Beer—Sugar—Oats

447Th Bomber Group 710th Squadron England

Charles Eyer First Most Desired Home Meal

1 bowl tomato soup
1 order of homemade potpie with meat and potatoes
Lettuce & tomato salad (side dish)
Raisin bread
Butter & jam
1 glass of ice cold milk
¼ piece of homemade lemon pie

May 12, 1944

   We were awakened at 3:AM. Had our breakfast at 4:AM. (eggs & bacon) were briefed at 5:AM. & took off 6:15AM. For synthetic oil plants at Bruxs, Chech. At 11:30AM. Near Frankfurt we were attacked by 109's (100–150). On their second pass at our formation they hit us in both wings and got our four gas tanks on fire. Seeing we could do nothing & knowing it would explode any minute we hit the silk. I landed in the back yard of a small village home. About 200 people were there to greet me in their own little way. I was searched and threatened by waving arms, guns, pitchforks and was called just about anything including Swine. I stood there in a cold sweat for I knew what happened to fellows before me that bailed out around Frankfurt. Two German soldiers were nearby and they came and took me away from the civilians. I was marched through the village where once more fists stared me in the face & once in a while I was spit at. I was put in a small stone building and guarded. In a short while Finch, Rakio & the Co-pilot were brought in. About 4:PM. They loaded us on a truck and took us to a German headquarters building. We were again searched and questioned. After that we were taken to a German interrogation center. There we were questioned and threatened so we would talk. I spent next night and most the next day in solitary confinement. Was sent to transient camp that afternoon.

* * * *

B. POW Postcards

   The following postcards were written by Charles Eyer while he was a prisoner of war in Stalag Luft IV. They were mailed home to his family and are a very dear possession of his family to this day.

Opposite: **This hand-drawn B-17 Flying Fortress bomber was inside Staff Sergeant Charles Eyer's POW journal, 1944–1945.**

Kriegsgefangenenlager

Datum: May 26/44

Dear Mother; A few lines to leave you know all is well with me. Say hello to all for me and keep that pot-pie ready. Don't forget my packages. I hope this card finds you all well. Take good care of yourself Momma and don't worry. Your boy, Chas.

* * * *

Kriegsgefangenenlager

Datum: May 28/44

Hi Skipper; How's my little bad boy? HA! HA! Was you worried about your Charlie? Well, just you take care of Momma and Poppa and, keep my bed warm. I am in good health Skipper and I hope you are the same. Take care of yourself and don't worry about your Charlie. I'll see you. Brother, Chas.

* * * *

Kriegsgefangenenlager

Datum: June 15/44

Dear Mother; A few lines to leave you know everything is going along fine. I hope you are all well and not worried about me. I also hope Poppa is feeling good. Say hello to everyone Momma, and take good care of yourself. Keep that chin up Momma and keep smiling. I am. Your boy, Chas.

* * * *

Kriegsgefangenenlager

Datum: 7/15/44

Dear Mother; A few lines to leave you know I am well and thinking of you always. I hope to hear from you soon. Give my love to all and I hope this card finds you all well. Don't worry Momma. Love, Chas.

* * * *

Kriegsgefangenenlager

Datum: 8/3/44

Dear Mother, A few lines to leave you know I am well. I hope you are not worried because I'm alright Momma and, passing time by playing games, drawing and taking sun bathes. Give my regards to all and I hope to hear from you soon. So-long Momma and God Bless You. Love-Your Son, Chas.

* * * *

Kriegsgefangenenlager

Datum: 8/6/44

Dear Mother, Just got up and had breakfast Momma. I'm feeling fine and will be going to Church services before long. How is everyone Momma? I'm praying that everyone is well. It's hard not hearing from you but, I won't worry too much Momma. I write as often as I am allowed and I hope you have received at least one by this time. Just keep that chin up Momma and don't worry. I'll see you soon, I know. What is Poppa doing just now? Does he still have his rabbits? Tell Skipper to train his little dog some tricks so I can have fun with him when I get home. Tell Whitey to keep the skates oiled up. We'll need them again before long. Love to all. Your Son, Chas.

* * * *

Kriegsgefangenenlager

Datum: 8/19/44

Dear Momma, A few lines to leave you know all is well with me. I hope you are all the same and don't worry Momma, I'll see you before long. Remember me to all. Good luck. Love Your Son, Chas.

* * * *

Kriegsgefangenenlager

Datum: 11/10/44

Dear Momma, I'd like to write to everyone back home but the quota for the month is 2 letters and four cards which makes it hard to write. You can write to me as often as you wish. In packages Momma send anything you wish. Candies, Dried fruit, Crackers etc. Momma Santa Claus time is coming fast so give Hannah fifty dollars for the kiddies' presents and don't forget Leon & Stinker. Love, Chas.

* * * *

Kriegsgefangenenlager

Datum: 12/12/44

Dear Momma. Up to date I have received nine letters from you. 1 from Johnny & Hannah, one from Helen Weber, one from Anna, two from Phylliss, two from Clem Cope, one from Fern & Doris, one from Cathryn Starr and one from Mrs. Behler. From Grace I have received thirteen. I'm still sweating out Stammy & Johnny Bachman. Your Son, Chas.

* * * *

C. Letter to Mother

May 7/45

Dear Momma,

After months of not being able to write this is indeed a pleasure. So much has happened lately that I'm really all besides myself. I heard today that the war is officially over. It's hard to believe after all these years but, I guess it got to end sometime. I can picture the happiness back home when you received the good news. On the 23rd of April I had a real shock, Momma. I was still in German hands and was staying at a barn with a group of other P.W.s. when who do I meet but, Bill Dalious from good old Hamburg, Penna. After these years in the army I meet someone I know. I was so happy to see him I couldn't sleep that whole night. We were together there two days before I finally recognized him. He is here with us now and is waiting to start home. We are really anxious to get moving. I have no idea when I'll arrive home, Momma, but roughly figuring I should be in your arms the early part of June. I told you when I left I'd be back, Momma. Well a few things happened I wasn't counting on and that sort of delayed me but, nonetheless I'm on my way now. We are to leave here on the ninth for France. How long we'll be there I don't know. All I can say Momma is I was a mighty lucky boy and I have but one person to thank for being able to write to you now without an injury to my body and not a scar. God was with me all the way, Momma. Without him I never would of made it.

I have so much on my mind, Momma. I don't know just what to say. The 26th of April we were liberated which was undoubtedly the happiest moment of my life. I saw my first Yank soldier at 3 PM while crossing the lines and pretty near went crazy with happiness. It won't be long now, Momma, and, I can't wait to hug you again.

The Germans had us on a forced march which started the 6th of February and ended the day we were liberated. That was eighty days of a living hell, Momma. We were starving gradually but, still had to keep marching. At times I thought the chips were up but, I had one person in mind and she was worth every last oz. of strength I had. When those moments came I looked to you, Momma, and remembered I promised you I'd be back. I marched on with the rest in silence and prayed one prayer after another. We marched about eight hundred miles, Momma, and now I know I must buy a car when I get back. All in all it was rough, Momma but, I believe I could of walked another eight hundred knowing it was leading to home someday. I'll tell you all about it when I see you, Momma, which won't be long now.

I hope you received word by now, that I was liberated, from either the government or Red Cross. Bill Dalious and I decided if either of us got a chance to write we would do so and leave you know that we met and were alright. I didn't get a chance to write but, Bill did just after he crossed the Elbe River and got to Bitterfield. I hope his letter got through. I'm terribly sorry I couldn't write more than I did during my stay here in Germany. I wrote every time I had a chance to, Momma, only those times were few as you know. It has worried me but now that's all over so I guess we can forget it.

I feel great, Momma. I eat like a little pig, and I'm so happy as an old lark. All I want to do when I get home, Momma is EAT. (Pies, cakes, pot pie, rabbit etc). I'll keep you busy, Momma just cooking. HA! HA!

Give my regards and love to all at home. We had dark days but, as you said, now the sun is shining once more. I'm on my way home so keep that runway lit up, Momma. I'm coming in. Will write again soon.

So-long Momma.
Your boy, Chas.

D. Liberation Journal

Charlie started this new journal, which he titled Liberation Journal on the day he was liberated, April 26, 1945, until he arrived in the harbor at New York on June 10, 1945.

S/Sgt. Chas. M. Eyer,
13080118
P.O.W. # 1226
446 Bomb Group. 710th Bomb Sqd.
(England)
S/Sgt. Chas. M. Eyer 13080118

P.O.W. #1226	LIBERATED
May 12, 1944	April 26, 1945

APRIL 26—Seen first Yank Soldier at 3 PM. Crossed the lines at Bitterfield, Germany. Sam & I traded soap for bread & syrup. We ate like kings while marching to the American lines. We could hardly believe we were free men. We received K-rations for supper and stayed at Bitterfield over-night.

Appendix D. Liberation Journal

April 27—Rode G.I. truck from Bitterfield to Halle. We spent the day getting settled. Was pretty sick during the night.

April 28—Got de-loused and seen my first show in over a year.

April 29—Stood roll call. Cut Sam's hair. Took a good shower & shave. Went to show. Raided mess hall in the evening.

April 30—Spent the day with Bill Dalious. Played cards, went to a show & talked about home.

May 1—Spent day at leisure. Made raid on Mess Hall. All doors & windows were locked.

May 2—Played cards with Bill. Had clothes washed. Rested in the evening.

May 3—Spent day at leisure. Cut Hough's & Jack's hair.

May 4—New clothes issued. Shower & shave & cut hair.

May 5—Moved to new area.

May 6—Helped fix up a stove. Cleaned windows, went to show in the evening.

May 7—Ate doughnuts and laid around in the sun. Went to show.

May 8—Wrote letters. Took a walk with Sam in the afternoon. Pulled raid on Mess Hall.

May 9—Pulled big raid on German Warehouses 2 miles from base at 5:30 AM, cookies, chocolate bars, meat etc. We ate the remainder of the day.

May 10—Left Halle at 9 AM. Flew on C-47 to Rheims, France (2 hrs. 40 min.) spent day getting situated.

May 11—Took shower & was issued new clothes.

May 12—Caught plane to Lucky Strike Camp near Dieppe, France (1 hr. 10 min.) staging area. Ate supper twice & hit the sack.

May 13—Spent day resting. Took sunbath.

May 14—Spent day resting. Met Capt. Van Every in the evening.

May 15—Spent day at leisure. Took sunbath.

May 16—Spent morning with Capt. Van Every. Wrote letters to home. Took a shower 2 miles from camp. Rode around in weapons carrier on my way back. Spent evening cleaning around the tent.

May 17—Spent morning washing clothes. Spent remainder of day lying around taking life easy.

May 18—Spent day visiting the boys from camp that just arrived. Went to USO show in the eve, and seen moving picture after the USO show.

Appendix D. Liberation Journal

MAY 19—Spent day taking sun bath. Went to show in the eve. With Sgt. Northrup & Sgt. Snead.

MAY 20—Rainy day. Spent day in sack.

MAY 21—Spent day getting new clothes issued.

MAY 22—Wrote letters, spent the day at ease.

MAY 23—Moved from C-24 Area to D-28 Area.

MAY 24—Took physical exam, Typhus shot, interrogated, received ribbons.

MAY 25—Payed partial pay of $50.00 in the afternoon. Drew PX rations. Saw show.

MAY 26—Moved back to Area C. Spent day fooling around.

MAY 27—Wrote letters. Went to show.

MAY 28—Wrote letters. Went to show.

MAY 29—Spent day at rest.

MAY 30—Wrote letters. Went to show.

MAY 31—Wrote letters. Seen show.

JUNE 1—1st. hitch (3 years completed) Lucky Strike Camp, France. Had Francs changed. Took quick physical, show down inspection.

JUNE 2—Was prepared to leave for boat. (Orders changed) seen show & wrote letters.

JUNE 3—Took sun bath. Was alerted to leave for boat.

JUNE 4—Left Camp Lucky Strike 10 AM. Arrived at Le Harve 1:30 PM. Boarded the U.S.S. Admiral Benson at 3 PM.

JUNE 5—Left Le Harve at 8 AM. Spent day in sack.

JUNE 6—Spent day in sack. Little sick.

JUNE 7—Started work in kitchen.

JUNE 8—Worked in kitchen. Spent rest of time in sack.

JUNE 9—Kind of rough. Got sick in the morning spent day in sack.

JUNE 10—Went to church service in the morning. Worked in kitchen. 1 to 7 PM.

Chapter Notes

Chapter 1

1. Craig Kleinsmith, *The Blue Mountain Legion* (Westminster, Maryland: Heritage Books, 2005), 275.

Chapter 2

1. 99th Bombardment Group Historical Society, *The Diamondbacks: The History of the 99th Bomb Group (H)* (Paducah, KY: Turner Publishing, 1998), 8.
2. Donald Miller, *Masters of the Air* (New York: Simon & Schuster, 2006), 121.
3. 99th Bombardment Group Historical Society, *The Diamondbacks: The History of the 99th Bomb Group (H)* (Paducah, KY: Turner Publishing, 1998), 8.
4. 99th Bombardment Group Historical Society, *The Diamondbacks: The History of the 99th Bomb Group (H)* (Paducah, KY: Turner Publishing, 1998), 8.
5. 99th Bombardment Group Historical Society, *The Diamondbacks: The History of the 99th Bomb Group (H)* (Paducah, KY: Turner Publishing, 1998), 8.

Chapter 3

1. 99th Bombardment Group Historical Society, *The Diamondbacks: The History of the 99th Bomb Group (H)* (Paducah, KY: Turner Publishing, 1998), 8.
2. 99th Bombardment Group Historical Society, *The Diamondbacks: The History of the 99th Bomb Group (H)* (Paducah, KY: Turner Publishing, 1998), 8.
3. 99th Bombardment Group Historical Society, *The Diamondbacks: The History of the 99th Bomb Group (H)* (Paducah, KY: Turner Publishing, 1998), 8.
4. 99th Bombardment Group Historical Society, *The Diamondbacks: The History of the 99th Bomb Group (H)* (Paducah, KY: Turner Publishing, 1998), 8, 9.
5. 99th Bombardment Group Historical Society, *The Diamondbacks: The History of the 99th Bomb Group (H)* (Paducah, KY: Turner Publishing, 1998), 8, 9.
6. 99th Bombardment Group Historical Society, *The Diamondbacks: The History of the 99th Bomb Group (H)* (Paducah, KY: Turner Publishing, 1998), 9.
7. 99th Bombardment Group Historical Society, *The Diamondbacks: The History of the 99th Bomb Group (H)* (Paducah, KY: Turner Publishing, 1998), 9.
8. Donald Miller, *Masters of the Air* (New York: Simon & Schuster, 2006), 92.
9. Donald Miller, *Masters of the Air* (New York: Simon & Shuster, 2006), 92.
10. Edward Jablonski, *Flying Fortress* (Garden City, NY: Doubleday & Company, 1965), 233.
11. Edward Jablonski, *Flying Fortress* (Garden City, NY: Doubleday & Company, 1965), 233.
12. 99th Bombardment Group Historical Society, *The Diamondbacks: The History of the 99th Bomb Group (H)* (Paducah, KY: Turner Publishing, 1998), 9.
13. Martin Bowman, *Clash of Eagles* (Barnsley, South Yorkshire, England: Pen & Sword Aviation, 2006), 80.

14. 99th Bombardment Group Historical Society, *The Diamondbacks: The History of the 99th Bomb Group (H)* (Paducah, KY: Turner Publishing, 1998), 9.
15. 99th Bombardment Group Historical Society, *The Diamondbacks: The History of the 99th Bomb Group (H)* (Paducah, KY: Turner Publishing, 1998), 9.
16. 99th Bombardment Group Historical Society, *The Diamondbacks: The History of the 99th Bomb Group (H)* (Paducah, KY: Turner Publishing, 1998), 9.
17. 99th Bombardment Group Historical Society, *The Diamondbacks: The History of the 99th Bomb Group (H)* (Paducah, KY: Turner Publishing, 1998), 17.
18. 99th Bombardment Group Historical Society, *The Diamondbacks: The History of the 99th Bomb Group (H)* (Paducah, KY: Turner Publishing, 1998), 9.
19. 99th Bombardment Group Historical Society, *The Diamondbacks: The History of the 99th Bomb Group (H)* (Paducah, KY: Turner Publishing, 1998), 9.
20. 99th Bombardment Group Historical Society, *The Diamondbacks: The History of the 99th Bomb Group (H)* (Paducah, KY: Turner Publishing, 1998), 9.
21. 99th Bombardment Group Historical Society, *The Diamondbacks: The History of the 99th Bomb Group (H)* (Paducah, KY: Turner Publishing, 1998), 9.
22. Edward Jablonski, *Flying Fortress* (New York: Doubleday & Company, 1965), 99.
23. Edward Jablonski, *Flying Fortress* (New York: Doubleday & Company, 1965), 102.
24. Martin Bowman, *Clash of Eagles* (Barnsley, South Yorkshire, England: Pen & Sword Aviation, 2006), 18.
25. 99th Bombardment Group Historical Society, *The Diamondbacks: The History of the 99th Bomb Group (H)* (Paducah, KY: Turner Publishing, 1998), 10.
26. 99th Bombardment Group Historical Society, *The Diamondbacks: The History of the 99th Bomb Group (H)* (Paducah, KY: Turner Publishing, 1998), 10.
27. 99th Bombardment Group Historical Society, *The Diamondbacks: The History of the 99th Bomb Group (H)* (Paducah, KY: Turner Publishing, 1998), 10.
28. 99th Bombardment Group Historical Society, *The Diamondbacks: The History of the 99th Bomb Group (H)* (Paducah, KY: Turner Publishing, 1998), 10.
29. 99th Bombardment Group Historical Society, *The Diamondbacks: The History of the 99th Bomb Group (H)* (Paducah, KY: Turner Publishing, 1998), 10.
30. 99th Bombardment Group Historical Society, *The Diamondbacks: The History of the 99th Bomb Group (H)* (Paducah, KY: Turner Publishing, 1998), 10.
31. 99th Bombardment Group Historical Society, *The Diamondbacks: The History of the 99th Bomb Group (H)* (Paducah, KY: Turner Publishing, 1998), 13.
32. 99th Bombardment Group Historical Society, *The Diamondbacks: The History of the 99th Bomb Group (H)* (Paducah, KY: Turner Publishing, 1998), 13.
33. 99th Bombardment Group Historical Society, *The Diamondbacks: The History of the 99th Bomb Group (H)* (Paducah, KY: Turner Publishing, 1998), 13.
34. 99th Bombardment Group Historical Society, *The Diamondbacks: The History of the 99th Bomb Group (H)* (Paducah, KY: Turner Publishing, 1998), 13.
35. 99th Bombardment Group Historical Society, *The Diamondbacks: The History of the 99th Bomb Group (H)* (Paducah, KY: Turner Publishing, 1998), 13.
36. 99th Bombardment Group Historical Society, *The Diamondbacks: The History of the 99th Bomb Group (H)* (Paducah, KY: Turner Publishing, 1998), 13.
37. 99th Bombardment Group Historical Society, *The Diamondbacks: The History of the 99th Bomb Group (H)* (Paducah, KY: Turner Publishing, 1998), 13.

Chapter 4

1. John McManus, *Deadly Sky* (New York: New American Library, 2000), 329.
2. John McManus, *Deadly Sky* (New York: New American Library, 2000), 330.
3. John McManus, *Deadly Sky* (New York: New American Library, 2000), 372.

Chapter 5

1. Donald Miller, *Masters of the Air* (New York: Simon & Schuster, 2006), 293.
2. Center for Air Force History, *Com-*

bat *Chronology 1941–1945* (Washington, D.C.: Center for Air Force History, 1991).
3. Center for Air Force History, *Combat Chronology 1941–1945* (Washington, D.C.: Center for Air Force History, 1991).
4. Center for Air Force History, *Combat Chronology 1941–1945* (Washington, D.C.: Center for Air Force History, 1991).
5. Center for Air Force History, *Combat Chronology 1941–1945* (Washington, D.C.: Center for Air Force History, 1991).
6. Center for Air Force History, *Combat Chronology 1941–1945* (Washington, D.C.: Center for Air Force History, 1991).
7. Edward Jablonski, *Flying Fortress* (New York: Doubleday & Company, 1965), 102.
8. Center for Air Force History, *Combat Chronology 1941–1945* (Washington, D.C.: Center for Air Force History, 1991).
9. Center for Air Force History, *Combat Chronology 1941–1945* (Washington, D.C.: Center for Air Force History, 1991).
10. Donald Miller, *Masters of the Air* (New York: Simon & Schuster, 2006), 265.
11. Center for Air Force History, *Combat Chronology 1941–1945* (Washington, D.C.: Center for Air Force History, 1991).
12. Donald Miller, *Masters of the Air* (New York: Simon & Schuster, 2006), 276.
13. Donald Miller, *Masters of the Air* (New York: Simon & Schuster, 2006), 267.
14. Center for Air Force History, *Combat Chronology 1941–1945* (Washington, D.C.: Center for Air Force History, 1991).
15. Center for Air Force History, *Combat Chronology 1941–1945* (Washington, D.C.: Center for Air Force History, 1991).
16. Martin Bowman, *Clash of Eagles* (Barnsley, South Yorkshire, England: Pen & Sword Aviation, 2006), 82.
17. Martin Bowman, *Clash of Eagles* (Barnsley, South Yorkshire, England: Pen & Sword Aviation, 2006), 81.
18. Martin Bowman, *Clash of Eagles* (Barnsley, South Yorkshire, England: Pen & Sword Aviation, 2006), 82.
19. Center for Air Force History, *Combat Chronology 1941–1945* (Washington, D.C.: Center for Air Force History, 1991).
20. Center for Air Force History, *Combat Chronology 1941–1945* (Washington, D.C.: Center for Air Force History, 1991).
21. Center for Air Force History, *Combat Chronology 1941–1945* (Washington, D.C.: Center for Air Force History, 1991).
22. Center for Air Force History, *Combat Chronology 1941–1945* (Washington, D.C.: Center for Air Force History, 1991).

Chapter 6

1. Donald Miller, *Masters of the Air* (New York: Simon & Schuster, 2006), 290.
2. Roger Freeman, *B-17 Fortress at War* (New York: Charles Scribner's Sons, 1977), 145.
3. Roger Freeman, *B-17 Fortress at War* (New York: Charles Scribner's Sons, 1977), 145.
4. David Dorfmeier, *C-Lager* (Paso Robles, CA: Self-published, 2016), 77.
5. John McManus, *Deadly Sky* (New York: New American Library, 2000), 204.
6. Donald Miller, *Masters of the Air* (New York: Simon & Schuster, 2006), 98.
7. John McManus, *Deadly Sky* (New York: New American Library, 2000), 70.
8. Kenneth Simons, *Kriegie* (New York: Thomas Nelson & Sons, 1960), 25.
9. David Dorfmeier, *C-Lager* (Paso Robles, CA: Self-published, 2016), 81.
10. David Dorfmeier, *C-Lager* (Paso Robles, CA: Self-published, 2016), 84.
11. Edward Jablonski, *Flying Fortress* (Garden City, NY: Doubleday & Company, 1965), 247.
12. David Dorfmeier, *C-Lager* (Paso Robles, CA: Self-published, 2016), 87.
13. Donald Miller, *Masters of the Air* (New York: Simon & Schuster, 2006), 382.
14. Donald Miller, *Masters of the Air* (New York: Simon & Schuster, 2006), 385.
15. Kenneth Simmons, *Kriegie* (New York: Thomas Nelson & Sons, 1960), 45.
16. Donald Miller, *Masters of the Air* (New York: Simon & Schuster, 2006), 382.
17. Donald Miller, *Masters of the Air* (New York: Simon & Schuster, 2006), 385.
18. John McManus, *Deadly Sky* (New York: New American Library, 2000), 221.
19. Donald Miller, *Masters of the Air* (New York: Simon & Schuster, 2006), 386.
20. David Dorfmeier, *C-Lager* (Paso Robles, CA: Self-published, 2016), 95.
21. David Dorfmeier, *C-Lager* (Paso Robles, CA: Self-published, 2016), 96.

22. Kenneth Simmons, *Kriegie* (New York: Thomas Nelson & Sons, 1960), 55.
23. Kenneth Simmons, *Kriegie* (New York: Thomas Nelson & Sons, 1960), 56.
24. Kenneth Simmons, *Kriegie* (New York: Thomas Nelson & Sons, 1960), 56.
25. Kenneth Simmons, *Kriegie* (New York: Thomas Nelson & Sons, 1960), 56.
26. David Dorfmeier, *C-Lager* (Paso Robles, CA: Self-published, 2016), 99.
27. Donald Miller, *Masters of the Air* (New York: Simon & Schuster, 2006), 386.
28. John McManus, *Deadly Sky* (New York: New American Library, 2000), 223.
29. David Dorfmeier, *C-Lager* (Paso Robles, CA: Self-published, 2016), 100.
30. David Dorfmeier, *C-Lager* (Paso Robles, CA: Self-published, 2016), 101.
31. David Dorfmeier, *C-Lager* (Paso Robles, CA: Self-published, 2016), 109.
32. John McManus, *Deadly Sky* (New York: New American Library, 2000), 218.

Chapter 7

1. David Dorfmeier, *C-Lager* (Paso Robles, CA: Self-published, 2016), 124.
2. Donald Miller, *Masters of the Air* (New York: Simon & Schuster, 2006), 394.
3. Stalag Luft IV 50th Anniversary, *Stalag Luft IV, 1944–1945* (Paducah, KY: Turner Publishing, 1996), 41.
4. David Dorfmeier, *C-Lager* (Paso Robles, CA: Self-published, 2016), 137.
5. David Dorfmeier, *C-Lager* (Paso Robles, CA: Self-published, 2016), 133.
6. David Dorfmeier, *C-Lager* (Paso Robles, CA: Self-published, 2016), 134.
7. Stalag Luft IV 50th Anniversary, *Stalag Luft IV, 1944–1945* (Paducah, KY: Turner Publishing, 1996), 8.
8. Red Cross, *Report of the International Committee of the Red Cross Visit of Oct. 5 & 6, 1944, Stalag Luft IV.*
9. David Dorfmeier, *C-Lager* (Paso Robles, CA: Self-published, 2016), 143–144.
10. Stalag Luft IV 50th Anniversary, *Stalag Luft IV, 1944–1945* (Paducah, KY: Turner Publishing, 1996), 8.
11. Stalag Luft IV 50th Anniversary, *Stalag Luft IV, 1944–1945* (Paducah, KY: Turner Publishing, 1996), 8.
12. Stalag Luft IV 50th Anniversary, *Stalag Luft IV, 1944–1945* (Paducah, KY: Turner Publishing, 1996), 31.
13. Stalag Luft IV 50th Anniversary, *Stalag Luft IV, 1944–1945* (Paducah, KY: Turner Publishing, 1996), 27.
14. David Dorfmeier, *C-Lager* (Paso Robles, CA: Self-published, 2016), 141.
15. Eugene Halmos, *The Wrong Side of the Fence* (Shippensburg, PA: White Main Publishing, 1996), 135.
16. Eugene Halmos, *The Wrong Side of the Fence* (Shippensburg, PA: White Main Publishing, 1996), 136.
17. David Dorfmeier, *C-Lager* (Paso Robles, CA: Self-published, 2016), 143.
18. John Hansen, *Walking Home from Germany* (San Bernardino, CA: Self-published, 2016), 42.
19. John Hansen, *Walking Home from Germany* (San Bernardino, CA: Self-published, 2016), 43.
20. John Hansen, *Walking Home from Germany* (San Bernardino, CA: Self-published, 2016), 44.
21. John Hansen, *Walking Home from Germany* (San Bernardino, CA: Self-published, 2016), 42.
22. David Dorfmeier, *C-Lager* (Paso Robles, CA: Self-published, 2016), 157.
23. David Dorfmeier, *C-Lager* (Paso Robles, CA: Self-published, 2016), 159.
24. Donald Miller, *Masters of the Air* (New York: Simon & Schuster, 2006), 400.
25. David Dorfmeier, *C-Lager* (Paso Robles, CA: Self-published, 2016), 158.
26. Eugene Halmos, *The Wrong Side of the Fence* (Shippensburg, PA: White Mane Publishing, 1996), 143.
27. David Dorfmeier, *C-Lager* (Paso Robles, CA: Self-published, 2016), 160.
28. David Dorfmeier, *C-Lager* (Paso Robles, CA: Self-published, 2016), 161.
29. Donald Miller, *Masters of the Air* (New York: Simon & Schuster, 2006), 403.
30. Donald Miller, *Masters of the Air* (New York: Simon & Schuster, 2006), 403.
31. David Dorfmeier, *C-Lager* (Paso Robles, CA: Self-published, 2016), 170.
32. David Dorfmeier, *C-Lager* (Paso Robles, CA: Self-published, 2016), 169.
33. David Dorfmeier, *C-Lager* (Paso Robles, CA: Self-published, 2016), 176.
34. David Dorfmeier, *C-Lager* (Paso Robles, CA: Self-published, 2016), 177.

35. John Hansen, *Walking Home from Germany* (San Bernardino, CA: Self-published, 2016), 47.
36. John Hansen, *Walking Home from Germany* (San Bernardino, CA: Self-published, 2016), 47.
37. Stalag Luft IV 50th Anniversary, *Stalag Luft IV 1944–1945* (Paducah, KY: Turner Publishing, 1996), 27.
38. Kenneth Simmons, *Kriegie* (New York: Thomas Nelson & Sons, 1960), 96.
39. Stalag Luft IV 50th Anniversary, *Stalag Luft IV 1944–1945* (Paducah, KY: Turner Publishing, 1996), 27.
40. David Dorfmeier, *C-Lager* (Paso Robles, CA: Self-published, 2016), 145.
41. Stalag Luft IV 50th Anniversary, *Stalag Luft IV 1944–1945* (Paducah, KY: Turner Publishing, 1996), 36.
42. Donald Miller, *Masters of the Air* (New York: Simon & Schuster, 2006), 396.
43. Donald Miller, *Masters of the Air* (New York: Simon & Schuster, 2006), 395.
44. Robert Smith and Laurence Yadon, *The Greatest Escapes of WWII* (Guildford, CT: National Book Network, 2017), ix.
45. Donald Miller, *Masters of the Air* (New York: Simon & Schuster, 2006), 398.
46. Donald Miller, *Masters of the Air* (New York: Simon & Schuster, 2006), 396.
47. David Dorfmeier, *C-Lager* (Paso Robles, CA: Self-published, 2016), 138.
48. John Hansen, *Walking Home from Germany* (San Bernardino, CA: Self-published, 2016), 42.
49. Donald Miller, *Masters of the Air* (New York: Simon & Schuster, 2006), 396.
50. David Dorfmeier, *C-Lager* (Paso Robles, CA: Self-published, 2016), 138.
51. David Dorfmeier, *C-Lager* (Paso Robles, CA: Self-published, 2016), 179.
52. John Hansen, *Walking Home from Germany* (San Bernardino, CA: Self-published, 2016), 43.
53. David Dorfmeier, *C-Lager* (Paso Robles, CA: Self-published, 2016), 165.
54. David Dorfmeier, *C-Lager* (Paso Robles, CA: Self-published, 2016), 173.
55. Stalag Luft IV 50th Anniversary, *Stalag Luft IV 1944–1945* (Paducah, KY: Turner Publishing, 1996), 13.
56. David Dorfmeier, *C-Lager* (Paso Robles, CA: Self-published, 2016), 181.
57. David Dorfmeier, *C-Lager* (Paso Robles, CA: Self-published, 2016), 152.
58. Kenneth Simmons, *Kriegie* (New York: Thomas Nelson & Sons, 1960), 163.
59. Stalag Luft IV 50th Anniversary, *Stalag Luft IV 1944–1945* (Paducah, KY: Turner Publishing, 1996), 8.

Chapter 8

1. David Dorfmeier, *C-Lager* (Paso Robles, CA: Self-published, 2016), 185.
2. David Dorfmeier, *C-Lager* (Paso Robles, CA: Self-published, 2016), 196.
3. David Dorfmeier, *C-Lager* (Paso Robles, CA: Self-published, 2016), 196.
4. David Dorfmeier, *C-Lager* (Paso Robles, CA: Self-published, 2016), 198.
5. Stalag Luft IV 50th Anniversary, *Stalag Luft IV, 1944–1945* (Paducah, KY: Turner Publishing, 1996), 11.
6. Donald Miller, *Masters of the Air* (New York: Simon & Schuster, 2006), 493.
7. Donald Miller, *Masters of the Air* (New York: Simon & Schuster, 2006), 501.
8. John Hansen, *Walking Home from Germany* (San Bernardino, CA: Self-published, 2016), 50.
9. David Dorfmeier, *C-Lager* (Paso Robles, CA: Self-published, 2016), 202.
10. John Hansen, *Walking Home from Germany* (San Bernardino, CA: Self-published, 2016), 50.
11. David Dorfmeier, *C-Lager* (Paso Robles, CA: Self-published, 2016), 202.
12. John Hansen, *Walking Home from Germany* (San Bernardino, CA: Self-published, 2016), 51.
13. David Dorfmeier, *C-Lager* (Paso Robles, CA: Self-published, 2016), 205.
14. David Dorfmeier, *C-Lager* (Paso Robles, CA: Self-published, 2016), 205.
15. John Hansen, *Walking Home from Germany* (San Bernardino, CA: Self-published, 2016), 52.
16. Donald Miller, *Masters of the Air* (New York: Simon & Schuster, 2006), 496.
17. David Dorfmeier, *C-Lager* (Paso Robles, CA: Self-published, 2016), 188.
18. Stalag Luft IV 50th Anniversary, *Stalag Luft IV, 1944–1945* (Paducah, KY: Turner Publishing, 1996), 21.
19. Stalag Luft IV 50th Anniversary,

Stalag Luft IV, 1944–1945 (Paducah, KY: Turner Publishing, 1996), 21.
20. Stalag Luft IV 50th Anniversary, *Stalag Luft IV, 1944–1945* (Paducah, KY: Turner Publishing, 1996), 21.
21. David Dorfmeier, *C-Lager* (Paso Robles, CA: Self-published, 2016), 219.
22. David Dorfmeier, *C-Lager* (Paso Robles, CA: Self-published, 2016), 222.
23. David Dorfmeier, *C-Lager* (Paso Robles, CA: Self-published, 2016), 225.
24. David Dorfmeier, *C-Lager* (Paso Robles, CA: Self-published, 2016), 228.
25. David Dorfmeier, *C-Lager* (Paso Robles, CA: Self-published, 2016), 229.
26. Stalag Luft IV 50th Anniversary, *Stalag Luft IV 1944–1945* (Paducah, KY: Turner Publishing, 1996), 22–26.
27. Stalag Luft IV 50th Anniversary, *Stalag Luft IV 1944–1945* (Paducah, KY: Turner Publishing, 1996), 20.
28. John Hansen, *Walking Home from Germany* (San Bernardino, CA: Self-published, 2016), 53.
29. David Dorfmeier, *C-Lager* (Paso Robles, CA: Self-published, 2016), 227.
30. Kenneth Simmons, *Kriegie* (New York: Thomas Nelson & Sons, 1960), 197.
31. David Dorfmeier, *C-Lager* (Paso Robles, CA: Self-published, 2016), 212.
32. Stalag Luft IV 50th Anniversary, *Stalag Luft IV 1944–1945* (Paducah, KY: Turner Publishing, 1996), 21.
33. David Dorfmeier, *C-Lager* (Paso Robles, CA: Self-published, 2016), 233.
34. David Dorfmeier, *C-Lager* (Paso Robles, CA: Self-published, 2016), 239.
35. Donald Miller, *Masters of the Air* (New York: Simon & Schuster, 2006), 502.
36. David Dorfmeier, *C-Lager* (Paso Robles, CA: Self-published, 2016), 245.
37. David Dorfmeier, *C-Lager* (Paso Robles, CA: Self-published, 2016), 246.
38. David Dorfmeier, *C-Lager* (Paso Robles, CA: Self-published, 2016), 243.
39. David Dorfmeier, *C-Lager* (Paso Robles, CA: Self-published, 2016), 241.
40. Stalag Luft IV 50th Anniversary, *Stalag Luft IV 1944–1945* (Paducah, KY: Turner Publishing, 1996), 12.
41. Stalag Luft IV 50th Anniversary, *Stalag Luft IV 1944–1945* (Paducah, KY: Turner Publishing, 1996), 12.
42. Stalag Luft IV 50th Anniversary, *Stalag Luft IV 1944–1945* (Paducah, KY: Turner Publishing, 1996), 20.
43. Stalag Luft IV 50th Anniversary, *Stalag Luft IV 1944–1945* (Paducah, KY: Turner Publishing, 1996), 11.
44. John Hansen, *Walking Home from Germany* (San Bernardino, CA: Self-published, 2016), 55.

Chapter 9

1. Stalag Luft IV 50th Anniversary, *Stalag Luft IV 1944–1945* (Paducah, KY: Turner Publishing, 1996), 37.
2. David Dorfmeier, *C-Lager* (Paso Robles, CA: Self-published, 2016), 281.
3. David Dorfmeier, *C-Lager* (Paso Robles, CA: Self-published, 2016), 284.
4. David Dorfmeier, *C-Lager* (Paso Robles, CA: Self-published, 2016), 285.
5. David Dorfmeier, *C-Lager* (Paso Robles, CA: Self-published, 2016), 271.
6. John Hansen, *Walking Home from Germany* (San Bernardino, CA: Self-published, 2016), 59.
7. Kenneth Simmons, *Kriegie* (New York: Thomas Nelson & Sons, 1960), 250.
8. David Dorfmeier, *C-Lager* (Paso Robles, CA: Self-published, 2016), 289.
9. David Dorfmeier, *C-Lager* (Paso Robles, CA: Self-published, 2016), 290.
10. David Dorfmeier, *C-Lager* (Paso Robles, CA: Self-published, 2016), 298.

Chapter 10

1. David Dorfmeier, *C-Lager* (Paso Robles, CA: Self-published, 2016), 298.
2. David Dorfmeier, *C-Lager* (Paso Robles, CA: Self-published, 2016), 299.
3. David Dorfmeier, *C-Lager* (Paso Robles, CA: Self-published, 2016), 298.
4. David Dorfmeier, *C-Lager* (Paso Robles, CA: Self-published, 2016), 298.

Bibliography

Ambrose, Stephen. *Citizen Soldiers.* New York: Simon & Schuster, 1997.

American Prisoners of War in Germany. *Dulag Luft.* www.stalagluft4.org.

B-17 Bomber Flying Fortress. www.b17flyingfortress.de/en.

Bowman, Martin. *Clash of Eagles.* Barnsley, South Yorkshire, England: Pen & Sword Aviation, 2006.

Center for Air Force History. U.S. Army Air Forces in World War II, *Combat Chronology 1941–1945.* Washington, D.C.: Center for Air Force History, 1991.

Congressional Record. *Commemorating the 50th Anniversary of the Forced March of American Prisoners of War from Stalag Luft IV.* Washington, D.C., 1995.

Dorfmeier, David. *C-Lager.* Paso Robles, CA: Self-published, 2016.

Eyer, Charles M. *Liberation Journal.* Self-published, 1945.

Eyer, Charles M. *POW Journal.* Stalag Luft IV. Self-published, 1944–1945.

Eyer, Charles M. Personal interviews with the author. Family videotapes.

Freeman, Gregory. *The Forgotten 500.* New York: Dutton Caliber, 2007.

Freeman, Roger. *B-17 Fortress at War.* New York: Charles Scribner's Sons, 1977.

Halmos, Eugene. *The Wrong Side of the Fence.* Shippensburg, PA: White Mane Publishing, 1996.

Hansen, John. *Walking Home from Germany.* San Bernardino, CA: Self-published, 2016.

Jablonski, Edward. *Flying Fortress.* Garden City, NY: Doubleday & Company, 1965.

Jackson, Robert. *Warplanes of World War II.* London: Amber Books, 2002.

Kleinsmith, Craig. *The Blue Mountain Legion.* Westminster, MD: Heritage Books, 2005.

Liddell Hart, B.H. *History of the Second World War.* New York: G.P. Putnam's Sons, 1970.

McManus, John. *Deadly Sky.* New York: New American Library, 2000.

Miller, Donald. *Masters of the Air.* New York: Simon & Schuster, 2006.

99th Bombardment Group Historical Society. *The Diamondbacks: The History of the 99th Bomb Group (H).* Paducah, KY: Turner Publishing, 1998.

O'Donnell, Joseph. *The Shoe Leather Express.* Self-published, 1982.

Simmons, Kenneth. *Kriegie.* New York: Thomas Nelson & Sons, 1960.

Smith, Robert, and Laurence Yadon. *The Greatest Escapes of WWII.* Guilford, CT: National Book Network, 2017.

Stalag Luft IV 59th Anniversary. *Stalag Luft IV, 1944–1945.* Paducah, KY: Turner Publishing, 1996.

United States National Archives & Records Administration. World War II Prisoners of War Data File, 12/7/1941–11/19/1946. www.aad.archives.gov.

War Department. *FM 27-10, Rules of Land Warfare.* Washington, D.C.: War Department, 1940.

War Department. *If you should be captured these are your rights.* Washington, D.C.: US Government Printing Office, 1944.

Watkins, Claude. "A Prisoner of the Luftwaffe." *American Ex-POW Bulletin*, April 2000.

Wikipedia. *RAF Rattlesden*. www.en.wikipedia.org.

www.stalagluft4.org. Military Intelligence Service War Department Report, 1944.

www.stalagluft4.org. Stalag Luft IV Monument.

www.stalagluft4.0rg. *Testimony of Dr. Leslie Caplan, The Evacuation of Luft IV*, 1947.

Index

absent without leave (AWOL) 65–67
accident 23, 26; bomb explosion 49–50
Adjutant General of Pennsylvania 186
USS *Admiral Benson* 205
Afrika Korps 32, 34
Air Medal 43, 184
air speed calibration 25
alcohol 36, 74
Algiers 59, 62
Altengrabow, Germany 169–170
Amazon River 32
American Legion Drum and Bugle Corps 185
ammunition 20; tracer bullets 91
Amundson, Lt. Steve 18
Anklam, Germany 155
anoxia 24
Arabs 35, 37, 47
Army Air Corps 12
Arnew, Sgt. Athel 135
Atkinson Field, British Guiana 31
Atlantic Ocean 32
Audrey 59

B-17 Flying Fortress 4, 6, 17–19, 24, 27, 50, 53, 75, 87
Bachman, John 186
Bagenstose, Cali 185
bail-out button 92
ball turret 20–21, 90–91
ball turret gunner 19, 21
Baltic Sea 112, 142
Bangor, Maine 68
barbed wire disease 124
Barksdale, Louisiana 22, 25
barns 161–162
basic training 14

Bataan Death March 142
Bathurst, Gambia 29
Battle of the Bulge 97, 127
Belém, Brazil 29, 31
Belgard, Germany 144
Benevento, Italy 57
Berlin, Germany 77–78, 80–81
Bible 82
Big Stoop 134–135, 144, 173
Biloxi, Mississippi 14
Bitterfeld, Germany 173, 175
Bizerte Harbor 43
Black Death March 173
Black March 173
block busters 46, 52
Bloomsburg, Pennsylvania 185
boiler room 186
Boise, Idaho 18, 22
Bombach, Lt. Col. Otto (commandant) 112, 135
bombardier 19, 41, 54
bombing run 91
bombs 52
Borinquén, Puerto Rico 29, 31
boxcar 109, 168–169
Bread March 173
breakfast 74
briefing 42
brig 65
brotherhood 29
Budden, Catherine 185

C-rations 73
camp inspection 132
Camp Lucky Strike 176–177, 179–180
Caplan, Capt. Leslie 158
Capua, Italy 57

casualties 75
casualty rate 61
cell 102, 104
Chicago, Illinois 22
cigarette camps 177
cigarettes 120–121
clothing 45
cold temperatures 24, 44, 46
cold weather 136, 143
combat fatigue 58
combines 147
Commandant Rigor Mortis 129
concentration camp 156
Constantine, Algeria 34–35, 40
co-pilot 18
court-martial 65–66
crash-landing 26

D-Day 74, 82
Dachau concentration camp 103
Dakar, Senegal 62
Dalious, Bill 163
Daniels, Staff Sgt. Farron 18
Death March 142, 173
delousing 181
"Diamondbacks" 31–32
Distinguished Unit Citation 50
dog tags 103–104
dogs, police/guard 110, 112, 121–122, 132–133
Doolittle, Gen. Jimmy 87
Dulag Luft 98–102, 105–106
Durchgangslager 99
dust storms 47
dysentery 163–164

East Anglia, England 70
Eastern Front 140–141
Ebstorf, Germany 168
8th Air Force 5, 70, 75, 81
Eisenhower, Gen. Dwight D. 10, 52, 74, 179
Elbe River, Germany 167, 172
electrocution 127
England 69–73
English Channel 93
escape 133–134, 148–149
Esmerelda 50
espionage 22
European Theater of Operations (ETO) 4
Eyer, Edgar 9
Eyer, Joellyn (Susie) 185
Eyer, John 10

Eyer, Kevin 185
Eyer, Lester 10
Eyer, Raymond 10, 179, 186
Eyer, Skip 186
Eyer, Walter 9

Fahnert, Sgt. Reinhard 112
Fallingbostel, Germany 156, 167
Fallon, Sgt. Charles 18
FBI 22
fear 62
ferret 130–131
fiftieth combat mission 59
.50 caliber machine gun 20, 22, 91
Finch, Staff Sgt. William 68, 85, 93, 95, 114, 138, 144
Fink, Sarah 9
fire 93
Fisher, Lt. Brayton 18, 52
flak 5, 48, 51
flak happy 48
Fleetwood, Pennsylvania 181
flight engineer 19
Florida 63
Flugzeugabwehrkanone 5
Foggia, Italy 53, 56
food 40, 42; lager 117–119, 121; march 156–160
Fort Lee, Virginia 13–14
Forty and Eight 109
447th Bomb Group 69–70, 86
416th Bombardment Squadron 18
Frankfurt, Germany 72, 85, 98–99
Franklin Street 9
free-fall 94
Frieberg, Germany 87, 96
Friedrichshafen, Germany 75
Frosinone, Italy 57
frostbite 45

Geneva Convention 98, 102, 117, 122
Georgetown, British Guiana 29, 31
Gerbini, Sicily 50–51
German fighters 50, 53–54, 77, 79–80, 85–86, 92; crash 128
German Missing Air Crew Report 87
Germany 9, 75, 87; civilians 96–97; soldiers 97; surrenders 176
Gestapo 103
Gooks Gulch 170
goon baiting 129
goons 130
Göring, Reichsmarschall Herman 53, 81
Gowen Field, Idaho 22

Index

Green Bay Packers 68
Greyhound bus 65
Gross Tychow, Germany 106, 112
ground crew 37–38
guard duty 38–39
guards, march 167, 173
guards, stalag 131–132
Gulf of Mexico 16
gunnery school 15–17
gunsight 20

Halloween 63
Hamburg, Pennsylvania 9–11, 163, 186
Hamburg Armory 185
Hamburg Army National Guard 9
Hannover, Germany 79
Hathaway, Sgt. Charles 68, 85, 93
health 135–136
Hitler, Adolf 171
Hohemark, Germany 99
home guard 144
Homestead Air Force Base, Florida 17, 27–29, 31
Hope, Bob 54–55
Hough, Staff Sgt. Ralph 68, 85

Iceland 68
infantry 13
infirmary, camp 135–136
Initial Point (IP) 91
International Red Cross 107, 112, 142
interrogation 99–103, 105
Ireland 68–69
Isernia, Italy 57
Istres–Le Tubé airfield 56
Italy 32, 44, 47

Jackson, Staff Sgt. Robert 68, 83, 85
Jacobs, Lt. Rudy 68
jail 97–98
Jamaica 63
Jankes, Lt. Leonard 68, 85
Joe Wisser's Restaurant 186
jungle 37, 62

K-rations 73, 176
Kasserine Pass 33
Keesler Field, Mississippi 14
Keller, Bill 186
Kiefheide, Germany 110
kitchen police (KP) 67
Knoebels Amusement Resort 185
kohlrabi 119, 159
kriegie 130

Kriegsgefangenenkartel 102
Kriegsgefangener 96
Kriegsmarine 106
Kutztown, Pennsylvania 63

lager 113; barracks 114; coal burning stove 114; kitchen 114
Lager B 114
Lake Constance 75
Langford, Frances 54–55
Laon, France 82
La Senia Airfield 35
latrines 115; radio 126
Le Culot, France 77
Le Havre, France 177, 180
Lehigh Valley Hospital 188
Leipzig, Germany 85
lice 164–165
life boats 56–57
Lippolt, Staff Sgt. Beauford 18, 21, 29, 38–39, 66
Lockhead P-38 Lightning 53
Luft Gangsters 99
Luftwaffe 77, 80, 82, 98–99, 103, 106, 112
Luxembourg 84

machine guns 16
Mae West jacket 45
mail 125–126
"the major" 27–29, 32, 40–41
malaria 63–64, 185
Malines, Belgium 84
maps 148
The March 173
march, forced 140; disease/illness 163; medical treatment 165
Marrakech, Morocco 30–34
Marseille, France 56
Mazu, Staff Sgt. Mike 18, 26, 39
Mediterranean Sea 31–32, 52
Messina, Sicily 48, 54
Middletown, Pennsylvania 25
migration 149
military police 65, 67
missing in action 106–107
Mitchell, South Dakota 27
Montgomery, Field Marshal Bernard 52
moonshine 35
Morrison Field, Florida 29, 31
mosquitos 62
Mulde River, Germany 173

Naples, Italy 53
Navarin, Algeria 35

navigator 18, 41
Nazi 112
New York City 181
90-Day Wonder 57
99th Bombardment Group (Heavy) 17–18, 22–23, 27, 29, 31–32, 34–35, 37, 41, 43, 47, 50, 52, 56
Noball, France 80
non-commissioned officers (NCOs) 19
Norden bombsight 5, 41
Normandy, France 5, 82
North Africa 31–32, 34
North Sea 93
Northrup, Sergeant 71–72, 138
Nuremberg trials 97

Oberursel, Germany 98–99, 106
104th Infantry Division (Timberwolves) 173, 175
121st Quartermaster Car Company 10, 179
Operation Overlord 74
Oran, Algeria 35, 40
Orlando, Florida 17
O'Rourke, Lieutenant 57
Orwigsburg, Pennsylvania 185
Oudna Field, Tunisia 47, 54
oxygen 24

P-51 Mustang 80
Pantelleria 46–47
parachute 93–95
pass 66–67
Pennsylvania Army National Guard 10, 179, 185
Pennsylvania Dutch 9
Philadelphia, Pennsylvania 13
physical examination 13
Pickhardt, Walther, Captain 112, 134
pilot 18
Pisa, Italy 56
plane, reconnaissance 172
Plexiglas 20
Pomerania 112, 141
"Poon Tang" 32
Potteiger, Dr. 64
Prendergast, Staff Sgt. John 68, 82–83
prisoner of war (POW) 96, 109, 112
PTSD 58, 182

quinine pills 64–65
quonset hut 71

radar stations, German 77
radio operator 19

Rainey, Lt. Col. Leroy 18
Rakiewicz, Sgt. Anthony 68, 85, 96, 114, 144
Rattlesden, England 70
Ratzebuhr, Germany 141
Reading, Pennsylvania 11–13, 64–75
Recovered Allied Military Personnel (RAMP) camp 177
Red Army 140–141, 155
Red Cross 76, 106; parcel 106, 112, 118–120, 136, 143
refugees 149–150
Rhine River 85–86
Richardson, Lt. Oran 68, 85
Rip's Corner 163; Rip Trexler's 163
roll call formation 129–130
Roman ruins 52–53
Rome 52–54
Rommel, Erwin 34
Rooney, Andy 21
Royal Air Force (RAF) 112
Russians 138–139, 141; POWs 151

sabotage 22, 47
Salerno 58
Salina, Kansas 27, 68
Salt Lake City 65
Salt Lake City Army Air Base Replacement Center, Utah 22
Sam 147
San Lorenzo, Italy 54
Schmidt, Sgt. Hans 134
Scholz, Lt. Nicholas 68, 85
Scott, Maj. Gen. Richard 186
scrounging 40
710th Bombardment Squadron 69–70
Shanker Ali 32–33, 48, 51, 56
Shoe Leather Express 173
shotguns 15
shower 111
Sicily 32, 44, 46, 52
sick wagons 153, 165–166
Sioux City, Iowa 23, 25–27, 66, 68
skeet shooting 15
slave laborers 99
snow 25
solitary confinement 100
spy 103–105, 108
SS troops 150–151
Stalag Luft IV 106–107, 109–110, 112, 142
Stalag XIA 169
Stalag XIB 167–168
stallion 59

Index

Stalzenburg, Germany 146
Stammlager der Luftwaffe 106
Starr, Milt 26, 81
Stars and Stripes 21
starvation 157
Statue of Liberty 181
still, alcohol 35
Stockheim, Germany 87
stooges 116
strafing attack 170
straggling 152–153
Strasberg, Lt. Jack 18, 48
strategic bombing 4
strip search 101
Super Duper Shit Scooper 115
Swinemunde, Germany 154

Tail-End Charlie 29
tail gunner 19
Tampa, Florida 15
targets of opportunity 47
Tarnow, Germany 156
tent 35–36
Terni, Italy 56
terror fliers 97
Terrorfliegers 97
Thistlewood, Capt. John 18
toilet, bomber 20, 46
top turret gunner 19
Torre, Annunziato, Italy 58
tour of duty 61
training 24, 26
trap shooting 15
Tunis 54
Tunisia 32
12th Air Force 32

Uelzen, Germany 168
United States Army Air Force (USAAF) 4–5, 10, 12–13, 19, 30, 75, 81, 94, 100
United States Marine Corps 5, 12
Upthegrove, Col. Faye 18, 54
Usedom Peninsula, Germany 155

V-weapon 77; V-1 rocket 80
Van Every, Capt. Harold 67–68, 78–79, 85
Vatican City 52–53
Villacidro Aerodrome, Sardinia 41
Volksstrum 144
Volturno River, Italy 57
Vorlager 110, 143

waist gunner 19
Walla Walla, Washington 22–23
War Crimes Tribunal 112
warning wire 116–117
Watertown, South Dakota 27
weather 27, 72–73
Wehrmacht 106, 151
Werley, Mike 184
Wetzlar, Germany 99, 106
White Cliffs of Dover 76, 79
women pilots 27
Women's Army Corps (WACs) 60
wounded airmen 82–83
"Wun Hung Low" 32
Wynsen, Capt. Henry 121

Yandum Field, Gambia 31
YMCA 123

Zwickau, Germany 85, 107

www.ingramcontent.com/pod-product-compliance
Ingram Content Group UK Ltd.
Pitfield, Milton Keynes, MK11 3LW, UK
UKHW041954140426
5217IPUK00015B/799